Kathryn Hanley
Christmas
1977

The World of the
PUBLIC SCHOOL

The World of the PUBLIC SCHOOL

Introduced by
GEORGE
MACDONALD FRASER

ST. MARTIN'S PRESS
New York

For information, write:
St. Martin's Press, Inc.,
175 Fifth Ave., New York, N.Y., 10010

Printed in Great Britain

Library of Congress Catalog
Card Number: 77-72369
First published in the
United States of America in 1977

Library of Congress Cataloging in Publication Data

Main entry under title:

The World of the public school.

1. Public schools, Endowed (Great Britain) --
Addresses, essays, lectures. I. Fraser, George
MacDonald, 1925-
LA632.W757 373.2'22 77-72369
ISBN: 0-312-89230-6

CONTENTS

ACKNOWLEDGEMENTS

The publishers are most grateful for the help and co-operation of the following organisations and for the illustrations they supplied: Charterhouse School: 1, 8, 11, 30, 36; Radio Times Hulton Picture Library: 2, 3, 6, 9, 10, 12, 13, 14, 17, 18, 19, 20, 23, 25, 26, 27, 29, 31, 35; Mary Evans Picture Library: 15, 24, 32, 33; Mansell Collection: 21, 28, 34, 37. In addition the publishers are very grateful to Philippa Lewis, who did the picture research.

Introduction
GEORGE MACDONALD FRASER

During the war a friend of mine was serving in an Officer Cadet Training Unit, preparing to be a second-lieutenant, when he and his comrades were called unexpectedly to a special parade; as they fell in, the frightening rumour went round that some of them were to be sent back to their units as unsuitable officer material.

'They can't do that to us,' said the cadet next to my friend. 'We're public school men!'

My friend, a grammar school boy, murmured, 'Speak for yourself,' at which his companion turned, looked him up and down, and said, 'Well, semi-public school.'

It has always seemed to me that that incident summed up more about Anglo-Saxon attitudes, class-consciousness, and the fine distinctions of our social and educational systems, than a course of lectures on the subjects. It is all there – as it always is, in a tone of voice, a look, a particular kind of accent, a way of laughing, a use of certain phrases, or even just a vague, unspoken sense of something exclusive. Everyone in Britain knows and recognizes it; sometimes it is nearly invisible, but it is always real. It is the difference between the boy, or man, who was at a public school, and the rest.

Many people – including some public schoolboys, and various social unfortunates who aren't quite sure whether they are public schoolboys or not but hope to God people will think they are – try to pretend that this distinction does not exist, that it is a thing of the past. They lie in their teeth, and they know it. The genuine division remains – perhaps not as obvious as it was, perhaps not as important, but still there.

I should say at this point that I doubt very much whether the young officer-cadet who spoke to my friend *was* a genuine public school boy, within the meaning of the act; if he had been, he wouldn't have said so; he wouldn't have needed to, and it wouldn't have occurred to him. If that seems to remove the point of the story, I must explain by defining what a public school boy is.

For the purpose of this book, he is a boy who has attended one of the Great Schools, or one of those slightly less famous boys' boarding schools modelled on them. There is a historical definition of which those Great Schools are, but in the present day they are Eton, Harrow, Rugby, Charterhouse, Winchester, Westminster, Shrewsbury, and ——. I leave the blank so that some readers can salve their social pride, and to save myself having to answer indignant correspondence. But it should be understood that there is only room for one more.

Beyond that inner circle, from which this book draws most but not all of its examples and case-histories, are round about twenty (thirty?) establishments which differ from the charmed circle only inasmuch as they don't belong to it; they are almost all boarding schools, with well-known names, substantial fees, traditions, etc., and only the charmed circle can say (or rather, make it plain without actually saying anything) that they don't quite belong in the same league. To the outside world they look virtually identical to the Great Schools – and in a way they are. Almost. They have the style, and only when they run into an Old Etonian is the difference properly apparent. (One way of identifying these schools is by their reaction if one of their old boys becomes Prime Minister; they will look satisfied about his achievement. When a boy from one of the Great Schools becomes P.M., no one takes a blind bit of notice.)

These, then, are the public schools proper – the small super-elite at the top, and then the larger group on the next tier, who frequently play the Great Schools at cricket. This is intended to be a realistic definition – in other words what most people mean when they talk about 'the public schools'. Technically, there are about 200 schools in the Headmasters'

Conference which are called public schools, but no one is going to pretend that Carlisle Grammar School (now defunct) was ever a public school in the same sense as Eton or Winchester, although it existed for centuries before any of the Great Schools was founded.

However, those thirty or forty top schools which I have defined as public schools proper, are not the end of the story. Beyond them there is a great body of minor public schools (to one of which I suspect the officer cadet belonged), great day schools, ancient local foundations, and private schools of one kind and another, most of them more or less in the mould of the big public schools, and of varying academic and social status. Some of the boys from these schools are virtually indistinguishable from those from the top thirty; others have no social pretensions whatever; still others, if they find an Old Harrovian in the same barrack-room, will try to get the bunk next to him. (The alumni of this last category are legion; when asked where they were educated, they will reply, with the insouciance of a rhino trying to waltz, 'Grockle's' or 'Bogborough', in a swift, defiant murmur as though they didn't want you to catch it, or hoped you would mistake it for something else. They tend to have a secret inferiority complex about Manchester Grammar School.)

The great day schools, incidentally, like Manchester G.S., and the merchant schools of Edinburgh, are in a sort of separate category from everyone else. One or two of them can truly be called public schools – Dulwich is the obvious example – but for the most part the simple fact of not being boarding schools sets them apart. It is worth noting, too, that there is a minute handful of boarding schools which are so exclusive and expensive that one seldom thinks of them as public schools at all, although they are. They seem to cater for the children of jet-set billionaires, oil sheikhs, and occasional royalty, and are frequently founded on progressive educational principles, rock-climbing, and good food, all of which disqualify them from our consideration.

So we are left with our top thirty–forty, by common-sense social definition, and a vast number of emulatory and like-minded establishments. In connection with which it is necessary to recall the passage in A.G. McDonnell's *England, Their England*, in which someone is praising the public schools, and the Major-General (who didn't go to one, being a prep-school-crammer-Sandhurst product) hastily interjects: 'Not only the public schools, but the public school *type*.' Our officer-cadet would have known exactly what he meant: all the privately-educated below the level of the real public schools may be considered, or consider themselves, the public school 'type' – it won't do them a bit of good socially, in those circles which really matter, but it is not unconnected with a great truth about the English public school mystique.

This is that its values, ideals, traditions, what can only be called its spirit, as well as its educational methods, have spread throughout our entire school system. This has happened principally because lesser schools have tried to emulate the great ones, but also because for the past century generations of British children, both boys and girls, have absorbed the public school myth – a myth in which there is a great deal of truth – from sources as diverse as Thomas Hughes and Kipling at one end of the scale and comics at the other; it might be make-believe for them to try to recreate it in their own local schools, but so far as they could, they did it, and their schools gave them every encouragement.

As a small boy I watched this process at first hand. I went to one school of unbelievable antiquity – officially it dated from only the twelfth century, but since its earlier records had been disposed of by waves of marauding Picts and Vikings, it is possible that those antiquarians who traced its origins to the arrival of Christianity may have been right. Naturally, its sense of tradition was immense, if largely unspoken, and any infant who wore its curious hollow-star symbol and distinctive colours was aware of a scholastic and cultural heritage which had survived siege and starvation by Robert the Bruce, to say nothing of late-comers like Cromwell. (It has gone now; what Bruce and centuries of raid and assault could not destroy has been killed almost overnight in the name of educational reform, but that's another matter.)

The point is that every year that old school would be invaded by scores of new scholarship boys from the local elementary schools, tough, belligerent, and frighteningly clever, and dyed-in-the-wool little reactionaries like myself would think, here's an end to traditional culture, the vandals are upon us. But not so; they came already steeped in the mystique of St Dominic's and Red Circle, they absorbed our rituals and hallowed, freakish customs, and the magic words of our cant, within hours they bellowed the school song (which characteristically was all about blood and defiance and the virtues of killing Scotsmen), they appointed themselves guardians of form and tradition – and never were more jealous custodians. They became so many Bob Cherrys in their assumption of public school ideals and attitudes, in their loyalty, team spirit, code of honour, and (even in our lowly backwater) snobbishness. It was only when they grew up and went, some of them, to Oxbridge that they discovered that the real thing was quite different. But for a time we too had dwelt on Big Side.

The school, as I have said, was partly responsible for this, but much of the credit, or blame, belonged to those fertile, anonymous writers for D.C. Thomson's tuppenny bloods, who with considerable skill (it is really worth studying as an exercise in social engineering) had adapted the world of Tom Brown's Rugby and Reed's Grandcourt to suit middle- and working-class children. The *Hotspur*'s Red Circle School was an amazing place, its boys sturdy, classless, decent young Britons of no recognizable background – one knew they weren't rich or upper class, because the occasional toff in their midst stuck out like a comic sore thumb. They played soccer – on one occasion, I recall, they tried rugby, and a philosophic debate whose niceties would have baffled Plato took place on the sporting ethics of kicking into touch – they had no homes or parents that one ever heard of, were financially illiterate, and behaved like hooligans. (My own belief is that Red Circle must have been either a fearfully expensive orphanage or a sort of fee-paying prep. school for Borstal.) But their code, their ideals, and their spirit were rock-hard in the Victorian tradition; there was just that hint of raffishness lurking somewhere to remind the discriminating that this was not quite the world of Hughes or the B.O.P.

If proof of this transmission of public school influence throughout our other schools is needed, consider the image of the school-master as depicted in even the lowliest comic papers in modern times. He wears a cap and gown – I question if one child in ten thousand in Britain over the past century has been taught by a man in a mortar-board, but there he is, and we know where he came from.

I am probably wrong, though, in speaking of this particular childhood influence as though it were still going on. I imagine that with the revision of educational values over the past twenty years, to say nothing of the arrival of the permissive society – and, to be quite honest, the deterioration in the standard of comic papers – it has probably decreased, possibly to vanishing point. Which some will mourn and others rejoice at.

But for better or worse, no one is going to dispute the overwhelming power which the public schools have exerted, and continue to exert, on our national life as a whole. For close on two centuries they have trained most of the men who ran (and run) our government, armed forces, civil service, church, law, commerce, and patronage; they have influenced virtually everything about our country – and, through the old Empire and the remaining Commonwealth, a sizeable part of the world as well. As I have tried to show, even the vast majority of Britons who never attended them have still been trained by their diffused lights and conditioned by their teaching.

Not all their bequests are as obvious as, say, their impact on Parliament and the army. Probably nobody on Liverpool's Kop or the terracing of Ibrox is aware that if it had not been for the boys of the Great Schools, who made the rules and taught the game to their fathers' employees, there would probably be no such thing as football; certainly not the game we know, which has run round the world like wild-fire. No World Cup, no Pele or Cruyff, no Match of the Day, no rioting in Barcelona (not for that reason, anyway). Football, of course, is of debatable importance in the destiny of mankind, but for what it is worth it provides an example of a human institution decisively shaped by the public schools. Whether the world should feel grateful to the muddied oafs who hacked and thundered across their Victorian meadows is beside the point.

For that matter, it is pointless at this stage to discuss whether the public schools have, on the whole, been a Good or a Bad Thing; it might make an interesting academic debate before it sank noisily in a morass of class prejudice, but it could reach no useful conclusion. Whether the schools have, or should have, a future is another matter, although it is not a question which is of primary concern in this book. Rather, it has seemed of interest to treat them as a peculiarly English phenomenon of great importance, past and present, and to try to examine them as a collective closed community, looking into their institutions, their history, their myth as opposed to (and as entwined with) their reality, their place in and relation to our society, their influence on their pupils and on the world outside, even the reasons for their existence. For there is nothing quite like them anywhere else, and they constitute a vital thread in our history, and, therefore, the world's.

Yet they are, and I hope I am using the word advisedly, something of a mystery to the public in general, and perhaps even to public schoolboys themselves. The phrase itself is evocative in so many different ways. 'Public school', as an informative comment in a board-room or mess, said in a casual, accepted way, speaks whole volumes; hear it in the mouth of a docker or labourer in a pub, usually with a slightly derisive grin, and you may be forgiven for feeling that a chord has been touched that would have rung responsively in the ear of Wat Tyler. Ask anyone in the land what he thinks 'public school' signifies, and you will get a different answer, and a catalogue of mixed truth and misinformation, political philosophy and misunderstanding, every time.

For instance, I have already attempted, rashly perhaps, a physical definition of the public schools. I doubt if it would find universal acceptance. And that is only the start. Consider again the pictures that 'public school' conjures up. A series of images occurs – small boys in Eton collars – stately buildings amidst immemorial elms – straw boaters – Bunter yelling 'Yarroo! Leggo, you beastly cads!' – Freddie Bartholomew getting his lumps from a gloating Flashman – stern, granite-faced Doctor So-and-so, in cap and gown, cane in hand, glowering at the trembling infant on the study carpet – fags burning toast – sex-starved adolescents indulging in unnatural vice – wastrel fifth-formers in the toils of unscrupulous bookies – singing of 'Forty Years On' – Twits of the Year sneering loftily at oicks – speech day with sunlight through stained glass – fist fights behind the fives courts – tuck-boxes and exeats – blotted letters home – footballs in the October dusk and the smell of cricket pitches and linseed oil . . . take your choice.

All the above, it may be noted, are straight out of public school fiction. They are also straight from public school fact. I remember, not long after I left school myself, being anxiously questioned by a mother whose twelve-year-old was shortly to be sent to a well-known public school; she obviously believed that it was tantamount to sending him to the galleys with his underwear clearly marked, that he would be beaten up, sexually assaulted, robbed, flogged, starved, and finally roasted over a fire. (Thank you, Thomas Hughes.) And yet the headmaster and matron had seemed very nice . . .

Of course I reassured her out of my scanty and imperfect knowledge. I had been a boarder at a big Scottish school, which is a far cry from the English article, but I knew quite enough to feel privately that her fears were not entirely unjustified. He would probably go through an initial experience which would be either mildly miserable or absolute hell, but he would settle down eventually and become reconciled to the place; he might even enjoy it. He would receive a good education, and valuable training – some of which I was shortly to appreciate myself, when I found myself in an army hut full of Durham gypsies and East End Londoners, and discovered that I was the only one who had the vaguest idea of how to make a bed, clean boots, look after my kit, discourage pilferers, and react promptly to a word of command. Those were, admittedly, special circumstances, but no doubt the advantages apply in most environments.

And there were other advantages which I did not need to tell her about, because she knew them already, and they were the reason she was sending the child away. She was getting him into the charmed circle, giving him the best possible start, ensuring him a place in the network, etc. That is the reason the public schools exist, resentfully tolerated by the masses (which are powerless to do anything about them anyway, unless they become Labour Cabinet Ministers, in which case they may well decide to send their sons to Winchester), and supported by an enthusiastic middle class who may not go to public schools – but are probably the public school *type*, and believe in freedom of educational choice anyway.

Is it worth it? Are the advantages worth the price which the child undoubtedly has to pay in being taken away from home? Obviously increasing numbers of people think the answer is 'yes', and as the quality of education in Britain sinks – as it undoubtedly has done – no doubt the waiting lists for the Great Schools and their adherents will become longer.

That being so, the essays in this book may be thought to have some relevance to the continuing debate on educational standards and the future of the British school system. They do not comprise a case for or against public schools – although any partisan should find plenty of ammunition in them. I would not expect the following random samples to pass unchallenged:

There is little reason to suppose that public school life does in fact breed homosexuals.

The patronising, effortless air of Wykehamists who (more than any other group) have brought this country to its knees by their foolish advice and policies ...

Excellent. Letters need not be addressed to the author of this introduction, but he would be delighted to see copies.

The policy has been to invite various respected writers with particular knowledge or experience to consider certain aspects of the public school system, past and present, in the belief that the whole will at least provide some insight into the world of the public school. It is not a work of history, although there is a good deal of history in it – how the system began, and its rise and dramatic development in the last century; the life of the Victorian schoolboy, and the discipline and custom under which he lived; the impetus his schools gave to sport, and its effect on the country and the schools themselves; the well-publicized, notorious institutions of fagging, bullying, punishment, ritual, and so on. But the attempt has been made to go beyond the history, and see the subject in a modern perspective. Thus, the place of the boy in his group society, the effect of his removal from parental to school care, are not matters which received more than superficial attention a century ago, but are of large significance today. Similarly, those unwritten laws of team spirit, group loyalty, and honour which governed school life can be looked at in a modern context, and the question asked: how much did they owe to reality, how much to legend, and are they still valid anyway?

Again, what has been the impact of the schools on public life, so far as it can be measured, and is it changing? What is the relationship between social class and academic achievement? How much has the great tide of school-story literature and lore revealed, how much concealed or distorted? How much have the schools themselves changed with the times, and how far have they preserved their traditional character and characteristics? (In this connection it is interesting to compare the reminiscences of two well-known ex-public schoolboys in modern times with the factual account of school life in the 1870s, and to listen to the slang of the modern

Etonian, with its archaic closed-community overtones.)

These are some of the subjects treated, and some of the questions raised, and it goes without saying that the treatment is not comprehensive, and that all the questions have not been answered. Some of them never will be, which is not to say that they will not be argued over with increasing vigour. There is scope and to spare for controversy, which one would expect from a collection of highly individual essays representing no common point of view; personally I disagree, with varying degrees of violence, with several passages by my fellow-contributors, but it would be a pretty worthless book on the public schools which produced any unanimity of opinion. Not all the writers are ex-public schoolboys – one of them is an ex-public schoolgirl, a necessary reminder that the preserve is not exclusively masculine.

But if there is no uniformity of view, perhaps there is just a hint of one common underlying tone – or maybe it is just an impression that comes from reading the essays as a whole. The point is made more than once, I think, that there is often a divergence between the point of view of the boy at school, and the man looking back in retrospect; an implication that men tend to forget, and that it is one thing to regard school from afar, and quite another to take a balanced view when Flashy has you by the neck. I don't think any contributor to this book can be accused of that insensitivity; while being in no position to speak for anyone but myself, I would guess that not one of them would willingly be translated back to the moment when, for the first time, he set out in his new blazer and squeaking shoes, his small stomach quailing as he approached that terrifying juvenile jungle, in the awful knowledge that home, mother, privacy, and familiar things – to say nothing of physical safety – were many miles and weeks away.

That possibly tells us something about the public boarding school system. I know I for one would not willingly face again the miserable dread of that first lonely walk from my housemaster's front door to the school itself, with my new woollen underwear hanging down below the level of my short trousers; it was raining, and strange, and a long way from home, and my drooping garments excited coarse comment. I knew then I couldn't face this alien, frightening world; I turned and ran – but only as far as a convenient bush, where I tore off those beastly drawers and hurled them into the River Kelvin with childish curses; they floated away, and my promises to my mother with them, and the next few years weren't bad at all.

But I know I was lucky; my acute unhappiness was over in a day or two, because I was at an unusually kindly and friendly school, in a small, close-knit house under the supervision of a magnificent housemaster and his wife. (For the record, I want to put his name down: John Coleman Smith, alias Coley, familiar to wartime Britain as the Indian Army voice which boomed out over the BBC each morning with his programme of PT exercises for the nation.)

From all that I have read and heard and seen in the years since, I honestly doubt whether most boys who are taken away to school, at an age when they would surely be happier at home, are quite so fortunate; for some, I'm sure, the initial unhappiness does not pass, and even when it does I wonder if the experience is, on balance, a good one. 'Many public schoolboys take an unconscionable time to grow up,' says one of the contributors to this book, and I believe he is absolutely right. Possibly they gain in other ways, but I wonder if the undoubted advantages of the system couldn't be achieved without the sacrifice of personality and individuality which I suspect the public schools often exact.

An easy, vague thing to say, and I have not the slightest notion how it could be done, or if it would be wise to try. Great, well-established, mysterious institutions like the weather, and Parliament, and the public schools tend to change, when they change at all, by unseen, gradual process, and I'm not sure that the public schools may not be the most permanent of the three. And one would be foolish to draw conclusions about a system which produced such extreme reactions as the following reflections by two English boys who became great English men, and who attended the same school, Rugby, within a few years of each other. The first, supposedly the 'Arthur' of *Tom Brown's Schooldays*, became Dean of Westminster; the other is a household name.

Most sincerely must I thank God for His goodness in placing me here to live with Arnold – *Arthur Penrhyn Stanley*

I cannot say that I look back on my life at a public school with any sensations of pleasure, or that any earthly considerations would induce me to go through my years there again – *Lewis Carroll*

I

Education of an Establishment

PAUL JOHNSON

The influence of the British public schools on national life is a subject clouded with emotions and mythology. It has always aroused high feelings. As long ago as 1810, reviewing a pamphlet entitled *Remarks on the System of Education in Public Schools*, the Rev. Sydney Smith, who had never forgotten his intense sufferings at Winchester, used the occasion to assail the readers of the *Edinburgh Review* with a comprehensive blast against the whole institution. He not only attacked its system of teaching and discipline but, in particular, hotly denied its claim to have produced Britain's great men: 'Great as the rage is, and long has been, for public schools, it is very remarkable that the most eminent men in every art and science have not been educated in public schools.' To prove his case, he listed a large number of non-public school men. Among poets, Spenser, Pope, Shakespeare, Butler, Rochester, Spratt, Parnell, Garth, Congreve, Gay, Swift, Thomson, Shenstone, Akenside, Goldsmith, Samuel Johnson, Beaumont and Fletcher, Ben Jonson, Sir Philip Sidney, Savage, Arbuthnot and Burns; among scientists, Newton, Maclaurin, Wallis, Flamsteed, Saunderson, Simpson and Napier; among historians, Clarendon, Hume and Robertson; among artists, Inigo Jones, Vanbrugh, Reynolds, Gainsborough and Garrick; among doctors, Harvey, Cheselden, Hunter, Jenner, Meade, Brown and Cullen; among philosophers, Bacon, Shaftesbury, Hobbes, Berkeley, Butler, Hume; among chemists, Priestley, Black and Humphry Davy; among generals, Marlborough, Wolfe and Clive; among lawyers, Coke, Hale and Hardwicke; among statesmen, Burghley, Walsingham, Strafford, Thurloe, Cromwell, Hampden, Ralegh, Russell, Temple, Burke, Sheridan and Pitt the Younger. He listed, indeed, a great many more famous characters, including Wolsey, More and Jeremy Taylor, and concluded that 'the English have done almost all that they have done in the arts and sciences, without the aid of that system of education to which they are now so much attached'. As a matter of fact, Smith, in his enthusiasm, was not always accurate. Thus, Sir Philip Sidney, whom he lists, was in fact at Shrewsbury, in the sixteenth century the most successful and famous public school in England; and Richard Brindsley Sheridan, who figures among his statesmen, was at Harrow, as Smith should have known. All the same, his list is formidable; and to it he might have added the men who, even as he wrote, were pushing through the first phase of the Industrial Revolution, none of whom went to public schools, and most of whom got their technical and scientific training at Dissenting Academies.

But despite Smith's disclaimer, the notion persisted, throughout the nineteenth century, that the public schools bred all Britain's talents; and the notion was constantly acquiring fresh testimonials, genuine or fraudulent. Thus, it was universally believed that the Duke of Wellington had said: 'The battle of Waterloo was won on the playing-fields of Eton.' True, the Duke had been to Eton, 1781–4, where one of his few recorded activities was beating up Sydney Smith's brother, 'Bobus' Smith. He did not like the school, declined later to contribute to its building fund and revisited it only when duty called. On one such occasion, in 1818, he noted a spot in the garden of the house where he had lodged. As there were no compulsory games in *his* Eton, he knew nothing of playing fields; but he did say, 'I really believe I owe my spirit of enterprise to the tricks I used to play in the garden.' In 1855, Montalembert, visiting Eton to gather material for a book about English politics, heard this anecdote, and presented it as '*C'est ici qu'a été gagné la bataille de Waterloo.*' This, in turn, was translated by Sir Edward Creasy, in *Eminent Etonians*, as 'There grows the stuff that won Waterloo.' In 1889, the story took final shape in Sir William Fraser's *Words on Wellington*, and has been repeated ever since.

But it is one thing to demolish mythology; quite another to form a just estimate of the influence the public schools have exerted, and still do exert, on public life. Before we can do so, a brief historical excursion is necessary. In the Middle Ages, very few members of the English ruling class attended school, public or private. Such places did, of course, exist. They were mainly attached to cathedral churches and minsters, which had foundations endowed for the training of choirboys and other clerical servitors, and whose schoolmasters and singing-masters were also allowed to earn money by taking fee-paying students. It is important to note that the charitable and the commercial have always been mixed, as we can see from the two great medieval school foundations, Winchester and Eton. William of Wykeham, the immensely rich Bishop of Winchester, founded Winchester College in 1382 as a new departure: a school with ten fellows, seventy pupils, a master and usher, with its own special buildings and separate endowment. It was an educational experiment on the grand scale. The boys, aged eight and upwards, were all to be *pauperes et indigentes*, and educated and maintained free, priority to be given (in this order) to founder's kin, then boys from the diocese, then those from parishes where the college owned property. *But*, provision was also made for accepting ten sons of noblemen and 'other worthy persons', as fee-paying boarders; and, almost immediately, other private fee-paying pupils of the master were admitted. Much the same story could be told of Eton College, founded by Henry VI in 1440, on roughly the same lines as Winchester, but on an even more ambitious scale. Again, there was provision for seventy poor scholars, drawn from parishes where the college had estates. They had to have an income of less than five marks a year (under £2). But in addition there were to be thirteen poor scholars, taught free in return for domestic services, and twenty fee-paying noblemen's sons – a number soon augmented.

All the same, few members of the medieval aristocracy and gentry were educated at Winchester and Eton. The normal form of training was in a large baronial household, or preferably a royal one. The staff of all baronial households included a grammar-master and a singing-master, attached to the castle chapel. So did the Chapel Royal, which had in addition a 'master of the henchmen', who taught the boys 'urbanity' and 'nurture'; how to ride, joust, wear harness (armour), speak and behave, the rules of precedence, manners and courtly conversation. At the establishment of the Prince of Wales, Edward IV's son, at Ludlow Castle, his tutor, Bishop Alcock, who also founded Jesus College, Cambridge, laid down that the Prince and other boys there should be taught 'in grammar, music and other cunning, and exercises of humanity, according to their births and ages'. Such castle and court chapels were the true public schools of the Middle Ages.

The elements of the modern system began to emerge in the fifteenth century, though curiously enough not in the collegiate foundations but in the Common Law Inns of Court, growing up just to the west of Temple Gate. Baronial and royal courts could not supply legal training; the Inns did; and landowning families turned increasingly to them to train their sons in professional skills as well as to round off their general education. Writing in about 1470, Sir John Fortescue, in his *De Laudibus Legum Angliae*, noted that at all the Inns, 'there is besides a school of law, a kind of academy of all the manners that the nobles learn. There they learn to sing and to exercise themselves in every kind of harmonies. They are also taught there to practise dancing and all games proper for nobles, as those brought up in the king's household are accustomed to practise . . . So for the sake of the acquisition of virtue . . . knights, barons and other magnates . . . place their sons at these Inns, although they do not desire them to be trained in the science of the laws, nor to live by its practice, but only by their patrimonies.' This custom spread. By about 1500 there were over 300 students at the Inns, which, in their courtly masques and amusements, gave birth to the Shakespearean drama. Sir Christopher Hatton, one of Queen Elizabeth's Lord Chancellors, said that since he was a youngster at an Inn the number of students had more than doubled, and from Elizabeth's time to the beginning of the Civil War, over 1000 members of the English ruling classes were, at any one time, receiving their indoctrination in the conventional wisdom at the London Inns. If we examine, for instance, the list of members of Queen Elizabeth's Privy Council (the nearest equivalent to a modern cabinet) in, say, 1580, we find that none went to colleges like Winchester and Eton, about half went to Oxford or Cambridge colleges, and virtually all attended an Inn for a year or more.

Yet with the decline of baronial households, the gentry and aristocracy felt an increasing need for institutions which provided basic academic education for their sons. Lord Burghley, as Treasurer and Master of the

Court of Wards, ran the last of the courtly household schools, for such scions as the Earl of Essex and the Earl of Oxford; after he died, in the 1590s, there was no real successor. The rich were already ousting the poor from Oxford and Cambridge. Professor Lawrence Stone ('The educational revolution in England, 1560–1640', *Past and Present*, xxviii, 1964) calculates that in the period 1575–1639, 50% of Oxford students were the sons of gentry; while W. Prest ('Legal education of the gentry at the Inns of Court', *Past and Present*, xxxviii, 1967) shows that as many as 80% of the places at the Inns, especially in the period 1610–40, were occupied by sons of landed aristocrats and gentlemen.

But the take-over of college and grammar schools was also beginning. Eton, Winchester and, from about 1640, Westminster appear to have constituted an upper tier of schools especially favoured by the ruling class. Then came the Merchant Taylors' and Shrewsbury, which at times had as many as 400 boys, followed by a number of grammar schools in large towns, with 100–150 boys. By the seventeenth century, most of these schools numbered the sons of gentry among their pupils. The process, indeed, aroused critical comment, especially at the universities. Writing in 1577, the topographer William Harrison noted 'the poor men's children are commonly shut out, and the richer sort received (who in time past thought it dishonour to live as it were upon alms) . . . Beside this, being for the most part either gentlemen or rich men's sons, they oft bring the universities into much slander. For, standing upon their reputation and liberty, they ruffle and roister it out, exceeding in apparel and haunting riotous company.' But it is important to realize that neither universities, nor collegiate or grammar schools, had ever taught children of the labouring poor, except in rare cases. The bulk of these schools were three-tiered, socially: a sprinkling of gentry at the top, a few 'poor scholars' at the bottom, and the bulk being formed by the sons of the middle class – prosperous tradesmen, merchants and shopkeepers, and substantial yeoman farmers – most of whom paid fees. Until the Civil War, the system appears to have worked well; there was a growing spread of literacy in England, and both grammar schools and the universities they fed expanded in numbers until they reached levels not again to be attained until the late nineteenth century.

With the Civil Wars and their aftermath, however, we entered a new phase of educational development, which saw the birth of the public school system as we know it. The Inns of Court ceased to be academies of gentlemen, and became virtually confined to the training of professional lawyers. At Oxford and Cambridge, the Anglican monopoly, the barring of Dissenters, and the exclusive concentration on a Latinized education led to a rapid falling off in numbers, and a long period of supine repose. Among the right-thinking members of the ruling class, however, the Oxbridge college appeared increasingly as the ideal establishment for rounding off the education of their sons. Hence they became its chief patrons, and Oxbridge activities in the eighteenth century were virtually confined to training state clergy and acting as a finishing school for the aristocracy and gentry. The grammar school, too, suffered, not least from a prevailing view among the ruling class that the civil commotions themselves had been caused by too much curiosity and book learning among the subordinate orders, and that literacy, at any rate among the poor, was a danger to stability and property. The Earl of Newcastle, echoing the conventional wisdom, warned Charles II: 'The Bible under every weaver and chambermaid's arm hath done us much hurt . . . the universities abound with too many scholars. . . . But that which hath done most hurt is the abundance of grammar schools and Inns of Court.'

Hence, in the eighteenth century, the great public educational foundations, both schools and colleges, became effectively limited to the scions of the upper and upper-middle classes. The corporations which ran them conducted their affairs in great secrecy, and with little or no regard to the general interest. Most town grammar schools shrank in size; some fell into almost total decay. The gentry and the aristocracy tended to send their sons elsewhere; or to have them privately educated by tutors, a tendency which persisted until the mid-nineteenth century. But among the old foundations, a few were still patronized by the great, and so began to stand out from the rest. Eton and Winchester never completely lost their reputation, though from 1660–1760 Westminster had the most *réclame*. In the eighteenth century, its King's Scholars were vastly outnumbered by fee-paying boys, and from among these it produced many illustrious statesmen, admirals, bishops and other ruling potentates.

Eton, however, remained the biggest, and at most periods could claim to be the country's leading school. Its numbers fluctuated from 425 (1720) to 244 (1745), 483 (1766) to 230 (1773). But the aristocratic element became very marked. In the upper school list of 1745, sons of noblemen, referred to as 'Mr', and baronets were differentiated from commoners; and of the 483 boys in 1766, fifty were noblemen, noblemen's sons, or baronets. The college's scholars fell in status, as for all practical purposes they were separated from fee-paying boys, who lived in comfortable town 'houses', and who did not have to share the spartan horrors of 'Long Chamber'. Indeed, the number of scholars often fell short of the seventy provided for in the college statutes. Aristocratic Eton proselytized. Thus, Harrow, founded as a local grammar school by John Lyon in 1571, under a succession of three Etonian headmasters, gradually superseded Westminster as London's most fashionable school, and built up a formidable aristocratic connection. This was not, strictly speaking, illegal, since – as in other foundations – the statutes allowed the trustees to admit fee-paying pupils at their discretion. But the intentions of the founder were clearly frustrated by a deliberate policy, for by the end of the eighteenth century Harrow had as many boys as Eton, but none was from the parish, educated free. Here, then, was a case of an old foundation purposefully transforming itself from a local institution into what was now known as a 'great school' (and, soon, 'public school').

These 'great schools' provided the smattering of classical education which distinguished House of Commons speeches in the last decades of the eighteenth century – what might be termed the unreformed House of Commons in its golden age. Perhaps half the leading statesmen of the period 1720–1832 went to one or other of the seven leading public schools (Eton, Harrow, Westminster, Winchester, Christ's Hospital, Shrewsbury and Charterhouse). Etonians included Bolingbroke, Fox, Pitt the Elder, Canning, Grenville, Grey, Walpole, Melbourne, Wellington and Durham. Among Harrovians were Palmerston, Sheridan, Peel and Spencer Percival. The mould was strengthened by the fact that so many leading M.P.s had been to Oxbridge, and especially to King's and Trinity Cambridge, and Christ Church Oxford; but it is important not to exaggerate the monopoly of the 'great schools'.

Thus, if we look at the composition of Lord Liverpool's cabinet of 1812, generally regarded as a phalanx of reaction, and a stern upholder of property rights and the 'ancient constitution', we find a mixed picture. Of thirteen cabinet members, Lord Liverpool himself and the Earl of Westmorland went to Charterhouse; Lord Mulgrave was at Eton; the Earl of Buckinghamshire went to Westminster; but these were the only representatives of 'great schools'. Lord Sidmouth (the former Addington) went to Canterbury Grammar School; Lord Eldon, a self-made lawyer, went to a local school in the North-East; while Nicholas Vansittart, the Earl of Harrowby, Viscount Castlereagh, C. Bragge-Bathhurst and Lord Camden were all educated privately. This last category meant either instruction by tutors living in the household or (sometimes in addition) residence in a clerical household which provided tuition for a small number of boys. This private pattern of education continued to be favoured by a large proportion of the ruling class until well into the nineteenth century, the reason being, usually, that the 'great schools' were thought to be violent and brutal places, where bad habits such as drink, gaming, borrowing and whoring were easily acquired.

Certainly they were violent. Eton had a number of 'rebellions', especially in 1768. Winchester had five rebellions in the period 1770–1818. There were also riots at Harrow, notably in 1771, and at Charterhouse, Shrewsbury, Merchant Taylors' and Rugby. On occasions troops (and at Eton the Brigade of Guards) had to be called in to overawe the boys. Thus in 1812 there was still a good deal of aristocratic prejudice against the public schools, to balance the common assumption, deplored by Sydney Smith, that they produced all the great men.

Gradually this prejudice was overcome, as the public schools, like virtually every other institution in Britain, underwent the process of nineteenth-century reform. The great age of the public schools, the period when they had their fullest impact on public life, was from 1832–1914, when virtually everyone concerned with the government of the country, whether statesmen, civil servants, senior clergy, the judiciary, the armed services, higher education or the learned professions, was drawn from their *alumni*. This historical phenomenon, which had no parallel in any other country, was the work not of any deliberate policy or series of decisions – there was no 'public school conspiracy' – nor even, to a great extent, of economic factors, but of a comparatively small group of professional pedagogues.

We have seen how ex-Etonian headmasters raised up Harrow socially.

The process operated elsewhere; indeed, public schools of a certain type and standard 'exported' themselves in exactly the same way as the early medieval monasteries. Thus Rugby, a local grammar school founded in 1567 by a grocer who had had a big success in London, owed its rise in the social scale not merely to the increase in value of the London properties which formed its chief endowment, but more particularly to the appointment of a headmaster with Eton experience; thus, by 1780, it had become a fashionable boarding school. In turn, Shrewsbury, another decaying grammar school, was proselytized by a Rugby master, and raised in the social scale. But a rise in the social scale almost inevitably produced (and to some extent was explained by) a steady rise in academic standards – it is another myth that Dr Arnold rescued Rugby from total eclipse. Able eighteenth-century headmasters also resuscitated two other old foundations, Christ's Hospital (founded 1552) and Charterhouse (1611), which differed from the others in that they were specifically created to cater for the needs of the children of 'needy' gentry, though admitting fee-payers. As standards improved, the 'needy' element was largely forgotten.

All these schools flourished primarily because they were well run and well staffed. Other schools with similar origins declined, for want of able heads. In the period 1770–1810, when the population of the city more than doubled, Manchester Grammar School's pupils shrank from 548 to 288, and the number it sent to Oxbridge fell from sixty-seven to twenty-nine (for each decade). A number of other large town schools also declined, during a period when *per capita* wealth and total population were rising fast. Some disappeared completely. When Samuel Butler became headmaster of Shrewsbury in 1798, it was on its last legs. There were only eighteen boys in the school. Butler was a powerful opponent of educational reform, and a man who believed strongly in strengthening the nexus between the ruling class and the public school; but he was also a formidable teacher and educational administrator, and by 1817 he had 130 boys at the school, a third of them, be it noted, free scholars on the foundation.

In short, though there was a distinct tendency for the upper classes to patronize the public schools because they were increasingly exclusive, and though there was a parallel tendency of the public schools to inculcate ruling class assumptions in order to increase this connection, the chief factor in the success of these schools was the quality of their training. In the first half of the nineteenth century, the public schools expanded, while their academic rivals, the Dissenting Academies, began to decline. The revival of academic standards at Oxbridge in the 1820s and 1830s obviously helped, for the public schools were the main, often the sole, channel of entry to most colleges. Not that public school academic standards were particularly high. The Royal Commission headed by Lord Clarendon, which was appointed in 1861 to inquire into nine schools (Winchester, Westminster, Eton, Charterhouse, Harrow, Rugby, Shrewsbury, St Paul's and Merchant Taylors'), and which reported in 1864, found much to criticize on the teaching side, especially as regards the lack of modern studies. Three years later, when reforms were under way, John Stuart Mill, making his inaugural address as Rector of St Andrews, sneered: 'Youths come to the Scottish universities ignorant, and are there taught. The majority of those who come to the English universities come still more ignorant, and ignorant they go away.'

But the schools were admired for the kind of boy they produced, and their numbers increased steadily. With an expanding market, taking in more and more entrants from the new middle classes, new schools were needed. All of them were based on the pattern set by the 'great schools', and after the 1830s were especially influenced by the methods of Arnold at Rugby. The attempt to create 'speciality' schools generally failed. Wellington, opened in 1856 as a memorial to the Duke of Wellington, was intended for the poor orphans of army officers. Its boys wore a German-style cadet uniform, designed by Prince Albert; but this was quietly abandoned after the school's first Vice-President, the Earl of Derby, then Prime Minister, arrived at the station to visit the school, and handed his ticket to the Head Boy, under the impression that he was a railway official! Within a decade, Wellington was a public school like the rest.

Some of the new schools made no bones about the fact that they were selling social class; thus Cheltenham and Malvern called themselves 'places of education for the sons of gentlemen'. But, as Bulwer Lytton pointed out in *England and the English* (1833), parents who sent their children to public schools in the hope of making useful connections ignored the fact that the overwhelming majority of boys were from middle-class homes anyway. One or two schools strove hard for educational change. Uppingham was transformed, after 1853, from a small grammar school into a go-ahead public school, by the efforts of Edward Thring, who introduced a modern curriculum with a special stress on the teaching of English and music; he also built the first school gymnasium in England. A number of institutions were created by Canon Woodard to bridge social divisions, or, more precisely, to cater for them separately; thus Lancing, which opened its doors in 1848, had two classes of pupils, who paid different fees, and used different halls (but the same chapel).

Rugby, with its Evangelical flavour, its stress on religion and godliness, epitomized the public-school movement in the Victorian apogee, 1840–70. Its boys, wrote Dr Moberly of Winchester admiringly, were noted for being 'thoughtful, manly-minded, conscious of duty and obligation'. Its very high tone ('On, to the bounds of the waste/On, to the City of God') was epitomized by Matthew Arnold's magnificent poem, 'Rugby Chapel', written in memory of his father. Rugbeians went on to become civil service reformers, earnest clergymen, campaigning lawyers, schoolmasters or, like Matthew Arnold himself, school-inspectors, thus helping to permeate the lower regions of the educational system – now expanding rapidly as a state enterprise – with Arnold's principles. The point was well made by William Temple, later Archbishop of Canterbury, son of a Rugby headmaster and a devoted Rugbeian himself: 'The great glory of Rugby is not the brilliancy of its results – it has few cabinet ministers and so on – but the incomparably high level of usefulness reached by its average products. Eton will produce, say, two or three Viceroys; Rugby will produce twenty or thirty first-class provincial administrators.'

With the 1870s, the system changed again. The notion of the nine 'great schools' aroused resentment among the excluded establishments, now numbered in scores, and the result was the establishment of the Headmasters' Conference, and the notion of a 'Headmasters' Conference School'. Following the report of the Clarendon Commission, and the subsequent Act of 1868, the opening of foundation scholarships to competitive examination strengthened the definition of schools as upper-class preserves. But, at the same time, more and more schools were included in the category, since the Age of Imperialism, from the 1880s to 1914, demanded vastly increased quantities of young men who could be described as a 'public-school product'. The introduction of school uniforms, the spread of compulsory competitive games, the growing emphasis on 'character training', and the influence of armed service and civil service standard exams, led to far greater emphasis on uniformity, both within schools, and between them.

Eton, as the largest, produced by far the greatest number of imperial administrators. Its connection with Westminster and Whitehall was very close. In 1878, it was only natural for the young George Nathaniel Curzon, President of the Eton Literary Society, to invite Mr Gladstone to address it on the subject of Homer, and for the Grand Old Man, shortly to become Prime Minister for the second time, to accept ('He said he considered himself bound to do anything for Eton'). Gladstone returned there on other occasions, on one of which he was shocked to observe the picture of a racehorse on the walls of Pop, the Eton Society of older, privileged boys; as a result, in 1894, when handing over Number 10, on completing his fourth period of office as Prime Minister, to Lord Rosebery, another Old Etonian, he begged him 'to address the college authorities on the current depravity of the school'.

Curzon and Rosebery, indeed, might be described as the quintessential figures of the Eton power-connection during its golden age – what was to be described, by an outsider cabinet minister, Iain MacLeod, seventy years later as 'the magic circle'. Curzon, claimed Sir George Sitwell, father of Osbert, Edith and Sacheverell, showed more skill and persistence at cribbing than any other schoolboy of the day. At any rate, he won more prizes during his five years at Eton than anyone in the whole history of the school – and afterwards went on to be Viceroy of India. Before he left to take up this post, in 1898, Lord Rosebery made a speech at a private dinner of Etonians, held also to celebrate the appointment of the Earl of Minto as Governor-General of Canada and of the Rev. J.E.C. Welldon as Bishop of Calcutta. 'What,' he asked, 'would Canada have done without Eton, when out of the last six Viceroys all but one are Etonians?' 'Our Alma Mater,' he continued, went on 'turning out the men who govern the empire almost, as it were, unconsciously'. The Etonians present, he concluded, were 'sending out three eminent men on three vitally important missions to different parts of the empire'. It was a 'stewardship nobly undertaken and triumphantly achieved, one which has helped to weld the Empire . . . to add to the glory and the credit of our mother Eton'.

But to most of the Etonian output, however (and still more to that of other public schools), life after school meant more humble jobs lower down the administrative ladder. The *Eton Boating Song*, the school song, is not a vainglorious but an emotional, almost a sentimental ditty. William Cory, the Eton master who wrote it in 1863, had in mind not cabinet ministers and viceroys, but subalterns and District Officers. Wandering on the Eton river one night, 'I thought of young men quartered in Indian hill-forts, droning in twos, or singly through a steaming night, miserably remembering their last row at Eton, pining and craving for lost youthfulness.' The extent to which the school connection helped the careers of such men is impossible to discover. It was probably of marginal importance only. Even in the Age of Imperialism, men became ministers and proconsuls largely through a combination of family connections and ability rather than by virtue of their Alma Mater. An Eton friendship or acquaintanceship might even be a handicap. When Curzon won the Prince Consort's French Prize in 1874, he helped to eclipse the performance of one St John Broderick, who had won it the year before. Thirty years later, Broderick, as Secretary of State for India, helped to secure Curzon's angry resignation as Viceroy, in circumstances which belied their apparent friendship, and which have never been satisfactorily explained. A long-sustained jealousy? Who can say?

Broderick was a member of A.J. Balfour's cabinet of 1902, which perhaps could be said to mark the apogee of the public-school dominance in British politics. Besides Broderick, Balfour himself, Lord Londonderry, Akers-Douglas, the Marquess of Landsdowne, Lord Balfour of Burleigh, George Wyndham, Gerald Balfour and Lord Windsor had also been to Eton. Lord Halsbury and the Duke of Devonshire had been educated privately, as had Lord Ashborne. Lord George Hamilton and Walter Long had been to Harrow; the Earl of Selborne to Winchester; R.W. Hanbury and Austen Chamberlain to Rugby; Lord James of Hereford to Cheltenham; and even C.T. Ritchie and Joe Chamberlain, who represented the commercial middle class, had been to the City of London School and University College School, both of public-school status. Virtually the entire governing group were products of the system.

Six years later, in 1908, when Asquith formed his first government, the public school grip on the cabinet was by no means so secure. The Prime Minister, like Ritchie, had been to the City of London School. In Lord

Tweedmouth, the Earl of Crewe and Winston S. Churchill there were three Harrovians. Herbert Gladstone, Lewis Harcourt and Lord Carrington had been to Eton, Sir Edward Grey to Winchester, Sydney Buxton to Clifton, Lord Loreburn and John Morley to Cheltenham. R.B. Haldane and John Sinclair, both from Edinburgh Academy, were products of the Scottish version of an English day school of public school standard. The Marquess of Ripon, educated by private tutors, represented an older aristocratic custom. But H.H. Fowler came from Southward Grammar School, Augustine Birrell from Amersham Hall, Walter Runciman from South Shields High School, and David Lloyd George from a church elementary school. John Burns, to complete the cabinet of twenty, had left school for work at the age of ten.

A decade before, Cecil Reddie, headmaster of Abbotsholme, a new type of progressive public school, had given evidence to a Royal Commission that Britain needed a three-tier system: 'the school for the Briton who will be one of the muscle workers . . . the school for the Briton whose work requires knowledge of the modern world . . . the school for the Briton who is to be a leader.' He further added that the respective leaving-ages should be fourteen, sixteen and eighteen. In a sense, that is the system which Britain has operated for the first three-quarters of the twentieth century – an elite of public schools, a leavening of independent grammar schools, and a mass of state schools. But political power is no longer the monopoly of the products of the top tier.

The historical process which has eroded the dominance of the public school product in the political field has been a very gradual one, and on the whole has come about more in consequence of other social and economic changes than as a result of deliberate policy. In 1944, to be sure, the Fleming Report on the public schools recommended that at least 25% of places should be set aside in these establishments for children from grant-aided primary schools, and their fees paid from public funds. Virtually nothing came of this proposal. The 1964–70 Labour Government set up a Public Schools Commission, whose first report appeared in 1968, and whose second, on independent day schools and direct-grant schools, was issued in 1970. It found, not surprisingly, that in all three categories of fee-paying schools 'their activities are based on the assumptions and aspirations of the British middle class, from which their pupils come and upon which their fees depend'. But the Commission has not, so far, been able to accomplish any change in the system by executive action. In terms of numbers and wealth, the British public schools have enjoyed a period of steady prosperity over the last thirty years.

What has changed, rather, is the greater liberty of access that non-public school boys, and increasingly girls, enjoy to parliament, the higher civil service, the judiciary, the command of the armed forces, and to positions of power and influence generally. The public schools, it can be said, have formed an effective rearguard or delaying action. Howard Glennerster and Richard Pryke, in *The Public Schools* (London 1964), produced some interesting figures of the percentage of places in certain bodies occupied by public-school products:

Conservative Cabinet (1964)	87%
Judges (1956)	76%
Conservative M.P.s (1964)	76%
Ambassadors (1953)	70%
Lieutenant-Generals and above (1953)	70%
Bishops (1953)	66%
Top execs. in 100 top firms (1963)	64%
Civil Servants above Ass. Sec. (1950)	59%
All City directors (1958)	47%
Labour Cabinet (1964)	35%

As we approach the 1980s, the percentage in every case is around or below the 50-mark. Present evidence suggests that, for the foreseeable future, the public schools will continue to make a significant contribution to public life, especially in the House of Commons, but that it is most improbable they will ever secure again the position of dominance they held until 1914 or even until 1945. A glance at the cabinet formed by Jim Callaghan in April 1976 gives an indication of the way things are moving. Of its twenty-three members, only three went to establishments classified as public schools by any criteria: Shirley Williams, from St Paul's Girls' School; John Silkin, from Dulwich College; and Anthony Benn, from Westminster, though his entry in *Who's Who* carefully omits this fact. No less than seven members of the cabinet went to grammar schools, ranging from fully-independent to non-fee-paying. Six went to fee-paying day schools, some of a special nature. Seven went to standard state day schools.

The pattern is varied, as varied indeed as our multifarious secondary school education system itself. What is significant is that the public-school element, which made up half of Attlee's 1945–50 government, and over a third of Harold Wilson's 1964 government, is now in a tiny minority. It is almost inconceivable that the public schools will ever again produce more than two or three members of a Labour government; and quite possible that they will fail to produce a majority in future Conservative governments – the trend is already there in Conservative shadow-cabinets.

Very likely the significance of this change has been exaggerated, just as, once, the importance of the public school influence was taken too seriously. Baldwin used to say he was always scheming to get more Harrovians into his cabinet; but this was an affectation to conceal more devious cogitations – indeed, the outstanding man he excluded in the 1930s, Winston Churchill, *was* a Harrovian. Even in 1902, when the public school tradition was paramount, it is likely that Arthur Balfour, in selecting his cabinet and allocating offices, was guided more by political and party considerations, and ramifying family relationships, than by any academic ties. The supposed influence of the public schools on our national life, especially in the period 1832–1914, was more a reflection of the cohesion and strength of the British landowning and commercial classes than of any intrinsic power in the spirit of Alma Mater. Equally, the decline of this influence since 1945 is merely one consequence of the progressive disintegration of our traditional ruling class.

Paul Johnson (Stonyhurst) is the author of many non-fiction books including *The Offshore Islanders, A History of Christianity* and *Enemies of Society*.

2

A Day in the Growth of Brown Minor

DAVID HOLLOWAY

It is some time in the late 1870s. The reforms outlined in the Reports of the Public Schools Commission of 1861 have been carried out in part, and so have the provisions of the various follow-up statutes of the late 1860s and early 1870s. The public schools, old and new foundations, are flourishing. The 'bad old days' of bullying and flogging are said to be over. The enlightened disciples of Dr Arnold hold headmasterships and there is no likelihood of another schoolboy rebellion like the one at Winchester only a decade ago. The old boys regard the new generation as 'softies'.

Softies? Well . . .

The time is exactly 6.30 a.m. The servant in College at Eton is calling out the time. The bell is ringing in the houses at Rugby, and the fags at Winchester are being called. A quarter of an hour later the bells will be ringing at Harrow and Charterhouse while the lie-abeds at Westminster and Shrewsbury have till 7 a.m. before the rousing shouts and bells are heard. Although the timings are slightly different, what happens then is much the same and does not need particularizing. Almost everywhere fags will be lighting fires and fetching hot water to fill the basins for their seniors who are still lolling in bed. At some schools fags will be cleaning their seniors' boots while at others they will merely be distributing the work done by the bootboys. Apart from Winchester, where the collegers sleep eight to a room, most of the boys at the older public schools will have the modified privacy of a cubicle, a study or a room, some even with their own basins. Where there is no provision for private ablutions, all boys will have to queue in front of what is called at Shrewsbury 'the swill', a long pipe with water gushing from it at various points, thus providing a quick and generally dampening wash. Everywhere there will have been a rush – stiff collars to contend with and lace-up boots. Most establishments will provide no early morning sustenance, though at Charterhouse the boys that are up in time may grab some milk and biscuits as they pass on the way to chapel.

At Winchester the first lesson is beginning at 7 a.m., where the whole school will be spending an hour studying or reciting the Old and New Testaments. At Eton in summer school will also have begun at seven but in the winter the first lesson will start thirty minutes later. At this school if there is to be an examination those taking part will have been allowed a cup of coffee before they start writing at 7.30. At Rugby the day begins with chapel at seven, as it will at 7.30 at Charterhouse and 7.45 at Westminster and Shrewsbury. Everywhere there will be a first lesson before breakfast, which will come somewhere between 8.30 and 9. How the meal will be taken will vary: the members of a House may all eat together in the dining hall or the sixth form, the monitors, the praeposters, the First Eleven 'Colours', or whatever the hierarchy of the particular establishment may consist of, may eat in a separate room or in their studies or common rooms. Whatever happens the fags, perhaps only boys in their first term but more likely those in their first year, will be in attendance. Sometimes the service will be personal with the fag making the toast and boiling the eggs for the senior who is his 'master', while at others (Eton and Rugby among them) there will be the rougher justice of the 'fag-call'. When the 'master' shouts all the fags in earshot – and there must be a jolly good reason for them not being within range – will have to answer the call, the last to arrive being given the task. The lucky ones will have to stand in line until they are dismissed.

In other schools a pecking order may exist. At Winchester, for instance, fags do not have to make toast for others at breakfast time, but the right to stand in front of the fire in the dining hall in order to hold out bread to be toasted will depend entirely on seniority in the school, so that juniors may have to wait twenty minutes while older boys dawdle in front of the fire, browning an extra slice of bread. Generally speaking breakfast will consist of tea or coffee (at Winchester only seniors will get tea) and bread and butter. Sometimes there will be cold meats as well, though in most places luxuries like jam and marmalade will come from tuck boxes supplied from home.

At nine, or a little later, school will begin again, or, for those schools where there has been no early morning chapel, a service will be held for everyone. This will be the most ceremonial occasion of the day. At Eton, for instance, the Queen's Scholars will march in in order of seniority. Almost everywhere the school prefects (or whatever they are called) will have taken some form of roll call to make sure that there is a full attendance. At some schools the prefect of the day (let off normal schooling so that he can fulfil his administrative duties) will have to spend the rest of the morning going round the boarding houses finding out the reasons for absence.

Everywhere there will be school until about midday, usually with a fairly short break in the middle of the morning. Fags will have carried their seniors' books to school from the boarding houses and will be ready to carry them back at the end of the day. At Rugby and the newer schools there will be the luxury of purpose-built form rooms, while those in older buildings will have to make do with the old method whereby everything happens in the big school hall and different teaching groups (sets, divisions, years) are at best divided from each other by a curtain. Each form has its own particular bit of hall, hence when later forms were given names the term 'shell' came to be used. This came from the fact that one set of boys at Westminster was taught at one end of the school hall that was shaped rather like a shell. The noise of mass instruction cannot help concentration and a master who has difficulty in keeping order and has a rowdy set of pupils can disrupt the whole school.

The curriculum is primarily classical, though the old boys are complaining that too many new-fangled subjects are being taught. At most places boys will still be called on to recite the lesson that they have learnt the night before, to construe Latin and Greek authors (translate them into English) and to write prose or verse in the ancient tongues. In general it can be said that two hours out of every three spent in morning school will be devoted to classics while one hour before dinner will go to Mathematics, Science or Modern Languages (French normally, though the progressive Harrow offers German as an alternative). On the days when there is afternoon school (we shall come to this later) roughly the same pattern of two-thirds classics to one-third modern subjects will obtain.

Generally speaking Mathematics, consisting chiefly of Geometry (the learning of Euclidean theorems by heart), will occupy three hours a week in school and three hours in preparation in the evening. Science will be a compulsory subject in only half the public schools and of the hundred and twenty-eight that are operating only thirteen will have laboratories of any sort (at Rugby these were at first in a small cloak room) and only eighteen more will have apparatus of any kind. Under the general heading of Science will come demonstrations of the elementary laws of physics plus some geology and astronomy. Where Science does not form part of the curriculum, there may well be lectures from visiting scientific speakers three or four times a year. Some of the boys of the 1870s are lucky for they are supplied with actual scientific textbooks which have just been published. They and (since Science is not a usual subject of study at the universities) their classically trained instructors have a more solid basis for learning the subject than ever before. French and German are not taught for conversational purposes but are studied, like Latin and Greek, for their grammatical structure, and texts for translation are not chosen for their literary value. In many places French will be dropped in the Sixth Forms so that those going to universities can concentrate on classics.

English literature is not taught at all in school, though in many places there will be a Shakespeare Society, often confined to senior boys, which will study the plays as a spare-time activity. Boys will, however, be expected to write correct English in their compositions on classical subjects and in their translations. History will form part of classical and religious instruction and therefore for the most part be confined to Ancient Times. Similarly Geography will not be considered as a separate subject, though map drawing, to illustrate the events described in Xenophon, Thucydides, Sallust and Livy, will be expected. The work of the drawing master, where he exists, will be largely concerned in ensuring neatness and exactness in map preparation.

The composition of each form is first decided by the entrance examination or a test set on arrival at the school. Later progress up the school will be determined by performance in termly and yearly examinations. In each form there will be a rigid order of seniority according to performance. Only Mathematics is regarded as a subject to be taught by a specialist; otherwise the day's instruction will largely be in the hands of one master. Although discipline is maintained if necessary with the cane, not only for inattention but for failure to supply an answer, the system of reciting a lesson and standing up to construe means that only a proportion of the group is actively involved at any one moment, so, if control is at all slack, there is plenty of time for gossip, the playing of noughts and crosses (sometimes on permanent boards cut into desk tops), the twanging of elastic bands stretched along a form and even, for the very daring, the introduction of animals (cockroaches and mice) to scuttle across the schoolroom floor.

During morning school the monitor of the day will tour the school with the punishment list. His purpose will be two-fold: he will be reading out the names of those to be beaten, or to see the headmaster for a rebuke, that day, and he will be collecting the names of sinners for future punishment. How this punishment will be inflicted will vary from school to school. At Eton there is still a punishment room and the birch is wielded while the victim is held by two of his peers. At Westminster minor offences are dealt with summarily by a birch on the back of the hand, while major public floggings (not all that frequent) are carried out in the school's traditional way with the boy being 'horsed' (hoisted on the back of another). And so on.

At midday, morning school will be over and all boys will have something like a couple of hours for playing games. In the winter these will largely consist of scratch games of football of some form or another, in the summer of cricket. In the spring term there will be gymnastics, athletics of some sort, fives (handball) and racquets. All boys will be expected to take part though enthusiasm is not necessarily demanded.

Dinner, the main meal of the day, is served at 2 p.m. or thereabouts. Sometimes the whole House will sit down together. Elsewhere the juniors may eat before the seniors. There will be a brief Latin grace and then a two-course meal, soup or pudding and meat. Harrow prides itself on offering a choice of meat. Winchester equally prides itself on serving only mutton to its scholars on four days a week. After the meal is finished, the activities vary according to the day of the week. Not all schools are the same, of course, but the general custom is that there are no afternoon lessons on Tuesday, Thursday and Saturday until the preparation periods in the evening. On Monday, Wednesday and Friday, there will be between two and three hours of lessons during the afternoon, again with a break, the pattern being exactly the same as in the morning.

On the afternoons without lessons, games are played. (Winchester, by the way, is more stern, allowing games only on Thursdays but also on Saints' days and on special Wednesdays; Shrewsbury too has an odd system whereby the head of the school may claim half-holidays for the playing of games in order to celebrate the award of university scholarships and other events.) In winter this will be the time for organized games of football. The pattern will be a senior game or two at the top and then at a lower level games between various Houses played by boys at different age levels. There will not be, as there were to be later, many matches with other schools as there is very little agreement about the rules under which football should be played. Eton has its 'field' game and, strictly for home consumption, its 'wall' game (not played by all but practised once a week or so by the adept for the big battle between the Collegers and Oppidans on St Andrew's Day). Winchester has a game played on a small netted field with trenches at either end which serve instead of goal posts. It is, incidentally, the daily duty of eight fags at Winchester to stand outside the nets of the two senior games in order to throw the ball back when it comes over. (At Rugby, by contrast, the only task which may not be given to a fag is fielding as a substitute for a senior at cricket.)

Rugby football, through the spread to other headmasterships of those who have sat at the feet of Dr Arnold, has now begun to become the generally accepted code for many schools. Carrying an oval ball rather than just kicking a round one is regarded as better character training. Indeed it is rugby football that is played between schools that are prepared to travel to meet each other. At Rugby itself, these 'foreign' matches against other schools are watched compulsorily by the whole of the rest of the school, with monitors armed with canes keeping order. Strangely these matches are not the ordinary game played at Rugby, for there are only fifteen players on each side. In the usual games at the school, in order to employ the largest number of boys, twenty a side is played.

Cross-country running of one form or another is the great activity for spring afternoons. Schools pride themselves on the barbarity of the courses that have been laid out and the number of ditches, usually filled with icy water, that have to be crossed. Often courses of varying severity are used and it will be up to the captain of games to choose the route to be taken that day. Eton is unusual in having a pack of beagles to follow on foot after real hares. Most other schools content themselves by giving human hares a ten minutes' start and sending a pack of boys after them, following the paper trail that the hares have laid.

In the summer term the choice lies normally between cricket and rowing, where there is a handy river. In both these sports there is much more inter-school competition. School sides will play cricket against each other and against visiting club teams. The best oarsmen will expect to take part in a regatta or two. But beneath the top level, summer games are taken far less seriously than winter football. True, there are House matches but very often there will just be casual 'pick-up' games. At Rugby, where there is no rowing as an alternative, cricket is not compulsory and it is perfectly permissible to go for a country walk or for a cycle ride. (The sin against the Arnoldian code is to be idle: a worship of games is not essential – yet.) Elsewhere one game of cricket a week is all that is demanded, and the other two games afternoons can be spent in walks or in botanizing. Even rowing was not necessarily a competitive sport. At Eton, particularly, it is thought to be quite enough to take a sculling boat or a pair-oared gig and just go for a casual turn up and down the river. The same is true of Westminster and Shrewsbury, though at Westminster it is no longer possible to launch boats near to the school and those who wish to row must board a steam pinnace at the House of Commons steps to go to the school boathouse at Putney. Swimming is also allowed where there is a suitable piece of water – a river or a pond. No one has yet built an artificial swimming pool. There is a Charterhouse story, possibly apocryphal, that shows how deeply rooted the fagging system is in the life of all public schools. A senior was in difficulties swimming in the River Wey. His response to the situation was automatic: 'Faaaag,' he called – and obediently a first-year boy dived in and saved him.

The late afternoon is a hard time for fags. In winter one duty will be to light the fires or stoke them if they are still burning. On games days hot baths will have to be filled from cans for the returning giants of the first teams. Messages must be run, and at schools where there is a suitable cooked-meat shop to hand, hot and cold food must be fetched to deck the senior tea tables. At Harrow, for instance, all kinds of hot food from eggs and bacon to sweet omelettes are carried back wrapped in paper, except for such delicacies as soup and jugged hare, which are transported in jam jars. Otherwise tea will be taken in Hall where pretty basic fare – inevitably cold meat and bread – will be provided and will be supplemented from private supplies.

At the end of games time, there will be a roll call, earlier in the winter than in the summer, when on half-days wandering around within bounds is allowed in the early evening. Then at most places from 7.30 p.m. till about 9 there will be prep. – the learning of the lesson for tomorrow's recitation, roughing out translations and the like. Seniors will tend to work alone or with the one or two with whom they share a study, while juniors at many schools will be gathered together in a large common room, or even in a form room, under the supervision of a senior. This will also be the time for writing 'lines', the inevitable school punishment for offences which do not merit a beating. (The lines, by the way, are the less taxing legacy of the original punishment, invented at Eton, of setting an offender the task of writing an epigram in Latin or Greek. The custom was dropped by mutual consent: if the offender was not witty and skilful, he found the task intolerably taxing, and if he were good at it, he could get away, under the rules of epigram writing, with being intolerably rude to the person who had set the punishment.)

The evening is the time too for the meeting of societies: debating clubs meeting about once a week can be found at most schools, so can glee clubs or choral societies. The botanists can listen to papers and the aspiring actors can rehearse Shakespeare. And there are the occasional communal indoor sports of a less intellectual kind. Most schools seem to take a malicious pleasure in making new boys sing. They have to stand on tables and sing a given number of verses. What happens to them varies from school to school. At some they will be beaten with or prodded by toasting forks for being tuneless or shy. Elsewhere they may be encouraged with cricket bats. At more humane establishments, displeasure may merely be shown by singing other songs loudly in order to drown an indifferent singer. At Shrewsbury such singing entertainments are supplemented by boxing matches between juniors, a couple of table tops serving as a ring. These matches are normally supervised by seniors and are condoned by authority. Indeed all such activities will be encouraged since idleness is the great crime.

At nine o'clock bread and cheese and beer are available. This is a voluntary meal and not everyone can be bothered to leave their studies to help themselves. Indeed at some schools only the seniors are invited to eat. Half an hour later someone in authority, usually the housemaster or a junior master on duty, will say prayers to the whole House assembled at some suitable point. More modern schools will have gas but where there is none boys will collect a candle to take to their cubicle or to put beside their beds. For the juniors it will be lights out at 10 p.m. and the seniors will be allowed another half hour. It will be the duty of the prefect of the day to see that all is quiet before he too goes to bed. The housemaster will make his final round soon after. It has been a long day and an unvarying day. Saturday is as much a full school day as any other.

Only Sundays are different. Even the fags do not have to stir then before 8 a.m. Schooling will be limited to a single period in the morning, almost universally spent in religious studies, but there will be three chapels during the day – morning, afternoon and evening, but only the last two will include a sermon. On Sunday there will be some moments that will not be organized. Boys will be able to write the Letter Home, and even read a book of their own choice. Where the housemasters are civilized (and married) some of the boys may go on Sunday afternoons to have tea with the family on the other side of the green baize door that divides the boys from the family in an atmosphere a little more homely than the world of school, though perhaps the diversions offered will be no more exciting than continual hymn singing or looking at illustrated books.

Then it is Monday morning again. What this will mean will depend on the boy and the school: the sensitive will flinch, the phlegmatic will endure and the conformists will enjoy themselves well enough – most of the time. And the holidays will come – eventually.

Afterword

In trying to give an overall picture of the daily round in the public schools of the 1870s, I am well aware that there will have been some differences between schools that I have glossed over, particularly in their use of language, so that I have tried to avoid local school slang. Prep., for instance, was called 'toy time' at Winchester and senior boys at Harrow dined in 'messes', but fundamentally what happened varied very little from school to school. I am conscious also that I have made very little reference to fighting and bullying, which were, Heaven knows, a part of the daily round – but not of *every* day's round. Probably the majority of boys would go through school without a serious fight or being involved in more than very occasional bullying, either as aggressor or victim. Equally, although there may have been daily punishment sessions, a boy could go through his school life without a flogging, from either masters or prefects. The daily round was humdrum, rather than terrible.

David Holloway (Colet Court and Westminster) is the Literary Editor of the *Daily Telegraph*, and is the author of books on exploration, social history, and English literature.

3
God, the Rod, and Lines from Virgil
PETER EARLE

Research into schoolboy history can be a rather frightening experience. For there, hidden behind the often stilted words of the autobiographer or novelist, are very real experiences which stir one's own memories of the miseries and joys of boyhood. The historian needs to be careful with these memories, both his own and those which he reads, for the history of schoolboy experience relies more than most history on anecdote and reminiscence in the absence of more immediate evidence. What is lacking in particular is the objective evidence of the outsider. Many writers criticized public schools in the nineteenth century, just as they do now. But few knew much about them. For public schools were secret places, isolated from the world and protected from that world by a code of secrecy and silence that was shared by masters and boys alike. No boy would tell his parents what really went on. If he had he probably would not have been believed. Masters too had a remarkable capacity for deception. They saw what they wanted to see and if they saw a little more they were not going to tell the world. Nowhere is this more obvious than in the minutes of evidence of the Public Schools Commission of 1864. Both the commissioners themselves and the headmasters and assistant masters whom they interviewed were public school men who well knew how to frame and answer a question without giving anything too damaging away. If there ever had been abuses these were always in the past. Flogging and bullying were both on the decline, if they still existed at all. Our doubts about the truth of these assertions are given some substance by the very few young boys who were called to give evidence. How were they chosen? Who was the one small boy from Winchester whom masters and commissioners felt safe to be cross-questioned? Presumably he was carefully selected. And yet, hardened schoolboy though he might be, his guileless answers indicate the existence of a pit full of horrors completely absent in the rosy evidence of his elders and betters.

The same problems of interpretation, the same suspicions of self-deception or deliberate falsehood, occur to the reader of the hundreds of memoirs, autobiographies and above all schoolboy novels which form the basis of our knowledge of the school life of the past. None of these are written by boys in our period. They are written by men, often very old men whose harsher memories have been filtered by time and who tend to view their own past with a mixture of heartiness, optimism and a sure conviction that their schooldays must have been the happiest days of their life. Such information poses many problems.

One thing we learn from such books is that public schools are always becoming better, more civilized, happier places. The typical public school memoir or novel is governed by an almost unavoidable chronological structure. The book describes the process by which a small boy becomes a man. But such books nearly always go further than this. As the boy becomes better behaved and more responsible so does the school itself improve, often as the result of changes which the individual writer claims to have introduced when he got into a position of power. Of course the impression of the writer is not always false. Schools certainly did change in the course of the nineteenth century. But such change was not always in a straight line towards progress and the historian is forced to doubt much of the optimism of his sources. For these sources often overlap in an embarrassing way. One writer's account of the bullying and general misery which existed when he was a fag overlaps with a slightly older writer's description of the same House in the same school at the same time as a haven of peace for the little boy. If the evidence of nineteenth-century autobiographers and novelists were to be believed there would have been no bullying or unpleasantness in public schools by Edwardian times. Unfortunately, this was by no means the case. Neither boys nor schools change as fast as optimists would like us to believe. The very realistic picture of life in one House at Harrow which appears in Arnold Lunn's novel of 1913, *The Harrovians*, shows a world which in many respects was even more unpleasant for the small boy than the Flashman-dominated Rugby of the late 1830s. The indiscriminate bullying and occasional roasting of Thomas Hughes' Rugby was one side of a picture whose reverse was an immensely happy and free existence. Bullying at Harrow in Edwardian times was systematically imposed by older boys who persecuted not only for the pleasure and the sense of power it gave them but also for the greater glory of their House, Harrow and the British Empire. Knocking small boys about imposed a discipline which in the long run would turn them into loyal, obedient men who would serve or fight for England with the same thoughtless self-sacrifice that they were expected to show when they played 'footer' for their House at Harrow. Or so the theory went.

The discipline imposed by big boys on small boys was only one aspect of discipline in the nineteenth-century public school. A boarding school is an astonishingly complex institution and the individual boy within it was subjected to several different systems of control, each with their particular sanctions and codes of punishment. Immediate and ever-present was the code of his own fellows, of the boys he lived and worked with. Such a code had nothing to do with the future government of the British Empire and little connection with the conventional school values of team spirit and obedience. Group loyalty was vital, of course, but the group was not the House or school. It was the collective body of small boys, a group whose immense loyalty to each other Thomas Arnold called 'the bond of evil' and whose first and last commandment was 'Thou shalt not tell'. No boy must tell prefect, parent or master, however awful the experience or appalling the conditions in which he lived out his often miserable life. God help the boy who did tell, for there are few things worse than the collective displeasure of small boys. Error was sometimes met with the terrible loneliness of a trip to Coventry but more often with the more amusing routine of continuous punishment, continuous pinching, kicking, tripping and pushing, the flick of the wet towel or the jab of the compass, continuous teasing and physical humiliation, continuous purloining of books and work to get the errant into trouble with his masters. There is no escape from such punishment at a boarding school, no mother to cry to, no outside world in which the boy is still a decent fellow. Even dreams bring hideous memories and the morning brings the reality of misery.

The rule of silence and the bond of evil protected the group from outside interference but it had its own internal ethos, an ethos of intense conformity and denial of a world outside the school. A new boy had to learn this ethos fast in order to survive. It was so easy to make a mistake in those first, kaleidoscopic days. The unfortunate exposure of a tradesman father, the affectionate mention of mother or sister, the tears of homesickness, unusual underclothes or, worst of all, the temptation to boast of former glories at prep or private school could lead to immediate humiliation and provide a handle for oppressors for terms to come. A boy must learn a peculiarly English form of self-discipline, to show no emotion even under the most trying circumstances, never to cry or lose his temper. He might be unhappy, but if he was he must be unhappy in a manly English way. Then he might be safe, as long as he wore exactly the same clothes and used the same secret schoolboy slang as everybody else, showed no enthusiasm for anything but games, ragging and dirty jokes, had no 'side' or 'swagger' and was not too good at work. Even then he would be tested. Could he fight and not scream when he was hurt? Could he outwit prefects and masters? Was he afraid to break the rules, to smoke or go out of bounds? He was not. Good. Smith mi. can pass into the ranks of the good fellows – for the time being at least.

Superimposed on the self-discipline of the group of small boys was the discipline of that strange institution, the body of prefects, half boys, half men, the marvel of the nineteenth-century public school and the future leaders not only of England but of half the red-tinted world. There were good prefects and bad prefects, those who used their power for good and those who used it for evil, but all were impressed with the power they had and the responsibilities it imposed, even if some of them only too often evaded such responsibilities. Few of them shared the values of the outside world or even of the masters, but they did think that the object of education was somehow to create a race of small boys at once less selfish and more obedient than they would otherwise have been. But they were boys themselves and thus reluctant to preach, knowing indeed that a sermon from a boy of eighteen was as ridiculous as it was useless. The answers to their problems were mercifully quite simple ones.

Small boys could be made to know their place and to be outwardly obedient by a constant diet of physical punishment, slaps, kicks, boxing of ears, backed up by the more formal discipline and ritual of the cane. Punishment could be simply for the universal crime of not respecting the superior status of the prefect, for guff or cheek or general insubordination. But the potential crimes available to small boys went much further than that. Generations of boys had developed an ever more complex code of rules and privileges which governed nearly every aspect of behaviour and which new boys must readily absorb if they wished to avoid the penalties for its infringement. Such codes varied from school to school but their similarity suggests a common ancestry. What was it that made two schools in different parts of the country have similar or identical rules of conduct, unrecognized by masters and rarely put into writing? Was it some anthropological law that determined the pecking order of the school jungle? Or was there a common origin? Did prefects reading schoolboy novels sigh with joy when they discovered yet another absurd rule which they could impose?

Whatever their origins these rules covered an astonishing range of subjects, the tilt of a hat, behaviour to masters, whom you might talk to and where and when. But they nearly all involved one vital element, being so framed that a boy's progress up the school could be measured by the number of rules he had to obey and the number of privileges he had earned. Here you must not talk in passages before your second year or whistle before your third. There the new boy must have his jacket fully buttoned up, undoing one button for every year that he had been in school. Thus even the most miserable small boy could look forward with pleasure to the day when he was an unbuttoned, whistling, passage-talking boy, a thought made even more delightful by the likelihood that one day he too would be able to punish a new generation of small boys for infringing these same regulations.

Whatever the crime, and there were hundreds, the punishment was likely to be the same. That 'slavish discipline of the rod' which has disgusted the faint-hearted and cast fear into the souls of the thin-trousered from Elizabethan times, had passed by the nineteenth century into the hands of boys as well as masters. The ritual, the nature and the vocabulary of beating of boys by boys varied as much as did the crimes for which it was imposed. In Lunn's Harrow a boy was prevented from rising after each stroke of his 'whopping' by being forced to bend underneath the half-open top drawer of a chest of drawers. He was then beaten with a cane on the buttocks, the accuracy of the 'group' being a point of pride to a new prefect. At Winchester we can find the 'great and glorious institution of "tunding" ', a classical word for a classical school, but one that simply meant whacking a small boy across the shoulders with an ash-plant or indeed anything else that happened to be available, such as a piece of firewood. But whether a boy was whopped or tunded, tanned or swished, he was beaten and beaten fairly often in the name of good discipline and for the honour of the House. Slackness must never be tolerated. Usually he was beaten in privacy or in the presence of two or three other prefects but occasionally, for very serious offences such as bullying without having received the privilege of bullying or for stealing, he was publicly beaten in front of all his fellows. The awesome spectacle of a 'hall-licking' at Rugby or a 'house-whopping' at Harrow could make a memorable impression on the bystander.

A boy who was obedient and nothing else would be a dull fellow and not much of an asset to his House. Duty was important but it should be channelled into somewhat more spirited ends. Fortunately there was an eminently satisfactory way in which both spirit and duty could be combined. Small boys could be made loyal and enthusiastic for approved ends by making a fetish of the one quality which they most admired and envied, physical strength. Make a hero of the athlete, make the greatest ambition of the small boy to acquire the status, hero-worship and privileges of the 'flannels', 'bloods' or 'colours' and half the job of discipline and character formation is done. Adults could preach the virtue of games, the leadership, pluck, endurance and loyalty to the team that they were supposed to instil into a boy. Boys did not need to preach. House spirit and the worship of games was easy to instil into the majority of boys and for that minority who hated games, who hated the mud, the blood, the guts and the endless toil and fear of the playing fields, there were methods of persuasion as big boy kicked and swore at small boy until, even if he still hated games, he would run until his lungs burst rather than be kicked any more. The Earl of Middleton was startled when he took a message to another House at Eton in the 1870s and saw a notice which read: 'Any lower boy in this house who does not play football once daily and twice a day on half-holidays will be fined half-a-crown and kicked.' His surprise was merely a reflection of the fact that Eton, although games-mad like all Victorian schools, was perhaps the most civilized of the great public schools. At Harrow there would have been no need of such a notice and a boy would be surprised if he only got kicked and fined for 'slacking at footer', since of all small-boy sins it was perhaps in the prefects' eyes the worst.

Some people might think that boys went to school to work and learn something, but this was not an important objective for the boys nor indeed for many of their parents, who despised cleverness as much as they admired leadership, pluck and manliness. But for most of the masters work was of course an important element in school life. They saw it as their job to drill into the unwilling heads of boys the rudiments of the classical languages. Little else was taught, at least in the first half of the nineteenth century. The curriculum in the lower classes at Harrow in the 1830s was entirely classics, thirteen lessons a week, five of which were in Greek grammar and five of Ovid. If thirteen hours seems very little we should remember that the object of lessons was not to learn but to repeat by heart to the master what one had learned out of school. Boys in the sixth form at Harrow got some respite from the classics. They had seventeen lessons a week, of which one was modern history on Thursdays and one was Euclid, Vulgar Fractions, Decimals or Logic on Wednesdays. The other fifteen lessons were Latin and Greek. Apologists for the almost total concentration on the classics approached the matter in different ways, though all held that it had something to do with discipline. Some thought that the classics were good simply because they were difficult. Others thought that the very nature of the dead languages with their rules and conventions imposed a discipline on the young mind. Most writers were extremely vague about the supposed values of an education which consisted almost entirely of 'droning recitations of incompletely mastered rules of grammar or passages from Latin literature'. Teachers were quite prepared to agree with critics that the boys in fact learned very little and might find that after ten years of Eton they were still unable to construe the Latin inscription on a tombstone. But this did not matter very much, as a writer in the 1830s pointed out. 'The scholar may give no outward show of learning, nor exhibit any useful acquirement, but he is undergoing a secret training which gives a regulated energy and a fine organization, fitting him to move hereafter with dignity and ease in any orbit of the intellectual world.' Whatever the process of the secret training the method of instilling it was no secret. For centuries it had been quite clear to pedagogues that the key to teaching Latin was the birch. It would be difficult to think of a man who had the reputation of being a great schoolteacher before 1850 who was not also a great flogger. Later the rod was to be restricted more to moral than scholastic offences. But in the first half of the nineteenth century the stereotyped view of the schoolmaster of old is essentially accurate.

Teaching was often carried out in one enormous schoolroom, each master, rod in hand, surrounded by his 'division' who repeated in turn what they were supposed to have learned. Good work was rewarded by a sometimes daily re-ordering of each pupil's place in the class, which together with twice-yearly examinations slowly moved the boy up towards the sixth form. Bad work met with instant chastisement, as did idleness, indiscipline and impertinence. The system of classroom punishments naturally varied from school to school, although all used various combinations of demotion, impositions and the cane. In some schools teachers could cane or birch in school, on the hands, shoulders or buttocks according to their various customs. In others, offenders were 'put in the bill' or 'sent up' for a ritual punishment by the Master of the Lower School or the headmaster. At Harrow in the 1830s the system was completely formalized. The first time an offender was sent up the headmaster set him three hundred lines of Latin or Greek to transcribe; the second he was flogged and demoted one place in the form. Each further offence was alternatively received with increasingly severe transcriptions and floggings until with the new term a new score commenced. The 'black book' at Charterhouse was an interesting variant. For each offence the boy's name went in the book. The third entry in one week led automatically to a flogging from the headmaster. Each week the boy started with a clean slate.

The transcription of lines or the alternative of learning by heart could take a very long time, as Dean Farrar's Eric was to discover when he was set to transcribe Virgil's fourth Georgic. As a result the hardened boy often preferred the quick pain of a flogging to the tiresome burden of an imposition done in his spare time. Indeed impositions got a generally bad press. Masters did not like them very much. Checking them or hearing them wasted their time, though a suggestion from the Royal Commission that the hearing time might be reduced by setting boys a shorter passage of something really difficult and dull like the *History of England* met with the laconic reply that 'no master I think would ever wish to hear the repetition through'. The commissioners themselves were extremely concerned that too many impositions might ruin the handwriting of England's future rulers, a worry which completely overshadowed any latent doubts that they might have had about the wisdom of so much corporal punishment. The main problem about beating in school was not really its quantity but the noise it made, a point made by the High Master of St Paul's when he welcomed the reduction of classroom punishments to six cuts with a cane on the hand. Previously, he reported, there had been 'a great deal of caning and striking the boys over various parts of the body; much more than necessary; besides which, the noise alone formed a great obstruction to the progress of the school duties'.

Dominating the schoolroom was a throne where sat a man of great majesty, the headmaster, who taught the sixth form and was the ultimate source of discipline within the school. His was normally a presence which could awe small boys with ease and turn them into quivering wrecks with a few well-chosen contemptuous words. Few knew him well before they began to rise into the upper reaches of the school but what they saw of him they feared, whether it was on one of those solemn occasions when he addressed the school about a breach of discipline or the more intimate and immediate fear of the long walk to his room to be flogged. A flogging by the headmaster is an ingredient in nearly all accounts of nineteenth-century schools and could be an impressive ritual, especially when it was, as in many schools, a public spectacle. Flogging could be merely the result of being sent up from school or appearing too many times in Charterhouse's black book, but it was also of course the ultimate punishment for serious breaches of school discipline. On these occasions a good headmaster could make a great show, delivering a passionate denunciation of the victim's particular sin before lashing into him with the birch. Everything had to be done just right. Each school had its particular ritual and particular instrument of punishment. At Westminster the victim was kept steady by one of his fellows, who hoisted him onto his back by the wrists and kept him suspended while the birch was applied. The same method was used at Christ's Hospital, the school with the reputation of having the most savage flogging of all since both hoister and flogger were beadles and hence had no pretensions to being gentlemen. At Winchester flogging was reserved for 'Bloody Friday', so the culprit often had several days of anticipation. Then, as school ended, he would be seized and forced to kneel while one boy unbuckled his braces and another held up his shirt 'and exposed to view about a foot of the small of the back'. Then the headmaster would lash him with the famous 'bibling-rod', a 'four-forked rod' made of four apple twigs fastened into a two-foot handle. When he had finished, 'the Doctor hurled the rod on to the ground, and marched in a stately fashion from the room'.

No discussion of flogging would be complete without mentioning Eton, where the almost daily 'switching' of those so unfortunate as to be 'put in the bill' was a source of constant amusement to their schoolfellows. The first sight could be alarming, as James Brinsley-Richards reports of the 1850s.

> I had never been chastised since I was in the nursery after the manner in use at Eton, and I thought the manner infinitely degrading . . . I never quite believed the stories I heard until I actually saw a boy flogged . . . It was on a cold rainy morning, when that corner of the Lower School where the block stood looked funereally dark. Several dozens of fellows clambered upon forms and desks to see Neville corrected . . . Two fellows deputed to act as 'holders down' stood behind the block, and one of them held a birch of quite alarming size which he handed to the Lower Master . . . Neville was unbracing his nether garments – next moment, when he knelt on the steps of the block, and when the Lower Master inflicted upon his person six cuts that sounded like the splashings of so many buckets of water, I turned almost faint. I felt as I have never felt but once since, and that was when seeing a man hanged.

Alarm and disgust soon turned to indifference. Indeed most boys who were able to make the comparison thought that a prefect's beating hurt much more than a flogging, although the latter might be more humiliating. A famous painting of a flogging at Eton in 1832 seems to bear this out. The scene is gruesome enough. There is the victim kneeling on the flogging block and behind him stand the two 'holders down', the one on the left posing with one hand on his hip and an expression on his face which could be interpreted as a smirk or a sneer of contempt. The master stands with the fearsome-looking birch raised well above his head, but he is tired, old, sad and very feeble-looking and one gets the impression that it is not really going to hurt very much. A boy had more to fear from a young athlete than from an old scholar.

School discipline took many forms, as we have seen, but the school itself did not complete the constraints under which the small boy lived. For beyond school lay home. The possibility of parental displeasure might normally have little effect on a boy's behaviour at school but the picture of the gentle, grey-haired, heartbroken mother praying for the soul of her erring son plays an important part in many Victorian schoolboy novels and may well have acted as an emotional control. More to the point was probably the threat of the 'letter to father'. This is well illustrated in the delightful letters home of a late nineteenth-century Etonian. He is constantly engaged in begging his sister to 'break it gently to Papa' every time he is 'swished', hoping that she will be in time to plead his case before the inevitable arrival of a somewhat different version of the story in a letter from his Tutor. The reiterated worry in these letters is that Papa may think that he is not 'trying his best'. What that 'best' involved we do not know. Parents' ambitions for their children in nineteenth-century public schools were not necessarily the same as in our own time. Many of the pupils at the great public schools were not faced with the thought of having to earn a living and scholastic attainments seem to have had a low priority in many parents' minds. Perhaps the best illustration of the sort of thing that most Victorian parents were interested in comes from the famous passage in *Tom Brown's Schooldays* when Squire Brown meditates what advice to give to Tom when he sees him off on the coach on his way to Rugby.

Shall I tell him to mind his work, and say he's sent to school to make himself a good scholar? Well, but he isn't sent to school for that – at anyrate, not for that mainly. I don't care a straw for Greek particles, or the digamma, no more does his mother. What is he sent to school for? Well, partly because he wanted so to go. If he'll only turn out a brave, helpful, truth-telling Englishman, and a gentleman, and a Christian, that's all I want.

Boys could well ponder on such ambitions. The ultimate sanction of both schoolmaster and parent was the boy's determination to avoid the disgrace of expulsion for a really shameful offence.

Finally we must remember that hanging over all Victorian schoolchildren was their own personal picture of the Victorian God. Whether their mental God was a great schoolmaster, a great athlete or the stern avenging tyrant of the Old Testament he had no compunction about sneaking or playing the detective and could do what no parent or master could do and look into the heart of a boy. Most writers assumed that pious talk in chapel had little influence on errant boys, fear of the rod rather than God being the more effective stimulus to good behaviour. But it is worth noting how regularly chapel and, in particular, Confirmation, with its emphasis on turning over a new leaf, appears in public school novels. Prosaic evidence of the effectiveness of this ritual can be seen from a Harrow master's assertion to the Public School commissioners that there was usually far less of both crime and punishment at the time of Confirmation.

Many influences thus came to bear on the public schoolboy, each designed to get him to conform to a particular set of values. That some of these values conflicted is only too obvious. The ideals of his peer group had little to do with either the ideals of organized religion or those of the archetypal schoolmaster. Indeed the boys were often extremely hostile to the proclaimed ideals of their elders. This was not a very satisfactory situation and the nineteenth century saw a gallant attempt by headmasters to subordinate all values within the school to their own. Great men, such as Dr Arnold of Rugby, were in the forefront of this movement and they certainly improved the schools. But their very successes carried the seeds of failure. For, in their attempt to bridge the gap between the adult world and the boy world, they were forced to adopt many boy standards of value, particularly the hatred of sneaking and the worship of games, and at the same time vigorously to restrict the freedom and individuality of the boy.

The nineteenth century starts with the schools in a state of virtual anarchy. The masters restricted their attention to teaching and to the punishment of idleness and indiscipline in school. Out of school the boys did more or less as they liked and attempts to constrain their behaviour could lead, and did lead on many occasions, to actual rebellion. What this could involve can be seen from a letter describing the end of the 1770 rebellion at Winchester, which began when the headmaster attempted to prevent the main body of Commoners from going to the assistance of some of their friends who had got involved in a fight with the townspeople.

> The riot I mentioned in my last, at Winchester, is all over, and no one expelled. It was a formidable thing, for they had several brace of pistols. It began, as I hear, by the landlord of the White Hart desiring some of the Commoners, who were drinking at his house, not to drink any more, but to go home . . .

The fighting was such that the Riot Act had been read. Perhaps significantly the Wykehamists were led by a boy recently expelled from Eton.

Intermittent riot and rebellion and a general state of lawlessness of the sort illustrated in this quotation lasted into the early decades of the nineteenth century. Public opinion was shocked. So, eventually, were the schools. Numbers were falling and they were hardly likely to attract the new rich of the Industrial Revolution to places like this. Clearly it was necessary to reinstitute some form of discipline. But how? Two main points of view came out of the debate. The first saw as the main problem the extremely low proportion of masters to boys. Some schools had only two or three masters and a handful of assistants to control hundreds of boys. The answer therefore was to increase the number of staff and to institute a regime of strict supervision and discipline, both within school and without. Such an approach found little support. It would be expensive. More important it was felt not to be English. English boys should be free to develop, free of the odious usherdom and regimentation that was felt to be particularly French or Prussian. The schools had been undisciplined for so long that it was thought that this fact alone was the main reason for their success in the past, a success which could be proved by the long list of successful and famous people who had attended them. It was the rough and tumble, the absence of restraint that gave a boy self-reliance and taught him to learn the best and worst about the world, about good and evil, before he moved on to a larger stage. All the same, some discipline was necessary and an alternative solution was put forward which was ultimately adopted in all the schools.

In the state of anarchy the popular and strong boys had risen to the top and had acquired more or less full control over the rest of their fellows. The answer was clearly to recognize this fact, to give formal approval to the system of boy power and boy government but at the same time to exercise some control over the choice of which boys wielded this power. The answer, in short, was the prefect system. School after school adopted this course from about the 1820s onwards. Headmasters now felt they had some control, especially after the general adoption of housemasters to replace the dames and private citizens who had previously managed the Houses where the boys lived. Headmasters selected housemasters, whose ideals of discipline were close to their own, and the housemasters in turn selected or approved the boys who were to be prefects. The boys were still in charge, out of school hours, but because they were carefully chosen and could be indoctrinated at leisure they would use their influence and leadership in the cause of good rather than evil. In many schools and under many headmasters there is no doubt that the new system worked more or less as it should do. But it had one basic flaw. Nearly all headmasters and housemasters recognized the boy code which stigmatized sneaking and spying as at the same time a betrayal of the trust implied in the office of prefect and as a moral offence of the lowest order. They therefore did not interfere and hence were at the mercy of their prefects, unless some accident should bring knowledge of evil which they could not ignore to their ears. Since the choice of prefects was nearly always restricted to the strong or intelligent there were never all that many boys to choose from and many disastrous mistakes were made. But the code of honour prevented most masters from ever realizing just how disastrous such mistakes were. They simply did not know or did not want to know what was going on, a situation made very clear in G.F. Bradby's brilliant novel, *The Lanchester Tradition*. The result could be the sort of boy tyranny which has been described earlier and, once it had been established, the essential conservatism of boys ensured that boy tyranny became the norm and not the exception.

Indiscipline in the early nineteenth century was seen to be not only the result of an uncontrolled boy power structure but also a consequence of the fact that boys could do as they liked out of school, so long as they turned up to pray, to eat and to sleep. The rest of the time was their own. What did boys do in their spare time? Some rolled hoops, some played marbles, some gambled, but they all played some sort of game and many were already taking very seriously such games as cricket and the various forms of football, even hiring professional coaches out of their own money to improve their performance. Masters had nothing to do with the organization of games. They were scholars who no doubt despised such boyish amusements as much as did the writer of an article in the *Edinburgh Review* of 1810. 'Of what importance is it in after life, whether a boy can play well or ill at cricket; or row a boat with the skill and precision of a waterman? Of what use is the body of an athlete, when we have good laws over our heads, or when a pistol, a post-chaise, or a porter can be hired for a few shillings?' Such adult values were soon to come under attack. Many critics of schools saw that the boys' love of games could be used as a method of control. A writer in 1835 made the point, though he used what must have seemed to many a somewhat unfortunate analogy.

> There is a school near London, consisting of about 130 boys, taken from the worst part of society, young thieves and vagabonds who are well governed by one man with an assistant. . . . In this school for vagrants the boys are employed in labour for the greater part of the day; the corresponding thing for a large school is systematic exercise.

Cricket and football would do for public schoolboys what stone-breaking did for hooligans, keep them out of trouble in the daytime and send them to bed exhausted.

It was not long before writers saw that organized games might have effects on the character of a boy that stone-breaking could never emulate. Indeed it was discovered that games taught all the manly virtues, self-reliance, loyalty, pluck and selflessness. The lesson was quickly learned. Schools hired young athletes as assistant masters, games-playing was made compulsory and the games themselves were systematized by the invention of codes of rules to prevent the anarchy and riot of earlier days. By the time of the Public Schools Commission in the 1860s, boys at Eton and Harrow were spending up to twenty hours a week playing cricket and the ethos and social structure of all schools was governed by the worship of the athlete, a worship awarded and recognized by masters, parents and boys.

The new emphasis on games had the desired effect. The life of boys was now regimented and controlled to an extent that never could have been achieved by usherdom. Prefects supervised the playing-fields as they did the dormitories and study rooms. Slacking became as great a crime as insolence or disobedience. There was no more rebellion. But the cost was high. The hero-worship of the athlete meant that once again it was the strong who were likely to rule. Housemasters found it difficult to deny the public opinion that stated that 'colours' and 'flannels' should have the privileges and the status of a prefect. Unfortunately, despite the nobility of games, not every member of the Eleven was a noble fellow. The cult of the athlete often led to an extension of boy tyranny. It also reinforced the naturally philistine outlook of the boys. Where heartiness and team spirit were admired, cleverness, art and individualism were likely to be despised. Many adult commentators were glad, proud of the fact that the English were a people who thought more of the team and less of self than continentals were supposed to do. But some were not so happy at the creation of a new ruling class of ill-educated stereotypes to whom no prize of adulthood could conceivably be equivalent to the thrill of receiving their school colours.

The combination of compulsory games and the prefect system solved the disciplinary problem of the nineteenth-century public school. But one wonders if such solutions did not mean that headmasters lost control by the very means by which they appeared to gain it. A writer in the 1830s laid down his ideal of the relationship between master and boys: 'Boys must not be allowed to form a distinct society for themselves. They are not sent to school to form a society for themselves; they are sent to live in a society framed and governed by the intelligence and virtue of a man whose profession it is to train boys.' Great headmasters believed this and acted on it but the compromise that they encouraged did in fact allow the boys to form their own distinct society. Games and the prefect system may have considerable virtues, as their apologists have always claimed, but they certainly reflect boy values and boy systems of control and not those of the adult world. Did the schoolmasters' capitulation to these boy values lead to the creation of a new English ruling class who would turn the adult world itself into a boy world, a world of old boys who loved playing the game but were most unwilling to think for themselves?

One wonders, too, what was the effect of so unrelieved a diet of corporal punishment. Critics thought the birch degrading and cruel but were not sure what long-term effects it had on a boy. Some held that the slavish discipline of the rod created boys who were servile and easily cowed. Others disagreed and thought the birch was simply counter-productive, producing an endless succession of martyrs whose friends admired the courage with which they bore their punishment and who 'grew up into an habitual contempt, and defiance of correction'. But the critics were definitely in the minority. Most contemporaries indeed hardly considered that there was a problem to discuss, flogging being in their eyes simply a natural part of the process of education. Strange to report, the boys themselves apparently shared these views. Two headmasters attempted to ban the birch in the first half of the nineteenth century but were forced by their own pupils to restore it. The English seemed to be proud of their scars, proud to have been birched for instance by the redoubtable Dr Keate, who once flogged seventy-two boys in succession in the library of Eton. Did the English have some strange affection for this instrument of punishment? Certainly the flagellant adventures of gentlemen in such establishments as 'Birchminster' play an important part in that strange hidden literature of the 'Other Victorians'. Pornography may not be the best guide to the deepest thoughts of a class but one wonders just who read these books and why.

Peter Earle (Cumnor House School and St Edward's, Oxford) is Lecturer in Economic History at the London School of Economics, and the author of many books on the downfall and deaths of the British and American ruling classes.

4
Fagging and Boy Government

MALCOLM FALKUS

Looking back to the short days of that Winter Half, I find that passages obsess my memory. Passages, narrow and wainscoted, down which we raced to the call of 'Lower Boy!'; passages where we lingered and gossiped in front of notice-boards; passages sweating with moisture after a game of passage-football; the complicated passages of other houses . . . (L. E. Jones, *A Victorian Boyhood*)

Setting up a Royal Commission generally indicates two things: profound public disquiet about the subject under scrutiny and equally profound ignorance about it. The Public Schools Commission appointed in 1861 and headed by Lord Clarendon was no exception. Concern about public schools had been growing steadily for decades, and few aspects of school life and government had escaped debate. Opponents and defenders of the schools joined battle over various moral, social, educational, political and financial aspects of the school system, though the strength of views expressed was as often as not in inverse proportion to knowledge about the subject. And when Lord Clarendon's team settled down to what turned out to be three arduous years of hearing and sifting evidence from those connected with public schools, they had much to enquire about.

The questions and issues raised by the Commissioners are a good guide to the areas causing the greatest anxiety. Almost the whole spectrum of school life was covered by detailed examination of headmasters, assistant masters, former pupils, schoolboys and others. Among these innumerable issues none aroused more public interest, passion and conflict of opinion than the subject of boy government in schools and its various aspects of monitorial powers of discipline and fagging.

Fagging is the subject of this chapter, though it will be necessary to refer to various related subjects from time to time. Three topics in particular will be examined. First, why fagging came to be such an integral part of the life of Victorian public schools; secondly what defects, real or imagined, produced such a pitch of public concern that grave, ennobled gentlemen like Lord Clarendon, Lord Lyttleton and the Earl of Devon spent many hours enquiring into matters such as whether a fag was obliged to lie in the bed of a senior to warm it for him, or whether a fagmaster could order a junior to poach an egg as well as make tea; and finally some picture will be given of what exactly life as a young fag was like in our great schools a century and more ago.

Surprisingly, fagging almost certainly did not exist in public schools in medieval times. Nor did boys legally inflict corporal punishment on each other. But we should recall how different those early institutions were, and how divorced the Victorian caricature was from the intentions of the founders. Indeed it was only during the course of the seventeenth and eighteenth centuries that fundamental changes produced what came to be the characteristic features and traditions of public schools, such as the fagging system. For one thing, the schools became dominated by boys from the upper classes, to the virtual exclusion of others. This was in sharp contrast to the early days, when foundation charters explicitly created the schools for poor boys in an age when the rich usually had private tutors. The change brought profound sociological consequences. The boys, drawn now from a socially homogeneous group, developed a pronounced group unity. This in turn elevated in importance such issues as conformity to the common characteristics of the group, and fostered a feeling of disregard and snobbery towards the outsiders. Being drawn from an aristocratic elite the boys in any case were prone, even more than other boys, to be intensely jealous of tradition and established patterns of behaviour, and tended to arrange their values in accordance with athleticism, loyalty and courage, rather than with educational achievement, artistic accomplishment, gentleness or humility.

Other changes reinforced still further the revolution away from the early conception of the schools. Almost by accident, and certainly by no pre-conceived plan of educationalists, the system of boarding and 'houses' became established. At first, apart from the 'collegers' established by the foundation who entered by examination, the fee-paying boys from distant homes usually boarded in the nearby towns. Gradually institutions catering exclusively for such boys were set up, and in time these came to be controlled by individual schoolmasters or in some other way drawn into the institution of the school. By the eighteenth century the arrangement whereby a school consisted of a foundation college and a number of other distinct Houses for non-collegers (oppidans, as they were called at Eton) was firmly established, and the educational and social impact of groups of boys living together away from home was as fundamental as it had been unplanned.

One other important change, gradual and unpremeditated, took place. As time went by the schoolmasters, for a variety of reasons, played a smaller and smaller role in running the life of schools outside the classroom. This left a considerable vacuum, a vacuum all the greater because of the remoteness of some schools and the poor state of communications in the pre-railway age. Necessarily the society of boys turned in upon itself, and the link between the boy and his home environment and standards became lost during term-time. Moreover the school year was much longer, and not until well into the nineteenth century did schools generally adopt a three-term rather than a two-term year. Under the old system a single term might easily last five and a half months. In all schools, therefore, though with wide differences among the institutions, the boys themselves became the rulers. The organization that evolved was based not upon educational or moral values, but upon the values of the boys themselves, and it reflected in essence the authority of the strong and experienced over the weak and raw.

By about 1750, therefore, life in public schools had effectively fallen into the hands of the boys who attended them. Boy government, based on hierarchy, conformity, and obedience to rules and traditions, was in the ascendant. And in schools, where a single decade sees an entire generation of pupils, traditions grew very quickly.

One of the principal manifestations of boy government was the emergence of the prefect-fagging system. Just when, or where, the system came into being is unknown. Most probably it grew simply from the prefect system, which in turn was based on seniority and stretched back to the earliest times when the founders placed responsibility on older and reliable boys to help in general school discipline. At Winchester fagging was well established in 1668, and by the middle of the eighteenth century every public school had an informal system operating whereby junior boys fagged for the seniors. The boarding element was vital. The great day schools, St Paul's and Merchant Taylors', had no fagging system, for they did not need it.

The historical background helps in the understanding and perspective of many of the fundamental characteristics of public school life. Boy government, with its respect for tradition and conformity, explains, for example, the elaborate rituals and initiations which became an integral part of the customs of most schools, also the highly developed schoolboy jargon which was idiomatic to the various institutions. Rituals were often irritating and trivial, and they were also frequently cruel and brutal. At Winchester in the 1840s the hands of new boys were scored with burning faggots, the 'tin gloves' initiation. At Marlborough in 1850 an eight-year-old new boy was strapped to a bench while the shape of an anchor was branded on his arm with a poker. At Rugby in the 1830s newcomers had to undergo 'Singing in Hall', being forced to sing solo before a jeering and hostile audience. A drink of salt water stirred with a tallow candle was the punishment for a less than perfect performance. All sorts of minute rules governed the everyday life of boys. In Harrow, for example, juniors could not have their umbrellas unfurled, their trousers were to be turned up, and their hats tilted forwards. Below a certain form not more than two could walk abreast. The new boy too had to familiarize himself with a mass of confusing slang. At Winchester to 'thoke' meant to loaf around, a 'jig' was a clever boy, a 'tunding' was a beating. At Westminster there was a considerable distinction between two types of thrashing, 'tanning' and 'tanning in way'. At Harrow a 'tosh' was a bath, a 'chaw' a cad.

And there was fagging. Uppermost, doubtless, in the mind of the young boy when first he entered his new school was the sort of person his fag-master would be. Many boys entered public school at a very tender age. Ten or eleven was common, while one Harrow entrant in the last century was only four. Some boys had attended private preparatory schools for a year or two before public school, but many had no experience of school-life, having been educated at home by a private tutor. After 1857 all boys would have read, or at least have known by hearsay, the terrifying episodes in *Tom Brown's Schooldays*. Certainly all boys would know of the fagging system, and knew also how capricious it might be.

The first day at school could be a terrifying experience. The long journey, perhaps by coach and four as ten-year-old Edward remembered his arrival at Rugby in the 1830s. The bleak, gaunt buildings – structures for giants to the eyes of a small boy. His own House, and a peremptory greeting from the housemaster, badgered on all sides in a welter of activity. The constant rushing and shouting of boys, the stream of arrivals, the cases, trunks, and boxes, cheery greetings of acquaintances, tear-stained faces of new inmates. Deep-throated roars of 'boy' or 'fag' from the awe-inspiring seniors. Edward, with his case and hat-box, was shown into a large room full of junior boys. The chattering stopped. The big boys crowded round. 'He shall be my slavey,' said one, and immediately fights broke out. After a time a servant came in and took the new boys to their rooms. They trudged through seemingly endless darkened passages lit only by candles and occasional gas flares on the stone staircases. Everywhere that characteristic school smell, occurring nowhere else, and never forgotten. There were six beds in Edward's room; being the only newcomer in that chamber he, of course, had the smallest one in the least favoured position. Ahead lay the initiations and the allocation of fags. The seniors lined up the new boys, inspecting them like cattle at a market. Edward trembled uncontrollably, fearful alike to be chosen by a bully or not chosen at all until no others were left.

Fagging, initiation, slang and other rituals were all an integral part of the complex boy society that developed in public schools, and during the seventeenth and eighteenth centuries almost imperceptibly innovation turned into custom and custom into tradition. But the process was not without checks. Occasional headmasters, concerned at the excesses of the societies they nominally controlled, tried to reassert schoolmaster authority. Sometimes they succeeded, but only for a time. The famous rebellions which all the major schools experienced in the late eighteenth and early nineteenth centuries were all either directly or indirectly the responses by boys to attacks by reforming headmasters on what they considered their established privileges. As early as 1768 Eton's praeposters rebelled against Dr Foster for refusing to allow them to punish juniors who broke bounds. At Harrow the boys revolted in 1771 because they felt they should be consulted over the appointment of the next headmaster: as a result the carriage of one of the governors was attacked and the school closed for nine days. Rebellions of varied intensity and significance continued everywhere, being particularly marked, revealingly, during the French Revolutionary period and again in 1818 when national unrest reached a new peak. But whatever the short-term results of the rebellions, the long-run effect was the more or less formal recognition of boy government in public schools, with prefects (or monitors or praeposters as they were variously called) having almost limitless powers within their spheres of school life.

From the last years of the eighteenth century the prefect-fagging system came to be officially recognized by a number of headmasters and so brought within the legal framework of school societies. Both Dr Goddard at Winchester and Dr Heath at Harrow (whose appointment had sparked the 1771 rebellion) acknowledged it, and by the opening of the nineteenth century it was a feature of most public schools. The basis of the system was that certain senior boys had a measure of authority over younger boys, an authority based on the customs and procedures of the boys themselves. Since the authority was, in theory at least, unsupervised and virtually unlimited it could of course easily degenerate into tyranny. When Dr Arnold instituted his great reforms at Rugby in the 1820s and 1830s he found the prefect system firmly rooted, and never attempted to abolish it. Instead he gave his monitors responsibilities as well as power. He placed great trust in the monitors, and in doing so attempted to bend the existing system to serve his moral purpose.

On two occasions headmasters attempted to abolish fagging. Dr Russell's reforms at Charterhouse after 1811 ended in disaster, rebellion by the boys and the reinstitution of stringent fagging. Samuel Butler, who became head of Shrewsbury in 1798, was an altogether more powerful and formidable character than Russell, and his reforms had a lasting effect. But although fagging at Shrewsbury never operated as strictly as in some of the other schools, the social subservience there of junior to senior continued nevertheless, and by the middle of the nineteenth century the select group of monitors were allowed to have fags. Indeed when a Shrewsbury monitor wanted a fag, he bellowed 'Dowl', a word supposedly derived from the ancient Greek for 'slave'.

Recognized by headmasters and sanctified by tradition, fagging became seen as a fundamental feature of public school education by the early nineteenth century. The system, it was said, taught the virtues of obedience to the fags and taught the exercise of authority to the fagmasters. 'I hardly know which is most useful,' gushed Dr Moberly, headmaster of Winchester, 'the habit of obedience which it requires from the lower boys or the exercise of authority on the part of the higher ones. It appears to me to be admirable on both sides.' Dr Butler of Harrow thought 'the only true way to govern boys is to train them to govern themselves'. Freedom from control by adults, never conscious policy in origin, was now seen as a positive virtue in teaching boys independence and authority. Fagging was a principle of limited government. The fag was protected by the custom of his assigned duties and by the attachment to a single master from the bullying which otherwise must prevail. Characteristic of the system was that most headmasters backed to the hilt the prefects in the exercise of their powers. To do otherwise would be to undermine the whole basis of authority. Thus in 1828 the headmaster of Winchester, Dr Williams, expelled six boys who rebelled against the authority of the prefects. At Rugby Arnold expelled a boy in 1836 who had resisted a whipping from a monitor.

Yet just as the system was becoming formalized, and even elevated into an experiment in moral government by Arnold and his followers, opposition became increasingly vocal. In the 1820s Sydney Smith wrote that the public schoolboy was 'alternately tyrant and slave', and another writer of the period thought fagging 'the most barbarous and senseless tyranny that ever was exercised by fools of a larger size over poor creatures of a less'. A contributor in 1829 to the journal *Westminster* thought that 'to black shoes under penalty of being beaten for non-compliance, is slavery in man or boy'. The system, moreover, inevitably produced tyrants, since fags 'when raised to authority cannot be expected to resist the malevolent passion for making others suffer in turn as they have suffered'. A writer in 1848 thought fagging made 'tyrants of big boys, poor oppressed little bedwarmers, message-runners, ball-fetchers, and shoe-cleaners, of the younger ones'. Concentrating its attack on Eton (by no means the worst in this respect) the *Edinburgh Magazine* noted in 1830 that 'by a tacit agreement between the stronger and weaker parties, has been established at Eton the system of fagging – the only regular institution of slave-labour, enforced by brute violence, which now exists in these islands'. Eton also came under attack in 1842 from William Thackeray: 'There are at this present time of writing five hundred boys at Eton, kicked, and licked, and bullied by another hundred – scrubbing shoes, running errands, making false concords and (as if that were a natural consequence) putting their posteriors on a block for Dr Hawtrey to lash at; and still calling it education.'

References to slavery by opponents of the fagging system doubtless struck a responsive note among liberals at a time when feelings over the slave trade itself were running at fever-pitch. Critics of fagging raised other issues too. Fagging resulted in the 'want of independence, both politically and in private life, which has characterized too many of our countrymen'. The system was good neither for fag nor for master. Good example rather than servility ought to characterize the relationship between older and younger boys. The problem was probably enhanced by the *mores* of public school life, which placed so great an emphasis on physical strength and athletic prowess: 'manliness' as the Victorians called it. Organized games became a marked feature at schools in Victorian times, and the growth was conscientiously cultivated by generations of headmasters who saw in such outlets a safeguard against less savoury pastimes. Yet the cult of sport further extended the idea of obedience to the 'captain', and those whose authority was based on physical superiority; and it ensured too that discipline continued to be enforced among boys almost entirely in a physical manner.

Opponents of fagging held that fagmasters became arrogant and bullying, and, in some cases, corrupted the morals of their fags. That a strong sexual undercurrent pervaded many schools is beyond dispute, though the connection with fagging is less clear. Fagging certainly brought older boys into social contact with younger ones at an early stage, and perhaps resulted in a speedier loss of innocence. This whole area of school life, though important, is naturally little documented, and Victorian writers scarcely ever went beyond veiled references and general comments. The

Public Schools Commission of 1861 studiously avoided the subject altogether. Yet occasional glimpses can be vivid enough. In the 1850s at Harrow the letters of John Addington Symonds, according to his biographer, show that 'it was the common practice for every good-looking boy to be addressed by a female name; he was regarded either as public property or as the "bitch" of an older boy'. The headmaster at the time was Dr C.J. Vaughan, who ruled Harrow from 1844 until 1859, and who is generally regarded as one of the great figures in nineteenth-century public school education. A writer in the 1880s extolled Vaughan's 'magisterial mind' and his great 'personal character for piety and Protestantism'. What only a handful knew until recently was that Vaughan's resignation from Harrow was due to the threatened exposure of his homosexual relationship with Alfred Pretor, one of his pupils. Vaughan was subsequently appointed Bishop of Rochester, only to resign after seven days on threat of exposure once more. He ended his days in quiet dignity as Dean of Llandaff. The astonishing capacity of Victorians to cover up such a scandal speaks volumes in itself. Public schools certainly had a private life, and contemporary silence on the most private of all subjects tells us more of Victorian attitudes and standards than it does of prevailing morality.

Up to this point the term 'fagging' has been used in only the most general way; the word has not been defined nor explained. When extremes are very great, to strike a balance between them may well distort the truth. The problem of discussing public school fagging in Regency and Victorian times is that any comment will have only a very limited application, or it will be so hedged with qualification as to be indigestible, or it will be so general as to be banal. Let it be admitted, therefore, that no comprehensive or coherent picture of fagging can ever be drawn. The system was as unsystematic as the boys who evolved it, and it was flexible enough to change subtly with feelings and attitudes of boys. Over a lengthy period of time one would naturally expect institutions to change in content if not in form, and in no school was the organization and operation of fagging immutable. The influence of different headmasters can be seen from time to time in the extent and function of the system. Some schools, like Charterhouse, Winchester and Westminster, had a tradition of strict and onerous fagging; in Eton and Harrow it was far less organized. At Shrewsbury only a select band of praeposters could have fags while at Charterhouse both sixth and fifth forms had the privilege. Some schools had no transition period between the time a boy was a fag and the time he was allowed to have one, while in others the fourth or fifth forms might neither fag nor be fagged. A fag might have one master and a master one fag; in other places fags served all the seniors. An individual boy, especially if he were a House or sports captain, might have three, four or even more fags for himself. Custom determined how fags were allotted, and what the duties and punishments were, and no two schools were alike in this. Moreover, the differences between schools were often mirrored within schools. It was common to find that the organization and duties of fagging differed widely between foundation and non-foundation boys. Houses, too, had varied systems: some strict, others lax. At Harrow, for example, some small Houses had no fagging at all, while others had a well-developed system with carefully defined procedures.

And beyond all such considerations were the boys themselves. A bully could terrorize a junior under any regime, while a boy with a kindly master could find fagging tolerable, or even enjoyable. Fags themselves reacted differently, of course. A sullen, unwilling boy could well invite bullying; a dreamy, unathletic youngster might be forever at odds with his stern environment. Perhaps it is no accident that literary men seem so frequently to have been unhappy at school. Anthony Trollope's years at Harrow were a perpetual torment, with constant thrashings and bullying from the bigger boys (his brother among them). Shelley, whose earliest extant writing is his name carved boldly on his Eton school desk, loathed his school. He rebelled continually against fagging, and suffered because of it. At one time he was hunted by vengeful fagmasters through the town.

On the other hand the vast majority probably came through the experience at public school with few lasting scars. Several factors softened the system. Based on seniority as it was (seniority based usually on time served rather than age), servility was finite. Even in the darkest moments a boy knew that the time would come when he would join the ranks of the elite and command the others. School society soon quashed independence or arrogance in the younger boys, and so bred a sort of insensitivity that was a protective cloak in the barbaric environment. The psychological urge in younger boys to hero-worship their seniors afforded another defence. It was quite usual also for new boys to have older brothers in the same school, although, as for Anthony Trollope, this might make matters worse. Families were much larger in Victorian times and frequently several boys from one family went to the same school: the repetition of surnames on war memorials at many public schools is a tragic reminder of this.

Defenders of fagging, and many had themselves been fags, could point to positive benefits. It inculcated the public school standards of obedience and manliness. Also, the system gave some measure of organized protection. Duties limited by custom could prevent excessive toil, while the fagmaster might take it upon himself to stop his fag being bullied. A writer in the 1850s praised fagging duties for 'the protection they afford to the weak, the restraints they impose on the unruly, the punishments they inflict on the vicious'. Fagging too brought senior and junior together in a manner impossible under any other system. Many masters aided fags with lessons and helped them settle down at school, and out of fagging grew many life-long friendships.

In the most general terms it would seem that the excesses of the fagging system were at their height during the early part of the nineteenth century. By the middle of the century the life of fags was getting somewhat easier and public school society as a whole was becoming more civilized. The process has continued, hastened, no doubt, by modern revulsion against corporal punishment and the spartan toughness which were part and parcel of a Victorian boy's education. In our own time fagging exists still in about two-thirds of public schools, but it is now a very pallid reflection of what it was in Shelley's day. Today the powers of punishment vested in prefects are restricted and controlled; housemasters play a far greater role in school society; and in the majority of schools the duties of fags are laid down and defined in the regulations.

But if fagging was tending to become less severe after the middle of the nineteenth century, there were still plenty of exceptions. In the 1890s a boy was driven to suicide by the frequent beatings meted out by his fagmasters. He dived under an express, leaving a note naming the three bullies. Perhaps nothing reveals more clearly the values of public school authorities than the particular headmaster involved, who asked the coroner's court for a verdict of 'insane' on the grounds that no boy in his right mind would have so ignored the schoolboy code of honour against sneaking as to openly accuse the three seniors. Even more salutary, because it could happen as late as 1930, is the case of a young fag, Charles Fairhurst. The day before he was due to return to Sedburgh after the Easter holidays he hanged himself in his bedroom. The reason for the tragedy, it transpired, was the misery caused by the fagging system at the school. At the call of a prefect each fag had to run; the first to reach the prefect was assigned the task and for this was awarded a mark. Each fag was expected to get twenty marks a week, and if he failed in this he was 'billed' – thrashed. Bullying at the school was apparently rampant, and the stress of constantly listening for the prefects' cry and the endless competition with fellow juniors led Charles to his death at the age of fourteen. The jury at the inquest, returning a suicide verdict, expressed the opinion that all fagging in public schools should be abolished.

The simple truth is that brutality and excesses could exist in almost any school at any period. How typical they were either of school or period is another question. Recalling his fagging days at Harrow in the 1830s a writer remembered years later how wretched were conditions in some Houses where fagging had become little less than tyranny. 'You fag indiscriminately for a fourth-form dunce and for a sixth-form praeposter, having to clean out study after study for your tyrants, and then return to your own with no heart to make it tidy, knowing it will only encourage them to have a violent "scrimmage" there at night. . . . And so the baited boy goes up every night to his bedroom, there to endure a new description of teasing; and it may be midnight, perhaps, before the victim falls asleep, to fight his battles over again in dreams, or sob on his pillow till morning awakes him from unrefreshing rest to another day of misery.' In some bedrooms 'floggings, smotherings, tossing in blankets, and every description of disgusting bullying, were of nightly occurrence'.

At all times, though, the majority of boys probably accepted fagging duties with a cheerful stoicism, like thirteen-year-old Samuel Rivers at Eton in the 1870s. He wrote home to his sister: 'I have been fagging a fortnight and three days and am quite accomplished. I can lay a table quite well and fry eggs. It will be very useful if I go into the Army. Oakton my fag-master is awfully jolly.' Three years later the wheel had turned full circle. 'I have got a fag this half, he is a fellow called Owen, but he is rather stupid and I have to tell him everything. Yesterday he made my tea without putting the tea in and then there was no boiling water in the boys' maids' kitchen, and I was nearly late for Chapel.'

Another fag's recollections of Rugby round about 1840 capture something else. Simpson has a breakfast party. George, his fag, armed with the princely sum of three shillings and sixpence, rushes into town as soon as he has got up and finished his early fagging tasks. What shall he buy? Simpson had sausages last time. A lobster. That would be something. And salad. That comes to one and ninepence. Duck eggs. Something rather aristocratic about duck eggs, and ninepence buys a dozen. And to drink? Tea? Coffee? A bit ordinary. Hot chocolate would be rather a swell thing, and it costs the remaining shilling exactly.

George borrows another fag to help prepare it; he will repay the debt tomorrow. The lobster is cut and laid out on the salad; the eggs cooked and laid around the plate; the chocolate steaming. Simpson and five grand fellows enter, Simpson looking a little anxious until he sets eyes on the table. He smiles at George and turns to his friends: 'This is my fag, the only fag in the school. All the others are idiots.'

Or Jones minor, at Eton in the last year of the century. 'My heart leapt up when Cockerell, who rowed in the Eight and was in "Pop", told me after prayers to put a can of water in his bath, or sent me a note for his friend George Lloyd. To be free, if only as a valet, of Cockerell's room, where the Rules of the Eton Society were framed in light-blue ribbon, and the white cap of the Eight hung upon the corner of a picture, was to taste privilege indeed.'

That a fag's life might be wretched can readily be imagined, but it is not easy to go far beyond imagination. The day-to-day life of the fag long ago has been recorded only infrequently. Reminiscences of the aged, though numerous, are often distorted by time, coloured perhaps by that English characteristic of veneration of youth and school, or, on the other hand, twisted by bitterness left from scarcely remembered wrongs. All school reminiscences, moreover, tend to pick on the exceptional, the remarkable, rather than the average undramatic happenings of boyhood. But certainly we know sufficient to get a very fair idea of what the lives of some particular boys were like in their schools during the last century.

Westminster and Winchester were perhaps the worst. In 1807 one eight-year-old new boy at Westminster found himself obliged to rise at six in the morning, brush his master's clothes and polish his shoes. Then he went to the pump in Dean's Yard for hard water for his master's teeth and to the cistern at Mother Grant's (a boarding-house) for soft water for the master's washing. In the interim he had to get himself up and prepare lessons for early school, which lasted from eight until nine. At nine he had to hurry back to prepare breakfast for his master: tea, toast, with sometimes things to cook as well. If there was time he might get breakfast himself before school began once more at ten, lasting until midday. Between twelve and one he was in the Usher's correcting room, preparing for afternoon school, and at one there was dinner in Hall (the food being very bad, we are told). At two o'clock began three hours further schooling. Between five and six the boy was engaged in buying food for his master's tea (bread, butter, milk, eggs, and other things) and then preparing it. From six until bedtime he did miscellaneous fagging such as tidying, carrying books, and taking various messages for senior boys who bawled out 'election' when they wanted to summon a fag. After two weeks of this the boy hid in the coal cellar instead of getting his master's tea. He was discovered two hours later and taken to his master, who knocked him to the floor with a 'buck-horse', a blow across the face struck with the fist. The fag got up, and was knocked down again repeatedly.

Such arduous duties were by no means uncommon. Also at Westminster young Dacres Adams in 1820 had to call his master and attend to him while he got up, and carry his master's books into school at eight. After an hour's school he went into a special room for half an hour to make birch rods. Breakfast followed, and then two hours school, for much of the time Dacres being obliged to stand by his master's desk in case he was needed to supply equipment or run messages. Playhour at midday was interspersed with taking messages for seniors, after which he had to prepare and cook dinner for his master. Sometimes he had no time for his own dinner; at other times he might snatch it during the odd four or five minutes. In the evening after school there was the usual tea-fagging and general fagging. Every fourth day his turn came to look after the ten Third Year boys in his chamber. Their candlesticks had to be cleaned, candles obtained, beds made, and clothes brushed. He had to clean the basins and fill the pitchers with water, and generally tidy and wash up. He had also to clean the fry-ing pans, saucepans, ovens and grid irons. On such days he had no time to have supper himself.

At Winchester in the 1840s every prefect had a 'valet'. The Junior Valet had to rise at 5.30 and call the others. He had then to light a fire and attend his particular master, brushing his clothes, bringing water, and similar duties. After morning service there was general fagging to be done for the seniors, who summoned fags with the cry 'junior'. Each senior had a 'breakfast fag' who would attend him and cook his meal. Between 9.30 and midday there was school, after which came games for an hour. During games the younger boys might well be expected to cricket-fag or football-fag for the seniors. This could be very tiring for it generally meant fielding or running to fetch balls that had gone out of play. In days before the widespread adoption of cricket nets and with fields often uneven and uncut such fagging was often the most unpopular of all duties. During football matches the fags were ranged behind the goal posts and along the sidelines, and were expected to stop and fetch the balls throughout the games. After games came dinner, then school once more from two o'clock until six. From six until bed-time came general fagging again. The Junior Valet had to light the fire and then prepare and cook supper for his master.

The situation at Charterhouse was little better. We know in some detail the fagging system there from a twelve-year-old boy who gave evidence in 1863 to the Public Schools Commission. This boy entered the school at the age of ten and, being a foundation scholar, lived in a foundation House consisting of forty-four boys. Seniors in the upper-fifth and sixth forms were entitled to have fags, a right conferred by the headmaster though in practice the privilege was rarely withheld and granted strictly in accordance with seniority. Fags were those in the 'petties' (lowest form) and the second and third foıms. Fourth form and lower fifth boys neither had fags nor fagged themselves. Generally speaking each 'Upper' had one fag, though if numbers were uneven a fag might have two masters or a master two fags. Those prefects not already with fags chose them from the new entrants (the most senior having first choice). One can well imagine the trepidation with which new boys faced this selection ordeal, the elation of being first selected, and the shame of coming last.

The new boy had two weeks to settle in before fagging duties commenced. Once started, the daily routine began at quarter to seven when he called his master (the fag himself being awoken by a man-servant). Sometimes if the master had particular schoolwork to prepare he might demand an earlier call. The fag usually had to call his master several times before he could eventually be roused. The fag then attended him, brushing and handing him his clothes.

Early school was from 7.45 a.m. until 8.30 a.m. At 8.30 the fags had to prepare breakfast for their masters; they would make tea and toast, and sometimes cook eggs and porridge. This meal was taken at 8.45, so there was little time for the fag to have any breakfast himself. He would get it at this time if he could, breakfast consisting always of bread and butter and milk. Breakfast-fagging lasted until 9.30, and quite often a fag went back to school without having eaten anything. At noon came games for an hour (unless it was Monday or Thursday, when there was sometimes singing), and during the summer this involved compulsory cricket-fagging. On half-holidays too there was compulsory cricket-fagging in summer and football-fagging in winter. Charterhouse had a game called 'football in cloisters'. During the game fags in goal were 'sent spinning head over heels for five yards along the stones'. During 'scrimmages' in the course of play 'shins would be kicked black and blue; jackets and other articles of clothing almost torn to shreds; and fags trampled underfoot'.

At one o'clock the boys had dinner, this being provided by the school with no additional fagging duties. Afternoon school was from two until four, after which the junior boys could play among themselves unless there was cricket-fagging required. After an hour or so (varying with the time of year) they were locked in their Houses, and from then until bed-time at nine o'clock had to perform general fagging duties and such school preparation as time permitted. The fag had to get his master's books, tidy the study, and generally run messages. The shout 'fag' brought the most junior boy in the fags' room running, and the lowest were therefore the most hard-worked. The number of messages and errands run by the junior fag might well be twenty in one evening, and when questioned by the Commissioners the boy admitted that he at first had longed to get away from Charterhouse.

At seven o'clock came tea, with exactly the same tasks as at breakfast. That is, the fag must prepare the master's tea and wait on him during the meal itself, which lasted until eight. And, as in the morning, the fags had to squeeze in time if they could to have their own meal. Lord Lyttleton asked the boy if the fags ate 'after the big boys, or before them?'. 'Both, I think,' came the reply. 'Whenever you can?' 'Yes.'

There were other duties additional to general fagging, and it so happened that the boy questioned by the Commissioners was both a 'fire-fag' and a 'cocks-fag'. He had been fire-fag for one term and his duty was to look after the largest of three fires; another fire-fag tended two smaller ones. These fires were lit each morning by the 'school-groom', and were then kept alight by the two boys. The fag tended his fire about six times during the course of the day, and on some of these occasions he had to carry the coal in a scuttle and build up the fire. The scuttle was enormous, some three times the size of an ordinary household one. Since he could not lift it himself he usually sought help from the other fire-fag and in turn helped the other boy when necessary. In this way the two were able to lift the scuttle and carry it about twenty yards or so to their fires.

The large fire heated the water-boiler, and so provided the hot water for washing in the mornings, and also the water required at breakfast, dinner, and tea. The fag had also to carry the hot water to the basins where the boys washed. If the fire went out, or the water was insufficiently hot, the fire-fag was punished. The boy had in fact been beaten on several occasions. Punishment consisted of being boxed on the ears and struck across the back. 'With the fists?' asked a Commissioner. 'With the fists.' 'How many blows on your back?' 'About nine, I think.' 'It was a thorough good thrashing?' 'I do not think it mattered.' Asked if he had neglected his fire, bringing the punishment on himself, the boy told the Commissioners 'I knew I had not; the boiler is not big enough for the water.'

He had been cocks-fag for a year. This duty involved cleaning three basins for the prefects four times a day for a week, and a rota of cocks-fags meant his turn came round every three weeks. During his duty week he had also to clean and dry the prefects' towels, each prefect having three towels a week: sometimes 'they drop them on the ground and they get dirtied'. Combs and brushes had to be cleaned and hot water poured into basins. Each morning and evening the cocks-fag asked every monitor if he wanted a bath or a towel, and if so had to provide them.

The life of a fag at Charterhouse was clearly tough, yet the boy told the Commissioners he was happy and, except for fire-fagging, did not find his tasks burdensome. There was apparently little bullying at the school and the boys were assured of about nine hours sleep.

This was in very sharp contrast to the horrific experiences of a Westminster fag, William Meyrick. William entered Westminster College at fifteen, and so brutal and degrading was his treatment as a fag that his father withdrew him a year later. On leaving, the boy wrote a detailed account of his experiences, and they are worth quoting at length, for no summary can do justice to the bitterness and veracity that ring from the prose of the sixteen-year-old.

He starts with Sunday evening.

We were supposed to be in college at a quarter to ten o'clock, in order to be able to attend prayers in the upper election room at ten minutes to ten. I, as a junior, always contrived to get into college at half-past nine, so as to be able to see that there was clean water in my senior's jug, or bath, as the case might be; and if there was not any there, to go and fetch some from the tap, outside the dormitory. I, also, as being that working junior, had to put round two matches to each cubicle belonging to the upper elections, and also to be able to give matches at any time to any of the election above me. After prayers I had to go to my senior and ask him whether he would take tea or coffee; if he did, I made him what was required, and then I was allowed to go to bed; being very lucky if, after having been obliged to make tea or coffee for my senior, I escaped personal chastisement from the monitor in the dormitory for not being in bed sooner. During the summer, there is a junior every morning who is denominated 'call'. His duty is to call every one in the election at the time he wishes; generally about five o'clock in the summer. There being eleven juniors in our election it did not come to one's turn above once a week . . . You had to ask them the time they wanted to be called just before prayers the previous night. During the winter two juniors were employed as calls. One was employed to call fellows, and the other one had to get up and light the fires in the upper and under election room, and get four kettles boiling before any senior or upper election boy came down stairs. The call up stairs had to pull the fellow out of bed; the earliest generally was half past 3 o'clock.

At Westminster, which was a relatively academic institution, some seniors not infrequently wished to be called very early in the morning to prepare their work, and the duty of rousing them fell on the boys on call. While getting up there were continuous cries of 'clock' from the seniors, at which upstairs call had to answer 'coming', and go and give the time.

Also cries of 'election', which was the summons to all fags to attend the seniors to run on various errands.

The boy continues:

> at 8 o'clock we go into school till 9 o'clock, we then take our senior's books down school, and go to breakfast in college hall; we there answer election and wait upon the seniors and the other elections above us, running out to the confectioner's for rolls, tongue, ham, &c., &c. There is a junior every day in college who has to stay in college all day. He is called 'watch', and his business is to answer 'election', and fag for everyone who comes into college during play hours; he has to keep the fires, see that the kettles boil, and attend to everything.

General fagging continued between morning and afternoon school, and in the evenings the juniors settled down to their various special duties.

> There is a junior who is called 'light-the-fire'; he has to see that the packets of tea, coffee, and sugar, and cans of milk are delivered in college, has to make three teas during the evening, has to sweep and keep the rooms in order, keep the fires up, and see that the kettles are boiling, run up with kettles to the seniors for washing their hands in the dormitory; no easy task to manage, with four kettles; to have hot water for all the upper elections, and to keep at the same time boiling water for tea, &c., &c. And if there is not a plentiful supply of boiling water always on the fire, you get licked in every direction, in fact, by everyone above you in elections, who wants boiling water and cannot get it, because it is nearly impossible to keep enough boiling, always ready, owing to the immense consumption. Every two minutes you have to fill the kettles, and you are very lucky if you have two minutes to sit down, let alone time to think about beginning an exercise, perhaps long, and requiring a great deal of care. This duty comes to a junior three times in a fortnight, and often many more times, because if any juniors have been playing in a foot-ball match, &c., the seniors sometimes say they need not do any work that night; so it often falls to the lot of other juniors, who have not been playing, to take the extra work, and I felt that very much last half. I was always doing extra work, because I happened not to be good at playing foot-ball; I did not care about it.
>
> There is also a junior who is called 'tenor'; he has to light all the lights all over college, and look after the upper election room fires. During the winter, when we have our 'lock-hours' at 6 o'clock, it is tenor's duty between 6 and half-past to go round to all the seniors and ask them whether they will 'please to take anything by orders'. If they want something, tenor writes it down on a piece of paper, and goes on to the next senior. Tenor is bound to take any orders from

any of the other elections, but he is not obliged to ask any of them whether they will take anything, except the seniors. Some or other of the upper elections are always giving tea-parties during the winter months, so tenor is always occupied getting orders and taking them in till supper-time, which is 7 o'clock, and he is very lucky if he has time to go to hall at all and get any supper. When tenor has gone round and got the orders from the seniors, he has to go up to college door and ring; and 'College John', who is waiting outside, reads the orders and gets them from Sutcliffe's or any of the shops near at hand. When tenor rings the bell for John, he has to cry out, 'Any more orders? John is going off.' One junior one day made a mistake and cried out, 'Any more orders? John is about to leave.' He was called into the upper election room immediately and very narrowly escaped 'tanning' for this breach of college discipline; as it was he was kept half-an-hour listening to the conceited trash of a tyrannical bully. During November, December, January, February we are locked up at a quarter to 6, and we come out of school at half-past 5. It is almost impossible to light all the gas in college in that time. At a quarter to 6 you have to answer your name in the upper election room, and if you are not there before he comes in to the room (generally a little before a quarter to 6) you have to submit to being struck like a dog, without a murmur or even a look. If you have not had time to light all the gas everywhere, you are called up by some senior or seniors, and have to undergo another degrading punishment. Often when you are hurrying about, lighting the gas, some senior will call you back and send you to fetch some petty trifle, without any consideration for you, and apparently with no other view than to get you a licking for not having lit all the gas. At 10 minutes to 10, when Mr Ingram comes in to read prayers, tenor has to go to the upper election room door and cry out, 'Phillimore ready, O'Brien ready, Bosanquet ready,' &c., &c., till he has been through them all. After prayers he has to stand at the upper election room door, and cry out, 'Struck 10.' Then the monitor of chamber replies something in Latin, which I never could quite catch; but very often the monitor keeps tenor standing at the door holloaing this out for five or 10 minutes, either too idle to reply, or with the laudable intention of delaying tenor in the performance of his other duties. Then tenor has to go round to all the other seniors, and ask, 'Do you want tenor, please.' Then if your own senior or seniors wanted tea or coffee, you had to make it for them. Then you had to put out the gas in the under election room and middle rooms, and then you were allowed to go up into the dormitory and undergo from the monitor of chamber some degrading punishment for not having been up in the dormitory before.

Tenor has to carry a watch about with him during the evening, and has to answer the time to the seniors when they holloa 'Clock', and to the 3rd elections when they holloa 'Time'. The seniors holloa 'clock' one after the other; a senior will holloa 'clock' and you will answer him loud enough for any one within 50 yards to hear him, but some other senior, although he be standing only three feet away from him, will holloa 'clock' a second after, and so they go on all evening; and the same with 'election': there is not 5 minutes during the evening without 10 or 12 'elections' being holloaed; and sometimes much more frequently, one after the other, a stream of them.

There are two juniors who are called 'put to rights'. At 25 minutes to 10 they have to ask permission from the monitor of chamber whether they may go and put to rights: one has to go and put the tables right and sweep the room up, and the other one has to put chairs for the seniors and chairs for the 3rd elections, and if there should be one chair too much, or one wanting, you are certain, after prayers, to be licked in such a way with a racket or walking stick that you cannot stand upright for the next day or two. Being 'put to rights chairs', as it is called, is a very hard duty; you have to run up and down to the dormitory to fetch chairs, because there are none in the upper election room, and you have got barely time to do it in. After prayers, 'put to rights chairs' has to carry up all the chairs again into the cubicles where he took them from and if the chairs are not exactly where they were before, you certainly have to undergo some ingenious punishment. Some new chairs, which were given to the under election rooms, were forbidden by Mr Ingram to be used in the upper election room, and the monitors had orders to see that they were not used there. They were obliged to be taken into the upper election by 'put to rights chairs' for prayers, but he had strict orders to take them into the under election room again directly after. He had to take them in again during the evening, about 11 o'clock, when the juniors are in bed (if they are lucky enough). Some senior wants a chair, goes into the under election room and takes one; next morning some senior finds one of these chairs in the upper election room, asks who was 'put to rights chairs' last night; when he is told he sends for the junior, and asks him why he left that chair in the upper election room last night. The junior says he certainly took them all out of the room last night. The senior says 'that is all bosh,' and gives him a brutal licking. After you have taken all these chairs up stairs, you have got to ask your senior or seniors whether he will take tea or coffee; if they do take it, you have to make it for them.

'Put to rights tables' is a rather lighter task. You have to clear up the tables and put them straight and sweep up the room and see that everything is neat and nice. One Saturday evening a junior, who was 'put to rights tables', had neglected to put a Bible on the corner of the table on which Mr Ingram reads prayers; the second election whose turn it was that night to see that the junior had cleaned the tables properly, and put the Bible in the proper place, had no time to tell the junior to go and get one, but caught up a Greek testament and put it there instead. Mr Ingram read prayers from his own book, as usual; and directly after prayers, a tyrannical bully of a senior, who saw that it was a Greek testament, called the second election, told him to fetch his (senior's) walking stick, and then, having made him touch his toes, beat him with this stick till it broke over his back, and then the poor fellow was allowed to stagger from the room.

It often comes to the turn of a junior to be 'tenor', 'light-the-fire' and 'put-to-rights', and perhaps to be one of the calls for to-morrow, and to have to get up at half-past 3 in the morning. All these duties are performed during the time we are supposed to be doing our work. There is not a night, but what you have one or other of these duties to perform, besides making teas for your senior, and answering 'election', and general fagging.

Punishments at Westminster were varied and brutal. 'Buckhorsing' was frequently inflicted on fags for such minor offences as not answering quickly enough to the call 'election'. There was also 'tanning', described by William Meyrick as 'hitting you on the back of the hand, or on the calves of the legs with a racket, or by making you put your hand on the table with an order to knuckle down, and hitting you over the knuckles with the sharp end of the college cap or book, or paper knife'. Caning was administered by the monitors. The junior had to touch his toes 'and they leather into you with the cane. Sometimes you tumble over, and then you have to stand up again.' The most feared and the most dangerous punishment was 'tanning in way'. The 'way' was a small place with a washbasin; the offending boy stood with one leg raised into the basin while the seniors in turn ran and kicked him from behind.

The terrifying revelations of William Meyrick show Victorian school life at its blackest. It was a harsh world, that minor universe of self-governing boys which made up the public school system. Yet for all the defects and enormities the schools have always attracted far more devotion and loyalty from alumni than recrimination. The very qualities inculcated in schools have no doubt helped. Traditions, even burdensome ones, became valued for their own sake. Despite the evidence of Meyrick and others, the Public Schools Commission found sufficient merit in fagging to recommend its retention, and fagging continues in most public boarding schools today.

Stoicism and bravery in the young allies with nostalgia in the elderly. School literature glows with glories and achievement sufficient to obliterate all but the deepest miseries. The public schools' peculiar virtues give their own protection: the 'stiff upper lip' and unwillingness to complain join forces with the felicitous ability of memories to soften suffering in retrospect.

Malcolm Falkus (Marist Convent, Paignton, and St Boniface's College, Plymouth) is a Senior Lecturer in Economic History at the London School of Economics. He has written extensively on modern British and international economic history.

5

Boy made Man

PEREGRINE WORSTHORNE

Much the most unpleasant part of my wartime military service was the period of army training, which proved far more arduous and dangerous than anything I experienced on the real field of battle. (No doubt I was lucky.) I hated and feared those sergeant instructors far more than I ever came to hate and fear the enemy. There was one particular assault course, for example, in the Welsh mountains, when a fellow officer-cadet was shot dead. In theory, it was a terrible mistake, and the instructors who were meant to be simulating real battle conditions with live ammunition had gone a shade too far, or rather too near. But in fact we knew them to be a sadistic and bloody-minded crew, and those supposedly make-belief bullets were just as much fired at us in anger – perhaps more so – than anything fired at us later by the Germans.

As for the sight of blood, that too – as far as I was concerned – has stuck in my memory as far more vividly and horribly to do with training for battle than with battle itself. There was that incident during bayonet practice in about 1943, when another lot of army instructors splattered us with great buckets of pigs' blood, while urging us on to the dummies with cries of 'Hate, hate, he killed your mate.' That, without doubt, was the most sickening part of my war. By comparison with this kind of training, battle itself, in the event, seemed amazingly civilized.

In just this way has adult life seemed amazingly civilized by comparison with the training for it, i.e. my years at an English public school. The theory, presumably, was to prepare one for, so to speak, the battle of life; to put one through a kind of dress rehearsal for the great drama of adulthood. But in my experience, adult life has proved to be child's play compared with those immeasurably more challenging years at public school. Never have I felt it so necessary to be a man as when I was a boy.

It is sometimes said that the English public schoolboy, like Peter Pan, never grows up; that the memory of his schooldays is so golden that he can never bear to adapt to the grey workaday world of reality. This was certainly the picture of Eton painted by Cyril Connolly in his celebrated *Enemies of Promise*. Adult life, for him, he implied, was a perpetual anti-climax. This was true for me, but in a very different sense. True, adult life has proved an anti-climax, but only in the sense that it has proved so much easier than one was led to expect; so much less awful than the reality schoolmasters threatened us with.

I remember, for example, complaining to my housemaster about being savagely punished for an offence which I had never committed. His reply was to tell me to stop whining – the sooner I learnt that the real world was an unjust place the better for me. But if unjustly picked upon in real life, one gets in touch with a solicitor, or writes to *The Times*, or to one's M.P. At school there was absolutely no protection, no Court of Appeal. Only at school was the human condition like Hobbes' state of nature – nasty, brutish, although far from short.

Not that I went to a particularly brutish public school. Rather the opposite. By the standards of the time Stowe was thought to be progressive. Most of the boys seemed to enjoy it. In the end, I did too. But the early years were unmitigated hell. Never in later life have I suffered such terror, such loneliness, such hunger, such pain, such oppression, such injustice; or had reason to believe that human nature was so vile. No doubt much of this suffering was my own fault. Other boys managed much better than I, for which they – not the public school system – deserve credit. The system itself was barbaric, operating in defiance of all the known rules of a civilized polity and therefore positively guaranteed to oppress the weak and the vulnerable.

There is a category of boy – and I belonged to it – who should not be sent to a boarding school. The category consists of boys whom other boys are likely to dislike. Needless to say, such unfortunate creatures are not going to have a good time at any school. But at least at day schools they go home in the late afternoons and at weekends. However miserable they may be during school hours each day, there is always the consolation that after lessons are over, they can escape their tormentors for a temporary respite in the safety of the home.

I sometimes think of this when I walk past any London school playground where the kids are theoretically enjoying recreation, shouting, laughing, chasing each other and generally larking around. It all looks so innocent, so much good, clean fun. But if one pauses a moment and looks a bit closer, what one sees usually is one boy, smaller than the others, being hunted. The pursuers may be enjoying themselves, but the victim looks petrified. But at least he, being at day school, knows that the 'game' is of relatively short duration. The bell for lessons will soon go, and after the lessons he is off home. But that was not the case for me at boarding school. After the playground 'game' the hunt continued in the changing room, and after the changing room, in the dormitory. Even nightfall provided no escape.

Or so it seemed at the time. The three-month term stretched before one like eternity. In those days – the 1930s – one never went home at weekends, as is now the practice, and only very rarely was one taken out by visiting parents – and then only to the nearby hotel where one was surrounded by other boys who managed to exude menace even with their parents. None of this mattered for the boy who was happy at school. But for the boy who was unhappy to the extent that I was unhappy, it was an outrageous fate.

I rather suspect that my mother realized this at the time. But it was impossible in those days to do much about it. All the boys of my class – rather upper – went to public schools and to be taken away was thought to be a momentous step, almost beyond imagining. In any case, Stowe was felt to be the mildest and sweetest school going. I would almost certainly be even more unhappy anywhere else. As for day schools, none of the right social kind existed in those days. Westminster, which then, as now, had day boys, would have been regarded as quite unsuitable socially. My father had been to Eton, as had my stepfather, and pretty well all my contemporaries were there too. By sending me to Stowe, enough conventions had been broken already; a day school would have been cranky to the point of madness.

But I had better begin at the beginning, since before one is sent to public school, one goes first to a preparatory school, which is a kind of apprenticeship for the apprenticeship. The first prep school to which I was sent, aged eight, a select and aggressively Roman Catholic establishment, was called Ladycross, near Seaford, Sussex. I was only there one term before my mother decided to take me away, as a protest against its hygienic conditions. I had caught impetigo, which is a disgusting skin disease, associated in those days with slum conditions, and my mother blamed this on the fact that there were no individual baths, just one big communal tub into which we were all immersed together once a week. That, at any rate, was the excuse for taking me away, although I suspect that my mother's real reason was more to do with religion than with hygiene. At about that time, she had begun to have doubts about the Catholic faith, and impetigo was seen by her to be extra evidence of the Church's backwardness and irrelevance to modern progress. Hung on the school bathroom wall there was a picture of a pink cherub, under which was inscribed: 'Mummy says, cleanliness is next to Godliness, but I say it is impossible.' This was a joke, of course, but my mother thought it a joke in bad taste, in the light of my impetigo.

So, after one term, I never went back to Ladycross, although to this day I still get letters from old Ladycross boys, who were my contemporaries there, inviting me to reunion celebrations, on the assumption that even so short a sojourn at such a beloved establishment must have left me with memories worth seeking to revive. One such old contemporary is a member of my London club and whenever we meet, he tells me the latest school news, although I have absolutely no recollections of the place except for having had my face covered there with blue paint, because of the aforementioned impetigo.

After Ladycross came Abinger Hill, near Dorking, which was a progressive, non-denominational establishment very much favoured by the avant-garde parents of those days, since the headmaster believed in the Dalton plan system of learning, which was then all the rage. This meant that the children could plan their own academic curriculum, it being left to them to decide which subjects to concentrate on most. My favourites were English and History, to the exclusion of the Classics and Mathematics. The idea was that one would work best at what one wanted to learn most. For some boys, with greater powers of self-discipline, this seemed to work quite well, but for me it was academically disastrous since, three years later, when the time came to take Common Entrance for public school, my progress in Classics and Mathematics was so minimal as to guarantee dangerously inadequate results.

But my years at Abinger Hill were, on the whole, relatively happy. The boys there were very much out of the ordinary, with a high proportion of eccentrics and sophisticates. I remember my lot of new boys included a rather fat eight-year-old whose *sangfroid* was such as to be unforgettable. Our first class was taken by the headmaster, who, in order to put us at our ease, read out an extract from, I think, one of Macaulay's essays. It was totally above my head but agreeable to listen to. After about twenty minutes he stopped, and asked us whether we had any questions. None of us had. We were all, naturally enough, tongue-tied, except for this fat eight-year-old, who was sitting next to me. To my astonishment, up went his podgy little hand. 'Yes, Edward,' said the headmaster, who was progressive even to the point of using Christian names, which in those days was highly unconventional. 'What is your question?' 'Not really a question, Sir,' said my neighbour, 'more an observation. I just wanted to tell you that with your voice you could fill the Albert Hall.' The boy's name was Edward Boyle.

Abinger Hill, as I say, was a progressive school and we did not wear a school uniform. Instead we wore open necked shirts, corduroy shorts, and cardigans, and sandals on our feet. For my first few terms this was a serious problem, since my mother, not wishing, understandably enough, to waste the expensive and more formal outfit she had been compelled to buy for me to go to Ladycross in, insisted on that being worn out first, before she would buy me the different Abinger Hill togs. So for my first few terms, I went around looking conspicuous, which is the last thing a little boy wants. At any other school such a fate would have been unbearable. But not at Abinger Hill, which was accustomed to eccentricity.

The headmaster, for instance, did not believe in corporal punishment. But this did not prevent him from beating us occasionally, although it was not called beating. It was called golf practice. And it was conducted in a jolly spirit. 'Take down your trousers, dear boy,' he would say. 'I have it in mind to practice a stroke or two, using your bottom as the ball, if you don't mind.' Then he would draw from his enormous golf bag some suitable club – depending on the nature of the offence – and apply it with a tremendous swing. I don't think this did me any harm except to put me off golf for life. It also put me off, at an early age, the deceits of progressive humbug.

But there was another eccentric at Abinger Hill – a boy, this time, who went too far. He was extremely precocious sexually, and took an excessive liking to me. But the liking took the form of threatening to strangle me. He was in the same dormitory as I, and night after night he would whisper how this project was taking shape in his mind, giving me all the details of how the dreadful deed would be done. He had, he said, made several botched jobs of the same general kind at other schools which he had attended, from three of which he had been expelled. But there was no need for me to be worried. There would be no mistake this time.

To begin with I was rather fascinated. He was older and bigger than me, and full of worldly knowledge. Detachable shirt collars were his hobby and he collected them, in all shapes and sizes, as other boys collected butterflies or stamps. His favourite was an outsize Van Heusen white evening collar, and it was with this, he confided, that I was to be privileged to have my neck wrung. He then proceeded to show me how, quite realistically. I was terrified. But I had been sworn to secrecy. I must never tell a soul about 'our' plan, since that would be a sign of childish immaturity. The torment went on for quite some weeks, until one day the date was fixed. I was to meet him in the woods at such and such a time.

It never occurred to me to go to the headmaster. The idea of seeking protection seemed out of the question. I was entirely under the boy's spell. So far as the school went, he was, in my mind, the dominant force from which there was no conceivable escape. So there was only one thing to do: run away. Nobody who has not been at boarding school can have much idea how radical such a solution would appear to a nine-year-old boy. My decision to run away was certainly the most courageous I have ever taken in my life. Running away! The phrase is, of course, absurd, since it suggests taking the easy way out, whereas running away from school was a monumental challenge. At that time in my life, I had never been on a train unaccompanied; had no idea, in any case, of how to get to the railway station some fifteen miles away. To this day, I have no recollection at all of how I did overcome the difficulties. I must have walked to the station and borrowed money there for a ticket to Waterloo. I do remember, very clearly, arriving at Waterloo, because at that point I made a decision which was later to cause me trouble. I went to the cinema there, which in those days used to show continuous newsreels, not because I wanted to, but because I dreaded going home. How could I possibly explain to my parents why I had 'run away'? Anything to put off that fateful confrontation.

Eventually, of course, I could delay no longer. To my infinite relief my parents were out to dinner, and the servants put me to bed. My mother, however, was summoned home soon enough, and through floods of hysterical tears I told my story. The relief at getting it off my chest was indescribable. I was told not to worry, to have a good night's rest, and she would see what was to be done in the morning.

Unbeknown to me, she then telephoned the headmaster and the conversation – which she recounted to me some years later – went something like this:

My mother: Sorry to be ringing you in the middle of the night, Mr So and So, but I am very worried about Peregrine.

Headmaster: Worried about Peregrine? Why on earth? The dear boy is doing very well. Of course he's fast asleep in the dormitories by now. It's long after the boys' bedtime, you know.

My mother: Fast asleep he may be, but he's not in the dormitory, headmaster, he's right here at home and I suggest you get up to London right away and explain what has been going on.

This the headmaster did, without a moment's delay, and I was woken in the small hours to repeat my story to him. He tried to bluff a bit. Hadn't I been imagining things? etc. In any case, when had I left school? How had I got to the station? He wanted to know the full details. So I told him, not forgetting to mention the newsreel film part. That gave him the opportunity. He turned to my mother with a smile. 'I think, Mrs Worsthorne,' he said, triumphantly, 'Peregrine may have been feeling in need of a little holiday, weren't you, dear boy?'

That damned newsreel. I could see that even my mother felt that it was rather a frivolous thing to do in the circumstances, casting doubts on the genuineness of my tribulations. How little grown-ups understand, I thought, not for the first time or the last.

But I refused to go back to school while X, my kinky admirer, remained. A few days later, I was told by my mother that she had heard from the headmaster, who had checked up on X. He *had* been expelled from several other schools for strange offences. My fears, in short, had not been made up or exaggerated. So X was duly removed and I was able to return to school.

The rest of my time at Abinger Hill was pleasant enough or, at any rate, comparatively uneventful. In fact I remember little about it, except for one other aspect. My brother and I were the only Catholic boys at Abinger, so special arrangements had to be made for us to go to Mass in a nearby Parish Church. This meant missing school breakfast on Sunday; no great loss incidentally, since, being a progressive school, its food was extremely cranky, consisting of lots of oatmeal mash, raisins, and things like that. The priest, taking pity on us, used to invite us round to his presbytery for post-Communion bacon and eggs and toast and marmalade. At no period in my life have I ever looked forward to Mass with such enthusiasm, or been so absolutely regular in attendance, never missing a single Sunday. Nor was this merely cupboard love. I became genuinely religious, and even read a lot of theology. Looking back on it there can be no doubt that those scrumptious breakfasts were at the root of my most intense period of religious experience, since the intensity declined as soon as I moved on to Stowe, where no comparable gastronomic inducements were available. (Rather the opposite: going to Mass involved a long and arduous uphill bicycle ride.)

But enough of these preliminaries. What about Stowe itself, where I went, aged thirteen, in 1936? It is a peculiarity of the public school system of education that it defies all the obvious norms of human psychology. First the child is sent to a preparatory school, the hierarchical ladder of which he is encouraged to climb. This I had done. Towards the end of my time at Abinger Hill, I had grown into a great swell, editing the school magazine, winning the top prizes for literary composition, becoming an all-powerful prefect, and generally developing the tastes and style appropriate to prestige and privilege. This was thought to be a good thing.

But on arriving at Stowe, as a new boy, one found oneself back at the bottom of the ladder again with a vengeance. So far as I was concerned, this was particularly traumatic, since I had done extremely badly in the Common Entrance examination, and therefore found myself in the bottom form for dunces. But I had not done badly because I was stupid, but because, as I have explained, Abinger allowed one to choose one's subjects and I had chosen to ignore the Classics and Mathematics, while concentrating, with some success, on History and English. But Classics and Maths were what counted in the Common Entrance exam.

So there I was at Stowe, very conscious of my intellectual superiority, in the bottom form, surrounded by loutish morons who quickly resented my pretensions. But even without this particular disadvantage, life would have been tough enough, since the sudden shift from being somebody during one's final term at prep school to being nobody in one's first term at public school is bound to be deeply unsettling. Such misfortunes obviously occur in adult life. A managing director disgraces himself and has to go back to square one as an assistant clerk. These tragedies do happen. But when they do, nobody ignores the terrible nature of the emotional strains imposed.

But with schoolboys it is thought to be absolutely normal and natural. Even beneficial. Good for the soul. Perhaps, in my case, it was. How can I tell? But the disturbance was certainly intense and protracted, to an extent that was absolutely excessive by any humane standards. I remember the first one or two terms with absolute horror. Presumably I must have given myself airs, which my contemporaries resented, and decided to punish by merciless bullying.

Two examples will suffice, since this is not a horror story. The instrument of torture used in the first was a laundry basket into which I was stuffed. Then the lid was shut tight, and the basket propelled down a long flight of steep stairs very fast, overturning several times on the way, like a plane looping-the-loop. The other brutality took place when one was having a bath, over the top of which was placed a row of soap racks, to hold one down. Then the scalding hot tap was turned on quite slowly. The more one struggled to get out, writhing in pain and terrified of being scalded, the more general delight was given to the gang of tormentors.

Needless to say, these were not nightly events. But there was no knowing when they were going to take place. Supervision by the masters in the dormitories was minimal, and the prefects, who were older boys, obviously felt that I deserved all that I was getting. In theory I could have complained. But not only would this have been a breach of the immemorial rule against sneaking, it would have been positively counter-productive, because the housemaster was himself even more certain than the boys that I needed taking down a peg or two.

In school stories, in this kind of situation, there is always a happy ending. The little fellow being bullied suddenly turns on the biggest of his tormentors, and, by giving him a black eye, earns the admiration of all, and the life-long friendship of the big tormentor. But I was much too cowardly to do anything of the kind. So instead, for about two terms, I lived in constant dread.

One is told that things like this don't happen nowadays at public schools. But they were not meant to happen even then. Stowe, as I have said, was not some antique Victorian factory for the production of stiff-lipped colonial administrators or army officers. It had been founded in the 1920s by J.F. Roxburgh, an educational pioneer who wanted to extend the frontiers of schoolboy freedom. So instead of being dressed up in tail-coats and stiff collars, or some other kind of old-fashioned uniform, we were allowed to wear the much more relaxed grey flannel suit. And Roxburgh himself made a point of remembering one's birthday. By such trifles, in those days, was it possible to build up a great reputation as a radical headmaster.

Roxburgh always struck me as a phony since, although he claimed to be running a progressive school, he did nothing to make sure that the housemasters lived up to his precepts. Mine certainly seemed to me to do nothing of the kind. He was called A.B. Clifford and nicknamed Fritz, because of his close-cropped hair-style. His passion was the O.T.C. (Officers' Training Corps), which he ran with tremendous enthusiasm. So far as I was concerned, Clifford *was* Stowe, since the character of the House was much more important than the character of the school. And the character of the House, under his influence, was philistine and by no means soft. My parents never realized this, because they were charmed by Roxburgh, and could not believe that anyone appointed by him could be educationally unsuitable.

But this is – or at any rate was – one of the problems of the public

Two images of the public schoolboy. Above, C.H.A. Benedict (Charterhouse) engrossed in watching a house match, c. 1908, and (*right*) the very model of a Victorian *Boys' Own Paper* hero, C.B. Fry (Repton), in the days when he was a Test cricketer, soccer international, F.A. Cup finalist and holder of the world long jump record.

The first term: Mr Roxburgh, headmaster of Stowe when it opened in 1923, welcoming new boys (*above*), and (*below left*) a Talbot Baines Reed hero being greeted at Stonebridge House with the question 'Are you a backward or a troublesome?' Anxious Victorian mothers probably preferred the comforting illustration from an 1897 edition of *Tom Brown's Schooldays* in which Tom consoles the latest arrival at Rugby, little Arthur, whom he has found weeping into his Bible.

In fact and fiction the public schools have become famous for eccentric custom and tradition. Above, the winner with his piece of pancake after the tossing-the-pancake ceremony at Westminster (1914). Below, a page of school slang from the Winchester *Word-book* (1891), and a boy touching the back of his head in salute to a master at Charterhouse (c. 1900). It is said that the boys used to wear their caps back to front and that even when caps ceased to be worn the custom of touching the peak continued.

L

LICET. adj. Allowed.

Ex.—Is it licet to sport bakers up to books?

LOB. The ball called a "yorker" by modern cricketers. It never meant an underhand ball.

LOBSTER. vb. To cry.

Probably a variation of "lowster," or "louster," a Hampshire word, meaning to make any unpleasant noise.

LOGIE. Sewage.

Connected with log occurring in log-pond and log-burn.

LONG-FORK. A stick used as a toasting-fork in College.

LONG-PAPER. Foolscap paper.

LUXER. A handsome fellow. (Obs.)

M

MAD. Angry.

Still so used in some parts of England, and universally in America.

Skeat says it originally meant "severely iujured"; and Johnson gives "enraged, furious," as a meaning.

St. Paul . . . . being exceedingly *mad* against the Church. *Decay of Piety.*

He would change the face of education, said a friend of Thomas Arnold, and he did. His influence was felt not so much at Rugby during his headmastership (1827–42) as in the second half of the century when his pupils carried his ideas and principles to other schools.

The spiritual forefathers of Pele, Best and Billy Bremner, (*below opposite*) the 1867 Harrow Eleven pose casually in their striped costumes with never a trade-mark or sponsor's name among them. Above, fives at Charterhouse in 1912, and the Eton Rowing Eight of 1863.

Runners in the four-mile steeplechase at Ardingly (1926), and (*below*) an enthralling incident in the Eton wall game.

The brutality of school discipline was well publicized by Victorian writers and illustrators, not without cause. Du Maurier neatly sums up a popular image – complacent, anxious, gloating boys, a cheerfully sadistic master, and a victim apparently trying to climb up the wall. Below, the birch and flogging-block, from *Recollections of Eton* (1870).

'Privations that would have broken down a cabin boy, and which would have been thought inhuman if inflicted on a galley slave,' wrote an Old Etonian reminiscing about school living conditions in the last century. But Eton's Long Chamber was probably no more spartan than the dormitories at Westminster (*above*) and Christ's Hospital School.

school system. Parents decide on a school for general reasons to do with its overall reputation, supposing that it is all of one part. I had been put, theoretically, in the care of the charming Roxburgh. But in fact Roxburgh played no part in my life, which was dominated in the early stages entirely by the awful Clifford.

Another deception had to do with the atmosphere of the place. To the visiting parents Stowe looked marvellous, being an eighteenth-century ducal palace on the scale of Blenheim. One can see how parents would be impressed with the thought of their young offspring being educated in such beautifully civilized surroundings, walking along the pillared colonnades, and around the Palladian temples, studying in the baroque library, eating in the great banqueting halls and so on. Roxburgh would show them round like the owner welcoming visitors to a stately home. He was a great showman. But my House, Grafton, had been the servants' quarters of the great palace, and was hideously bleak, with barrack-room dormitories and no space for private rooms, except for the senior boys. Presumably my parents were shown it, just as they must have been introduced to Clifford, but only after their eyes and ears had been so enchanted by the general charm of the place as to overlook the particular squalor of my particular House and the character of my housemaster, under whose shadows the greater part of my early life at Stowe was doomed to be spent.

How did I survive? At this point it is necessary to refer to my physical appearance at that time; to the fact that I was a rather pretty boy. I remember becoming aware of this asset first in school chapel, because my eye kept on being caught by the school's most fashionable master, who was in charge of one of the sixth-form classes. He and his wife were famous for running an exclusive and sought-after salon where on Sunday afternoons they entertained all the brightest older boys. Needless to say, being myself in the lower forms, such intellectual company was wholly beyond my range of expectations. So why was he looking at me with such obvious interest?

No, it was not a homosexual attraction; or rather not that in any simple sense. My looks were of the rather romantic, sub-Byronic kind, and he and his wife liked to gather about them anybody who looked in any way stylish or aristocratic or out of the ordinary.

It has to be understood that Stowe was an entirely self-contained community, stuck in the middle of the countryside, miles away from any town. Apart from a very few masters' wives there were no women. (Except for servant girls, about which more later.) Such feminine grace or charm as existed was supplied by pretty boys, and it was to fill this gap that, to my infinite surprise, I was invited to this famous salon.

This great event, which happened in about my third term, transformed my Stowe life, since it enabled me to escape the confines of my philistine House. Of course there was an element of latent homosexuality, since in a sense my role was to flirt with the older boys, or rather help to create that element of sexual adventure without which all social gatherings lack intensity. I do not recall ever being propositioned. But at the same time I was aware of this dangerous possibility. I used to dress up for the occasion, trying to look romantic with a cloak and floppy hat.

None of it was at all harmful. In fact, for me, it was an immense blessing. As a junior boy, I naturally took little part in the conversation, but enough to be able to demonstrate that I was more, so to speak, than just a dumb blond. Slowly but surely, through this door of the Sunday salon, I began to enter into the intellectual life of the school, under the patronage of these older boys, whose goodwill may not have been entirely innocent. But there was never any question of their asking for their pound of flesh. Such coarseness would have been wholly out of keeping with the highly civilized rules of the salon, where homosexuality was implicit but never rampant.

This was largely true, in my experience, of the school as a whole. Romantic friendships abounded, but only occasionally were they physically consummated. In addition there was a certain amount of straight carnal groping. But the only experience of the latter kind which I can recall had to do with a fifteen-year-old contemporary who has attained fame and fortune in adult life as a jazz singer and writer. He seduced me with incredible despatch on the art room sofa one afternoon. Our paths were to cross again many years later when we both appeared on a television programme. He was defending permissiveness, and I attacking it. After the show his very young new wife, who was accompanying him, along with a claque of other layabout hippies, gave me a contemptuous dressing-down as a typical example of buttoned-up, inhibited, bourgeois, kill-joy Puritanism who had obviously never enjoyed the true joys of sexual freedom. 'It might interest you to know, madam,' I was able to reply, 'that you and I have more in common than you care to recognize. We were both seduced in our teens by George Melly.'

From my own point of view, it was certainly an advantage that in those days girls played no part in Stowe life. Being endowed with neither academic nor athletic distinction I was able to win friends and influence people by virtue of an exceptional personal appearance. But quite apart from this personal consideration, it seems to me that the absence of girls also served a more important general good. Most boys, it had to be admitted, in the latter years at boarding school, suffered severe sexual frustration. Homosexuality was a poor substitute for what their adolescent instincts were truly yearning for. This was certainly true in my case. But as a form of substitution we fell upon romantic literature – novels and poetry – with a ferocious and insatiable appetite. Never afterwards have I read with such concentration as during those last years of boarding school, since never in later life was one to be so spared the supreme and irresistible distraction of female temptation.

It was, of course, an unnatural condition. And it may, by depriving adolescents so totally of girls' company at that vital age, have caused ex-public school men a lasting difficulty in their relations with women later. But at the time it was a remarkable way of building up an intensity of feeling which exploded in the mind instead of in the body. If there had been girls around I do not think it would have been the same. We would have learnt more about women, true, but less about much else.

Strictly speaking, of course, there were girls around, masses of them. But they were servants, known as 'skivesses', who did all the domestic work. I do not recall ever exchanging a single word with one of them, or knowing any of their names although they served all our meals, made our beds and so on. They were not at all the kind of *Upstairs Downstairs* servants we were used to at home in those days. They were coarse, unskilled labour from some industrial town, bussed in and bussed out by the day. In our class-distorted eyes, they were not really human. But many of them must have been sixteen or seventeen, the same as many of us, although we treated them as if they belonged to a different species. Very occasionally a rumour would circulate that some boy had been caught 'going with' one of them. This did not come under the heading of immorality. It was not felt to be wrong so much as disgusting, rather like eating manure.

Which brings me inevitably to the subject of class. Stowe was not a grand school. It was mostly made up of the sons of professional or business people, with just enough 'honourables' to make the list look respectable. In my time there was even a boy baronet. But there were also a number of very obvious non-gentlemen who were the sons of what were then called the 'nouveaux riches'. It is no good pretending that this did not matter. It mattered enormously. Class consciousness was a fact of life. I was at once aware, for example, that most of the boys in my dustbin of a House were exceedingly common; not at all the kind of people one would ever expect to meet at home. They spoke with funny voices, used brilliantine, had never learnt to ride or shoot, had home addresses in industrial cities, referred to their parents as Mum and Dad. Worst of all, their feet smelt. Presumably Major Clifford liked to fill his House with such types; or perhaps Grafton, being such a bad House, could get no other. In any case there they were and I felt exceedingly ill-done-by to be among them.

Of course this was monstrously snobbish and the memory of such feelings now makes me blush. But in self-defence I must plead that it would have been peculiar if I had felt anything else, since in those days the gap between gentry and manufacturers was still immense. And not only between gentry and manufacturers. Even the local doctor at home, or the solicitor, were never treated as equals. They were not expected to use the servants' entrance, as would have been the case a generation earlier, but they were certainly politely kept at a distance. I remember an occasion, at the beginning of the war, when my grandmother, the daughter of an Earl, had occasion to summon a Harley Street dental surgeon up to her house in the country. I was staying with her on holiday at the time and there was much family discussion as to whether he should be allowed to eat with us in the dining-room, or given his meals somewhere in between the dining-room and the servants' hall. In the event, as a wartime concession, he was allowed to eat in the dining-room. But coming from that kind of background how could one be expected to feel at ease with the children of Midlands tradesmen?

The most recognized social problem at the public schools is that of one or two lower class guinea-pigs made miserable by being out of place among a lot of toffs. My problem at Grafton – that of being a kind of 'guinea-pig gent' in a cage of common gorillas – was much rarer but scarcely less awkward.

Needless to say, like all class problems, it had its funny aspects. My mother once sent down to school a London tailor for the purpose of measuring me for a knickerbocker suit – then a perfectly normal form of country apparel – which she wanted me to wear during the next holidays. I was then about fifteen and the plan seemed to me quite reasonable. Indeed, being fond of clothes, I rather looked forward to the occasion. The tailor duly arrived, and we proceeded to go about our business in the school tuckshop annexe which had a large plate glass frontage opening on to the main school thoroughfare. In no time at all there were a hundred ribald eyes glued to the window in menacing mockery. The beknickerbockered spectacle I presented aroused fantastic scenes of mob hostility, as if I had deliberately set out to provoke a riot, by behaviour of obscene irregularity. But how was I to know that a knickerbocker suit, to eyes accustomed to the suburban purlieus of Liverpool, Manchester or Birmingham, was the equivalent of a red rag to a bull?

I have not written anything yet about the actual process of education. My problem here is that I can remember very little about it, until a miracle occurred; or what seemed at the time like a miracle. The year was about 1941, and most of the young masters had gone off to the war. (Not 'Fritz' Clifford, who stayed behind, alas, unlike the master of the salon, who was to win the MC.) To take their place, a number of amateur schoolmasters arrived, who were either too old for military service or in other ways unsuitable. One of these was John Davenport, then about thirty, and already a famous – or rather notorious – London literary character as well as a former Cambridge boxing blue, whose exploits included unceremoniously lifting the then Lord Chancellor on to the mantelpiece at the Saville Club as the only way to stop him boring the company to death.

At the time, of course, one knew nothing about him, except that he was very small, stout and utterly unlike all the other masters. I saw him first in the school library, looking rather dejected, and apparently – or so he recounted later – approached him with the comforting information that life at Stowe was not as awful as it seemed at first sight. He was amused, even touched, and we became great friends, which meant that I spent a lot of time listening to him talking, particularly about literature and history, but also about all the people he knew, Cyril Connolly, Dylan Thomas, Dadie Rylands and so on. Soon he formed a little circle around him of boys he liked, or was amused by, and he would even take us to dinner at the local hotel in Buckingham where we would be given claret and burgundy. Not really given, since John Davenport never had a bean, then or later. So when the bill arrived, he would pass it on to us saying, 'never too soon to learn how to settle these tiresome things,' which we were only too happy to do, in view of the pleasure received.

It is scarcely an exaggeration to say that John Davenport was my education. It was certainly entirely owing to his stimulating company that I was later to win an Exhibition at Cambridge. Two books, in particular, which he told me to read – Tawney's *Religion and the Rise of Capitalism*, and Edmund Wilson's *To the Finland Station* – made all the difference. But more important, he gave us intellectual confidence, since his pleasure in our company, which he much preferred to that of the other masters, was enormously flattering. Fritz Clifford deeply disapproved; so did Roxburgh. Davenport broke all the rules, as he did all his life, right to the bitter end a few years ago. I remember being in his room at Stowe one evening, after he had immured himself there for days on the excuse of having gout. The rather bullying school doctor arrived, sent by the headmaster to check up on the suspected malingerer. John was dispensing port, as well as being in mid-flight of fancy, and, furious at being interrupted, shouted at the doctor: 'Get out of my room, you second-rate little provincial apothecary.' Such Johnsonian rudeness made a great impression.

John did not last long at Stowe. But long enough for my purposes. There were also, as a result of the war, the famous Shakespearian scholar, G. Wilson Knight, and Martin Cooper, who was to become many years later music critic of the *Daily Telegraph*. But these innovations, which transformed Stowe for me, were not chosen by Roxburgh, but by the accidents of war, and I owe Hitler gratitude – not my *alma mater* – for the privilege of having been taught by them.

* * *

Needless to say, the above does not purport to be a fair or balanced account of my public school education. No doubt there were many splendid aspects of it which I have failed to mention. But these I simply cannot remember, since the whole experience was dominated by those first few terms. Perhaps I am making too much of them. After all, there is nothing unique about being cruelly bullied at school; or in having a housemaster whom one despised and hated exercising total power over one. When one thinks of all the far worse things that happen to some people in life these schoolboy tribulations obviously should pale into insignificance.

But they don't. The memory refuses to blur. And the reason, I think, is that for anybody fortunate enough to be born into the old ruling class in Britain, those first terms at a public school were the only time one learnt what life is like for the weak and vulnerable; what it is like to suffer permanent fear and hunger; what it is like to experience savage injustice without any real chance of restitution; what it is like to be dependent on the arbitrary whims, fancies and prejudices of the powerful; what it is like to be subjected to humiliation and persecution by the forces of law and order, or at least with their connivance.

At every subsequent period of life the cushions of class have protected me from most of the unpleasant sides of living in society; have smoothed the rough edges of conflict and competition; have provided protection from the more primitive worries that beset the human condition. Such first-hand knowledge as I have of life in the raw, of life red in tooth and claw, I owe entirely to my early terms at Stowe.

Neal Ascherson, the radical journalist, tells the following story at my expense. As members of a Press party visiting Poland some years ago, we were taken to see Auschwitz. Driving away afterwards, numbed by the horrors of the concentration camp, nobody spoke for a long time. The silence became oppressive, until it was broken by me saying: 'I have never been so glad to see the back of anywhere since leaving public school.' Of course this was an exaggeration in the worst taste. But it was not a joke. Auschwitz did remind me of Stowe. Viewing that scene of desolation and terror and despair, my memory searched for the nearest approximation to such things in my own experience, and Stowe, for want of anything worse, came at once to mind.

This is not necessarily a complaint or a criticism. In some ways, lessons in pain and suffering are more important for a ruling class than lessons in

Latin and Greek. In those pre-war days, paradoxical as it may sound, only a private, boarding-school education, in an institution cut off and self-contained in its own cocoon, could artificially create conditions in which the sons of the wealthy were taught these primary lessons; were deprived, for a year or two, of the advantages of privilege which, ever afterwards, their class would guarantee them.

Nowadays, of course, this case for private education is far less cogent. Manhood is hard enough, even for the most fortunate, without imposing on them this special boyhood burden. But egalitarians who want to destroy the public schools should not imagine that this will be a deprivation for the upper classes. It will, if my experience is anything to go by, be rescuing them from a very special form of discrimination, none the less grim for being immensely expensive and highly exclusive.

Peregrine Worsthorne (Stowe) is Associate Editor of the *Sunday Telegraph*. He also appears on television and radio, and is the author of *The Socialist Myth*.

6
The Individual and the Group
ANTHONY STORR

As a former public schoolboy, I cannot be entirely objective about this type of education, since my own experience is bound to prejudice me; in which direction, I leave the reader to judge. Moreover, since I left school in 1938, there have been many changes in public schools. Most of these changes have tended to make public schools less authoritarian and more egalitarian. But many of the most characteristic features of public school life remain the same; and, since human nature does not change much, the advantages and disadvantages which boys encounter in that life also remain the same.

What I have to say applies chiefly to boarding schools taking only male pupils; that is, to the archetypal public school of which most people think when public schools are discussed. There are, of course, excellent public schools which take both sexes and which have day-pupils. But these schools do not constitute the majority of public schools, and do not present in such clear-cut form the problems with which I shall be concerned. I am therefore omitting them from consideration.

Nor shall I consider in detail the formal education which public schools have to offer. Although some state schools offer facilities which are as good as, or better than, some public schools, the latter tend to provide both a higher proportion of staff to pupils and a wider range of subjects.

In addition, extra-curricular activities like music, art and games are generally better provided for in public schools. I must leave these important aspects of school life to experts in education.

My concern is with the social structure of the public school; with the hierarchy, the prefectorial system, the aggregation of adolescent boys in groups and their segregation from their families. Does the public school system promote growth toward psychological health and maturity, or does it produce 'old boys' who never grow up? Are public schoolboys aided by their experience to become independent, self-reliant and confident? Or are they moulded into a rigid pattern which precludes true autonomy?

Let us look at the advantages of the system first. Most boys, from the age of seven or eight until well after the onset of puberty, prefer the company of their own sex and age-group; and there are sound psychological reasons for this preference. For it is in interaction with their peers that boys learn the most important lessons of how to live in society. Of course the atmosphere of a boy's home is of paramount importance, especially in the earliest years of his development; and no one will be inclined to deny the value of having loving parents who both provide affectionate support and who also constitute models of male and female. However, psychoanalysts and others have tended to overemphasize child-parent relationships at the expense of peer relationships; and research into the development of both human children and their nearest relatives, the subhuman primates, has demonstrated that play and other interaction with contemporaries is also vital for normal development. Indeed, in the case of Rhesus monkeys, even the bad effects of severe maternal deprivation can be largely alleviated if the motherless monkey is allowed enough play with contemporaries at the right time in its development.

Whilst it is clearly unwise to extrapolate directly from monkeys to man, this type of research has stimulated psychologists to take a new look at the process of socialization in human children, and to attribute more importance than heretofore to the influence of other children upon normal development. Human children are capable of making some response to contemporaries from as early as eighteen months old; and they need the company of their peers right through childhood into adult life if they are going to develop happily. Public school life comes, of course, well towards the latter end of that long period of development, but is none the less important for that.

Both adolescents and pre-adolescents need to consort with their own sex in order to confirm their sense of sexual identity. Boys and girls generally go through a period in which the characteristics of their own sex are exalted whilst those of the opposite sex are denigrated. Thus boys regard girls as 'silly', and girls look on boys as 'rough'. Although many schools now provide sexual instruction, what children learn from their contemporaries is more important. Boys need to find out that others have the same sexual doubts, interests, feelings and preoccupations; and to share with their companions the curiosity, anxiety and fascination which sex arouses in those not yet mature enough to experience its full force. Boys who do not experience this mixing with contemporaries during adolescence, including the exchange of sexual information, smutty jokes and other obscenities, often have little idea of the normal range of male sexual experience; and it is common to find that adults who consult psychiatrists on account of sexual difficulties have believed themselves, in adolescence, to be abnormal solely as a consequence of isolation. Such a belief leads to loss of confidence in masculinity, with resultant difficulties in making sexual relationships.

Nor is it only in the sphere of sex that interaction with contemporaries and near-contemporaries of the same sex is important. Human societies, like many societies of other primates, are hierarchies governed by conventions of dominance and submission: that is, by aggression canalized and controlled in ways which are ritualized and socially acceptable. These conventions have to be learned, and it is vital for boys to do so if they are to become confident in society. That is, boys have to learn when to stand up for themselves and when to give in; when to fight and when to yield. It is important to find out by experience that bullies are sometimes cowards; and that the diffident may have hidden sources of strength. We know from the study of other primates that monkeys who are first reared in isolation and then introduced to a group never learn how to handle their own or others' aggression. They will put themselves at risk by challenging superiors, or cower from those whom they need not fear. Because they have never had the opportunity, they have never learned their place in the hierarchy. Exactly the same is true of boys. Boys who have difficulty in mixing habitually 'get it wrong'. They appear either arrogant or cowardly; often both at once. Because they have not learned any generally accepted way of relating to superiors or inferiors, they alternate between dominance and submission in an awkward fashion, often antagonizing both older and younger boys without intending to do so. For the average boy without particular difficulties in social relationships, public school society provides a valuable microcosm of what is to come. In after-life, it is important to have the feel of how to get on with superiors, equals and inferiors in a society which, however democratic, is unavoidably hierarchical; and the small society of 'House' and school gives opportunities to learn which may be lacking elsewhere.

'Day-boys' are at a disadvantage in this respect, for they do not have the same opportunity of social learning during leisure-time activities, and often have to waste a considerable amount of time in travelling which might be better spent with their schoolfellows.

In addition, the five or so years at public school provide opportunities for rising through the hierarchy with increasing responsibility for the welfare both of individuals and the group which are obviously more extensive than those obtaining in day schools. Some schools allocate to each 'new boy' an older companion who will show him round, an early exercise in caring for the less experienced: and, in the last year or so, many boys have the opportunity of becoming 'prefects' or 'monitors' with a good deal of responsibility for discipline.

Public schools also provide a greater variety of older males on whom the developing boy can model himself than is likely to be found at home. Day schools provide such models too; but the opportunities for making use of them are less. It is natural for youths to have heroes: older boys or masters to look up to and upon whom to base themselves. Boys discover their own capabilities by observing the capabilities of others and then emulating them: or by having drawn out (*educere*) of them potentialities of their own which they may not have dreamed that they possessed. A boy's father is generally the first important exemplar of the masculine which he encounters: but few fathers are such all-round characters as to exemplify everything a growing boy requires; and older boys and masters widen the scope of the possible, providing alternative routes to becoming a man which are highly valuable. In a good public school, there will be a range of models from athlete to academic; enough variety of men to meet the needs and canalize the aspirations of a wide spectrum of boys who are differently endowed by nature and by nurture.

Whilst there is no doubt that the collective life of a public school promotes the well-being, happiness and masculine development of those who will later look back on their schooldays with pleasure, it is also true that such a life is restricted, conventional and limited. 'Progressive' parents deplore public school life because it offers so little opportunity of interaction with the opposite sex. In my day, this was certainly minimal. The housemaster's wife and daughters, an elderly 'matron', and, for bolder spirits, the girls in the local Woolworths were all the feminine company we ever encountered. A more liberal spirit now encourages occasional meetings, perhaps even dances, with local girls' schools; and public schools have been known to put on plays in which the female roles are actually played by females. It is, I believe, undesirable that boys should spend two-thirds of the year virtually segregated from female company. Knockabout extraversion is not the whole of life, and feckless, rough-and-ready companionship, agreeable though this may be, does not comprise the whole of human relationship. Mothers, sisters and other feminine company, although less important at this stage of a boy's development, are salutary in demonstrating that masculine interests and preoccupations are not the only ones which count.

However, the conventional belief that segregation in an all-male society necessarily impairs confidence in approaching the opposite sex in later life seems to me improbable. The man who later becomes most sure of himself with women is the man who was first sure of himself with men. Nor is there necessarily a great deal to be said for the perpetual presence of girls as working companions in a school setting. Girls mature faster than boys, both intellectually and emotionally; with the consequence that the mix between adolescents of opposite sex and the same chronological age is sometimes an uneasy one.

It is often alleged that, if boys are largely segregated from girls, the image that they have of the opposite sex will continue to be unrealistic. Mixing with girls, it is supposed, will diminish the tendency to regard them as strange, alarming or unapproachable, by making them into 'human beings' who cannot easily be put upon pedestals. However, I rather doubt if this ostensibly sensible prescription is fully effective. It is true that if a boy is reared amongst sisters and goes to a co-educational school he is likely to regard the girls with whom he mixes as not too different from himself. It is harder to fall in love with those one is used to, or incest would be commoner than it is. But, let the boy once fall in love, and the girl whom he selects will take on all those qualities – mysterious, enthralling, special, magical – which he has so far failed to discern in the girls with whom he has mixed. In other words, the beloved will, in his imagination, be sharply separated from all the other girls whom he has encountered, and regarded as a different order of being so long as he continues to be in love. For the image of woman we project upon the beloved when first we fall in love seems to derive from an innermost sanctum, sealed since early childhood, which has scarcely been penetrated or influenced by day-to-day contacts in later childhood and adolescence.

Habitual mixing with the opposite sex during adolescence does have advantages. An all-male world is unnecessarily crude and rough; and there seems no particular point in underlining the tendency towards segregation of the sexes which, I have suggested, occurs spontaneously in any case. But the advantages are not so great as the passionate advocates of co-education would have us believe. More especially, it is unlikely that the presence or absence of girls in the life of a boy who is old enough to be at a public school has much effect upon whether or not he will later become predominantly heterosexual or homosexual.

Homosexuality in public schools is a controversial topic. It is known to be widespread, though highly subject to fashion. There is something of a conspiracy to deny the prevalence of homosexuality which is shared by parents and staff. Snobbery and the desire for their children's advancement tend to blind middle-class parents to the fact that they are exposing their boy to an environment in which homosexual encounters are likely. Housemasters and other staff, even if not homosexual themselves, which they often are, have strong motives to play down the incidence of homosexuality, and succeed in deceiving themselves about it.

When I was at school, a boy was expelled from College (the scholars' 'House') for homosexual practices. I am told that the headmaster, a clergyman with a slight stammer but considerable presence, summoned the other members of College into chapel. With unctuous gravity he condemned the sin; but, assuming a liberality made false by the fact that he had himself expelled the boy, forbade condemnation of the sinner.

'If you meet X in the street, do not shun him,' he urged. 'In spite of what he has done, he must not be treated as beyond the pale.' Since the boy in question was reasonably popular, no one had considered shunning him. The general attitude was that X had been unlucky to get caught. College, at that period, was going through an active homosexual phase, and X was far from being alone in his misdemeanours.

Headmasters of today are no doubt better informed, less disingenuous. At least one College contemporary of the expelled boy himself became a public school headmaster. But the motives for denying the prevalence of homosexuality remain the same. It is certainly possible to pass through a public school without ever encountering homosexuality or even hearing of it: but one or two active homosexuals in a House can rapidly start a fashion; and parents should assume that their boy is as likely as not to come across it.

In fact, though they do so for the wrong motives, parents are probably right to ignore the phenomenon. No one would wish his son to become permanently homosexual, a way of life which, in spite of changes in the law and greater public tolerance, is less likely to bring happiness than heterosexuality. But there is little reason to suppose that public school life does in fact breed homosexuals.

Whether or not one believes that the factors causing a predominantly homosexual inclination in adult life are genetic or environmental, there is no doubt that those factors have made their main impact long before a boy is old enough to enter public school; in most cases, before he goes to preparatory school. Whilst homosexual contacts at public school may sometimes postpone the development of heterosexual interest, or serve to bring out or underline a latent homosexual inclination, there is little reason to fear that such contacts will have much permanent effect in altering the direction of a boy's sexual interest. This is not to say that such experiences are unimportant. Although most homosexual encounters at public school are transient, some are highly romantic, and others part of passionate friendships which become of lasting value. In more sinister fashion, small boys can sometimes be cajoled or bullied into homosexual affairs by older boys who exploit them; one example of the abuse of the hierarchical structure which characterizes adolescent male society.

In my day, this structure was ludicrously rigid. The only comparable society is that described by Saint-Simon at the Court of Louis XIV. Every 'year' had its privileges, marked, as at Versailles, by minute particulars of dress; and newcomers were forced to learn these trivial distinctions as soon as possible after arrival in order not to offend their superiors by infringing them. Indeed, there was a great deal to learn in those days, including a ridiculous, esoteric language so extensive as to require a printed glossary.

Hierarchies are inevitable, both in public schools and elsewhere. But their ill-effects can and should be mitigated by democratic principle. This was not the case in my school in the 1930s, where it seemed that authority actually encouraged the class distinctions of age, position in school, year of entry and so on. When the youngest boys in a House are discouraged from consorting with the older boys, the opportunities of learning from the latter are diminished; and the risk of exploitation and bullying is increased by the fagging system in which younger boys act as servants to their elders. This rigid hierarchy with its insistence on trivial privilege and the master-slave relationship implicit in fagging are manifestations of adolescent insecurity. The confident do not need to boast of badges and rank, nor to show contempt for those beneath them. But adolescents, hovering uneasily between childhood and manhood, seize avidly upon anything which seems to increase their self-importance and reinforce their shaky sense of worth by showing contempt towards their inferiors. Thus, whilst a second-year boy might hit a first year with impunity, any attempt of the latter to retaliate would be treated as *lèse-majesté* and would simply invite more savage blows.

This is not the place to regale readers with horror stories of bullying or sadistic caning. Such things occur; and many writers, with good reason, look back upon their days at public school as by far the worst period of their lives. But writers tend to be exceptional, and their experience is not that of the average. I shall return to the problems of the exceptional later. For the moment I am concerned with the boy who passes through public school with enjoyment, or at least without serious distress. Has this all-male society other disadvantages which we have not, so far, considered?

One, which varies greatly from school to school, is lack of privacy. In some public schools, boys are given the privilege of a 'study' – either a room of their own, or one shared with two or three others – from the time that they enter the school. In others, studies either do not exist, or are only achieved towards the end of a boy's time at school. Public schools dislike privacy because they fear that it may encourage homosexuality. At my school, not only was it a crime to enter the dormitories during the day, but the lavatories had no doors. Defaecation was a public ritual performed after breakfast, with the next in the queue for one's lavatory seat observing the operation and urging one on to complete it as soon as possible. Some boys found this distasteful. The precautions taken to prevent boys ever being together in couples had the effect of making it equally difficult to be alone, except in special situations like the practice rooms of the Music School; and even those doors were furnished with spyholes.

As studies of kibbutz life have shown, collective living has its advantages. But it cannot be said to promote individuality.

The balance between individuality and collectivity is not an easy one to attain. Man is a social being who cannot usually find happiness in isolation and who, as we have seen, needs to learn social skills throughout the long period of his immaturity. On the other hand, the regimented hierarchy and absence of privacy so characteristic of public schools may justly be accused of encouraging conformity to a point where individuality is stifled.

Privacy is, or should be, an important part of growing up. Adolescents ought to be allowed secrets; secrets from parents, secrets from teachers, and secrets from each other. More especially, those who are destined to be creative need solitude in which to pursue their private phantasies; drawers in which to lock away their diaries and embryo fictions; places where no critical eye can penetrate to undermine, discourage or destroy.

Edward Gibbon once wrote: 'Conversation enriches the understanding; but solitude is the school of genius'; and, whilst it would be stupid to expect public schools to tailor themselves to the supposed requirements of genius, they could certainly do more to promote the flowering of individual talent by making privacy available to those who need it.

So far as I know, no study exists which shows what proportion of men of originality have been educated at public schools. It would be an interesting subject for research. Schools sometimes acquire reputations which become perpetuated as stereotyped labels in spite of the fact that schools often change quite rapidly as a result of changes of senior staff. Winchester, for example, long had a reputation for producing excessive conformity: judges, civil servants and the like, but few persons of dash or originality. Yet, even in the days when this label was applied, Winchester had educated men as different and as non-conformist as Oswald Mosley, Stafford Cripps and Richard Crossman.

I think it probable that public school life does have some withering effect upon the unusual boy, in the sense that it may delay his discovery of his own path. Certainly, many public schoolboys take an unconscionable time to grow up. Although often prepared to take administrative and other responsibility, they tend to remain childish emotionally, immature in their personal relations.

One reason for this may be that the contrast between life at boarding school and life at home is too extreme. Although the collective life of boarding school offers the opportunities for maturing as a male among males which we have already discussed, boys who go to them tend to be one person at school, another at home. Because they are only with their families for a small proportion of the year, boarding school boys do not have the same opportunities as do day-boys for growing and maturing in relation with their parents. This means that they tend to preserve, as if in cold storage, an immature relationship with parents and other members of the household at home, and to slip back, more than they need, into a childish role during the holidays. Unless a boy is with his parents a good deal, he may keep the image which he formed of them as a small boy, and fail to relate to them as people. Public schoolboys seem especially prone to mother-fixation; a disability which may be partly consequent upon the lack of women in the school environment, but which is more probably the result of being absent from the mother during critical periods of growing-up. To learn to see one's mother as a woman, and thus as a real person, is more difficult for a boy to achieve if he is seldom with her.

We have discussed some of the advantages and disadvantages of public school life as they affect the maturation of the average boy without coming to any very definite conclusion. Indeed, without considerable research, definite conclusions are out of place. We do not have the evidence which would make possible a rational comparison of public school education with other varieties. On the face of it, many boys enjoy their public schools. The opportunities offered are wide; the advantages considerable. Not much harm, and some good, is done to most boys who attend them.

For the well-adjusted, average boy who has learned, in much earlier childhood, to mix well with his peers, the psychological pros and cons are outweighed in importance by wider social and political considerations. Should public schools be preserved as examples of excellence in education which the State should strive to emulate, or should they be abolished as being elitist institutions which foster class divisions? Such questions are outside my brief, and I leave them to others to discuss. I must, however, return to some consideration of those who hated their public school, and believe that the regime did them serious harm.

There are many intelligent, sensitive, valuable people who look back upon their public school as upon a concentration camp; who have been haunted by nightmares that they might have to return there, and who only cast off the shadow of school, if at all, when well on into middle life. I shall argue that, as in the case of those who become predominantly homosexual, the fault is not primarily that of the school, but is to be attributed to various circumstances in the life of a boy long before he is old enough to go there. A more perceptive recognition of the problems with which this minority is faced would, however, save a great deal of unnecessary misery.

Many, perhaps most, boys who enter public school at the age of thirteen have already been to preparatory schools as boarders. This means that they have been sent away from home for about two-thirds of each year from the age of eight or nine. I believe that most of those who find public school life intolerable have failed to adjust to preparatory school life also; and I also believe that a good deal of damage might be prevented if those boys who were notably unhappy at a preparatory boarding school were not necessarily condemned to go on to a public boarding school. Moreover, I believe that some boys who fail to fit in when they enter public school at thirteen might well have welcomed boarding if they had not been sent away from home to a preparatory school too early.

Parents in other countries find the English practice of sending their eight- or nine-year-old children away to boarding schools incomprehensible. They believe, with reason, that many boys of eight are not ready to exchange the shelter of home for the less supportive, less personally considerate regime of boarding school. Of course, some children leave home cheerfully, and settle well in their new environment. Others, coming from homes where children are not understood or harshly treated, or in which the parents are at odds with one another, may be thankful to exchange home for an environment less stressful. But this is not true of all. Those children who, because of temperamental difficulties or an unfavourable environment, have not learned to mix with other children in early childhood often fail to do so when they are sent away to school, and are doubly miserable as a result. They may very well be miserable at day school; but at least there is home at the end of the day. At boarding school there is no escape, no respite from the crowd; and boys, like other animals, have a built-in tendency to torment and persecute anyone who does not fit in with the group or who appears to be different from themselves.

When children, for whatever reason, have failed to make social relationships with their peers before the age of eight, well-meaning parents welcome their attainment of that age, since they believe that sending them away to boarding school will furnish the companionship that they so clearly need. As I have said, this sometimes works; but very often it does not, and the isolated child becomes still more unhappy than he was before leaving home. It is also important for parents to realize that not all boys who appear to adjust to boarding school are as happy as they seem. Many children, especially at the age of eight or nine, still assume that what their perents decide is not only right, but an immutable part of reality to which they must adapt. They do not conceive that there could be any alternative. A boy is often sensitively aware that his parents are doing what they believe to be best for him and would be seriously distressed if they were to realize that he had not 'settled down' or was unhappy. And so boys write those cheerful, boring, uninformative letters: 'We beat Breckfield 2-nil. . . . it is very sunny today . . . I got 17 out of 20 for geography . . .', and entirely conceal the fact that they are miserable. This tendency to conceal unhappiness in order to spare the parents' feelings is powerfully reinforced by the assumption, common amongst children, that, if they are unhappy, it must be their own fault. How could it be otherwise, when they know that their parents are lovingly wise, and have made financial sacrifices to give them the best possible education at the best possible school? It is not uncommon to find that kindly, well-disposed parents have been entirely unaware of their child's unhappiness at school, and have been horrified, at a later date, to hear of it.

There seems little reason to persist with the practice of sending eight-year-old children to boarding school, even if they are already good mixers. There is strong reason for parents to avoid doing so if their boy has not already had the opportunity of forming adequate social relationships. Children who fail to mix with their fellows fail for various reasons. Some children, brought up in a limited neighbourhood, have been unable to find companions. Only children, it is clear, are particularly at risk. Others have had an upbringing which has made them so different from most children that their assumptions and way of life are too dissimilar to allow them to mix. I have known children to have so 'Christian' an upbringing that they have been quite unable to stand up for themselves and, in acting literally upon the injunction to turn the other cheek, have merely spurred on their tormentors. Boys who have physical disabilities or who suffer frequent illnesses often feel at a disadvantage, and fail to benefit from the 'country air' of the school to which their loving parents despatch them.

We are only beginning to find out, through painstaking research, how socialization takes place in the small human. At present the evidence indicates that the process starts very early, even before the age at which children are generally sent to nursery school. It appears likely that if, as a pre-school child, a boy fails to mix with his peers, he will have a difficult and painful time learning to do so later, and may therefore require the loving support of home for longer than most other children. Parents who send isolated children to boarding school do so at a risk which must be constantly scrutinized. Some children will happily make up for what they have missed; others will become profoundly miserable, or develop psychosomatic illness or other symptoms. In an essay on public schools, it may seem inappropriate to devote space to what happens before a child is old enough to go to one, but it is actually vital to do so. Those who have been unhappy at public schools habitually blame that particular regime for what in fact went wrong much earlier. I am sure that some boys should not be sent to public boarding school, but this is not to say that public schools ought instantly to be abolished. What is needed is a far more discriminating process of selection, not based upon parental wealth. Public schools offer standards of education not easily matched elsewhere. We must ensure that those boys who go to public schools are intelligent enough to reap the educational rewards. We must also be certain that they are socially mature enough to tolerate the public school community.

Anthony Storr (Winchester) is Clinical Lecturer in Psychiatry at the University of Oxford. He is the author of six books on various aspects of psychiatry including *Human Aggression*, *Sexual Deviation* and *The Integrity of the Personality*. He is also a regular contributor to the *Sunday Times*.

7

Manly Little Chaps

GEORGE MACDONALD FRASER

'I would rather have a boy a thief than a liar!' Thus the stern Victorian patriarch in one of R.M. Ballantyne's novels, listening in disgust to the excuses of the scapegrace son whom he has caught returning from a poaching expedition with the evidence sticking out of his pockets. The lesson is clear: the crime itself was less deplorable than the attempt to escape the consequences by prevarication – an interesting outlook, since it appears to cut clean across the Briton's sacred respect for property, and suggests that the sin against self (dishonourable lying), although not punishable at law, was morally much worse than sin against another, even when it involved crime.

Of course, they weren't the patriarch's pheasants, but his next-door neighbour's. Whether in fact he would have preferred a truth-telling son who decamped with the family jewels, to one who just fibbed a bit but kept his hands out of the till, is debatable. He might well say so – and perhaps, in his heart of hearts, he might even believe that he meant it. For lying, moral dishonesty, especially in the interests of personal safety, strikes at the root of that which Western man holds most dear – or says he does: personal honour.

It is a mysterious and paradoxical thing, is honour, as Falstaff, his mind wonderfully concentrated by the approaching terrors of the Battle of Shrewsbury, discovered. It can be, in the phrase of Sabatini's Venetian, 'the big, round, fat, senseless word' which, even when sincerely pursued, can shield a deal of dishonour and even provide occasion for villainy; or it can be something which ruffians and rascals still prize above their immortal souls – as in the case of the old Viking, last survivor of his kind, who was told that he should be baptized a Christian for his own salvation. Very good, he said, but what about his old ganger comrades, who were already dead; were they beyond absolution? Yes, said the priests, they were doomed to damnation. 'Then I will not be baptized,' said the old Viking. 'I will go with my people.' A pirate, scoundrel, murderer, intractable sinner – and a man of unquestionable honour.

As most people understand it, honour in its simplest and purest form is embedded in truth – in telling and living the truth, according to one's honest lights. Ask the Victorian patriarch – or for that matter, anyone who prides himself on his integrity in whatever time – if there is anything nobler than telling truth, and he would probably answer no. And yet here we find honour's greatest paradox, for while truth is supposed to enshrine all that is pure and good, it is a fact that every schoolboy knows, that there is nothing so dishonourable as to tell the truth in the wrong circumstances and for the wrong reasons. Truth is absolutely no excuse – indeed, it is regarded as the ultimate hypocrisy – when it infringes honour's first and simplest principle, which is that you do not carry tales.

If there is an unwritten law, this is it. Perhaps because it is central to child life, and has become enshrined in the true and fictitious history of the public school system, it is sometimes called 'schoolboy honour' – nowadays, interestingly enough, in a slightly deprecatory way. But if the so-called public school spirit embodied it, the law is something much more basic; a child learns it as soon as he or she is old enough to be insulted, robbed or hit. The toddler roaring for its mother, with one hand stemming the tears and the other pointing in denunciation at the assailant, grinning uneasily in the background, discovers, at first gently, later more sternly, that whatever wrong you may suffer, it is not the done thing to tell about it.

We can generally judge the importance of a thing, real or abstract, by the number of popular synonyms for it. Tale-telling has some beauties, both verbs and nouns: sneak, tell, inform, grass, peach, nark, rat, sing, squeal, squeak, and my personal favourite, the superb Scots word 'clype'.

There are no more offensive terms in the language, as we all remember from childhood – memories of jeering infants making scissor-movements with their fingers and chanting: 'Tell-tale tit, your tongue shall be slit,' or, in Scotland, the whiningly repeated 'Clype-clash, clype-clash'. Other sins might be excused, or at least lived down, but let anyone get the name of tale-bearer, and he was damned everlastingly. It is as old as time.

There are some abandoned souls who can endure it, of course; a few even seem to glory in it, but not many. Even Falstaff, who would have sung like a canary under pressure, still recognized informing as the unforgivable crime. 'If I be ta'en, I'll peach for this!' – when he found himself abandoned in the Gadshill hold-up, it was the ultimate threat, the measure of his desperation. Only one who really knew what honour meant, having studied it warily, as practical man and philosopher, from all angles, and who was scared stiff into the bargain, would have shouted it aloud.

From being in the human tradition, associated with group loyalty, initiation ceremony, and secret mystery, and possibly, in the Protestant ethic, with martyrdom and the refusal to deny faith in order to escape physical suffering, the idea of honourable silence (the Mafia has a word for it, '*omertà*') was a natural pillar of the Victorian public school code. How far it was actually practised, and still is, we can only guess, or judge from our own experience, whether at public school or not. Probably quite a lot. But in the myth of the public school at least – and in its effect, the myth was quite as important as the reality – it was paramount. Is there a school story (or a true school memory) which does not contain the picture of the terrified child, possessed of inside information (which he wishes to heaven he didn't have) being grilled by authority, and still keeping his trembling mouth shut? We all know it; we have all been there; we have all clammed up (mostly, anyway) for our various reasons, and honour has at least been one of them. Not necessarily the main one, but present, in however tattered a form, buoying us up against our better judgement and base natural instinct.

I remember breaking a lamp at school, throwing stones, and lying truth out of England to escape the consequences, while my associates joined in the conspiracy of silence. (Or did they? The crime was eventually laid at my door, and how that happened without someone turning stool-pigeon, I can't imagine. I have my theories, still.) On another occasion, the legend on the art-room door was defaced, the word 'art' being supplied with one lovingly-executed initial letter; a friend and I, gleeful but innocent witnesses, were haled before our housemaster, a truly terrifying man, who demanded if we knew the culprit. I doubt if he expected us to tell him, for when we stood mum, grinning in sheer panic at our own nobility, he simply said: 'You know, but you won't tell me, is that it?' and dismissed us. He wasn't looking displeased, either, and while I don't suppose he murmured 'What staunch little chaps, to be sure,' as the door closed, I know he would have held us in contempt if we had squealed. Thus authority hobbles itself.

It occurred to me, then, that in fact it took no courage at all to observe the code, provided you were dealing with a gentleman. If, on the other hand, he had said, 'Right, you little swine – talk, or I'll half-kill you,' would our lips have remained sealed? Probably; if not for honour's sake, at least for fear of the odium we would have received from our friends, and possibly their reprisals. And our housemaster's character and hope of maintaining discipline would have vanished. Perhaps authority is not so stupid after all; it knows it has to play by the rules, too.

Victorian novelists, recognizing that virtue is nothing if it doesn't involve sacrifice, took care of this by ensuring that Jack Champion, in refusing to split on a pal, suffered for his honourable silence. They contrived situations where he took the blame and punishment himself, usually on behalf of a weaker younger brother or friend (or sometimes even an enemy – preferably a drunken, gambling, bullying, sneaking lout who is going to have to be rescued from drowning before he is shamed into confessing and so putting noble Jack in the clear). How often has Harry Wharton stood pale and tight-lipped, in the tradition of that small, obnoxious infant on the stool being asked by the Roundheads when he last saw his father? Time without number. Why does he do it? Because honour demands no less – and there is, too, a comforting glow to martyrdom, especially when it is public.

This comes out strongly in everyone's favourite scene from *Tom Brown's Schooldays,* where Tom is roasted in front of the schoolroom fire by that fine young chap Flashman. When the housekeeper comes on the scene, and finds Tom unconscious and done to a crisp, she observes 'There's been some bad work here,' which must have been the understatement of 1837, and demands to know who is responsible. Of course, no one will tell, including Tom, who is smouldering but silent all the way to the sick-room. So elevated are his torturers by his manly conduct ('he's a staunch little fellow') that some of them even reform ('I'm sick of this work . . . what brutes we've been') and beg his pardon. (Not Flashman, of course; Hughes knew his man better than that.)

It goes without saying that Tom takes on increased stature and virtue by his suffering and his refusal to denounce his enemy. But the incident points up something else, which obviously never occurred to Hughes – where does the code end and common sense begin? Nowhere, in early Victorian days, apparently. Dr Arnold knew about the incident, but did nothing, which seems odd. There was no enquiry, no hint of action by authority at all. One would not expect a Victorian headmaster to call in the police, and if he had, what would have been the result? Probably nothing – Flashman would have been safer from denunciation by his enemies than by his friends. Yet, if he had pursued his roasting activities *outside* Rugby School – perhaps grilling a yeoman farmer over a wood fire for an afternoon's diversion – he would have been in court in no time, with witnesses giving evidence for all they were worth. Is it only in the enclosed society, then, that the code can truly operate, and stand up to extreme pressure? How far, in fact, can it stand up when it comes into conflict with the law?

Quite a long way, in my own experience: the police were called in at my own school to investigate an incident, and met a wall of silence, although everyone knew the culprit. (I have often wondered if any master knew, too; I imagine not.) It was an acutely embarrassing occasion, all round, but the police eventually just had to go away. *Omertà* indeed. It is probably at this point that Sabatini's Venetian would intervene to remark that here was an instance where the code of honour was not honourable at all, and might even have to be broken for honour's sake.

It depends, of course, on the circumstances; schoolboys operate most of their unwritten institutions with a fair amount of common sense, and know when enough is enough. But I suspect – and hope – that the old concept of honour and group loyalty remains stronger among them than it does in society as a whole; these are not good times for honour, in public or private life, as the newspapers inform us daily.

What does emerge, from any study of school honour, whether at first hand or through the medium of Greyfriars, Talbot Baines Reed, the *Hotspur*, etc., is that the code can work only as long as it remains unwritten and is sensibly, if slightly, elastic. And as long as its concept of honour is true, and is operated by honourable men, or boys. This becomes evident when one considers the truly fearful mess which emerged at the U.S. Military Academy at West Point.

It appears that West Point has a written code of honour, which sets out some more or less excellent rules, most of them, one would have hoped, entirely unnecessary for the guidance of young men aspiring to be army officers. The cynic might remark that there is something amiss with an establishment which feels that it needs to tell its pupils that they will not lie, cheat, or steal. However, this is the relatively harmless bit of the code; what matters is that it goes on to lay down that no cadet will tolerate anyone who lies, cheats or steals. In theory, this may sound reasonable; in practice at West Point it produced a situation which would have made our Victorian patriarch turn away in blank disbelief. For it appears that under the 'honor code' a cadet is *obliged to inform* on any other cadet who has breached the code; to put not too fine a point on it, West Point demands of its cadets that they shall rat on their friends, and makes this a point of honour.

If this sounds unbelievable, one can only quote the remark attributed to the commandant of cadets. Really it ought to be engraved in letters of brass somewhere, so that all those simpletons who thought they knew what honour was, can ponder it. For what the commandant was reported to have said was: 'It's not natural for an eighteen-year-old to tell on his friends. It's something that has to be instilled.'

Comment is surely superfluous, but it is instructive to consider the defence which supporters of the 'honor code' advanced – that it is essential that one officer in action should always be able to rely on the word of another. One always thought they could, as a matter of course, without any written code to prompt them; armies have been functioning for several millennia, on at least as high a level as the American one, without 'honor codes' to guide them. And it might by some be considered questionable how far an officer can rely on a comrade who considers it an honourable duty to tell tales. Dr Arnold and Flashman might both wonder

—and for once find themselves in harmony—whether West Point was any place for a gentleman.

However, interesting though it may be to ponder a moral standpoint which evidently holds that a man can be made honourable by forcing on him a code that is in itself an affront to honour, it adds little to our understanding of English public school behaviour. West Point is not an English public school, although there are interesting parallels to be drawn, not least in the matter of bullying, which at one time at the Point was systematized to a remarkable degree, evidently in the belief that it helped to inculcate discipline. English public school bullies needed no such excuse; all the evidence suggests that they bullied for sheer love of it, and it is a nice question how far this squares with the concept of schoolboy honour.

The answer plainly is that it did not infringe the code, much, in Flashy's day, and presumably still doesn't. It may be a bit off, or caddish, but it is not considered dishonourable; the infliction of physical and mental cruelty on the weak and helpless, while utterly opposed to the knightly, chivalric notion of good behaviour, may be easily excused as playfulness, or thoughtlessness, or boisterous high spirits – everyone knows it is nothing of the sort, of course, but the conventional excuses persist as strongly as the convention itself. The upper-class Englishman is a bit of a bully, and that is all there is to it. He is not a coward – it was one of the Victorian myths, perpetrated originally, I suspect, by Hughes, that bullying and cowardice went hand in hand, which they don't. Nor is the Englishman cruel, in the usual sense of the word; he doesn't really understand cruelty, so that while he may experience considerable enjoyment in watching one boxer bash another into a bloody pulp, or in torturing fish or slaughtering birds, the cruel aspect of these pursuits doesn't properly come home to him.

But he does enjoy a bit of bullying for its own sake, as Kipling pointed out, proving the point by thereafter enumerating schoolboy tortures with considerable relish. Kipling, of course, had been bullied at school – who hasn't? And who, by the same token, would confess to having been a bully himself?

Fortunately, and honestly, I can't – I was removed from my English school (where I was bullied, mildly) before I had grown big enough to start bullying myself, and sent to a Scottish school where bullying was non-existent. So far as I can judge, the traditional belief that Scottish schools are virtually free from bullying is in fact true – I don't pretend to speak for its few schools which are faithful imitations of English public boarding schools – although why this should be I cannot imagine. It may be that bullying requires a sense of knowing when to stop, which the Scot hasn't got, and knows he hasn't got, when it comes to physical violence.

However, consideration of Scottish schools raises an interesting point connected with schoolboy honour – theft. Without going so far as to suggest that Scottish schoolboys would lift the teeth from your head, one can propose that their attitude to personal effects is more communistic than that of their English counterparts. The English boy, like the English man, does have a respect for private property; a study of English public school history indicates that while 'boning', 'winning', and other forms of borrowing school books and items of equipment, were common enough, private valuables were fairly sacrosanct. This, however, did not apply to food, either belonging to the school or to other boys; one of the first lessons Tom Brown learned was to guard his potatoes and sausages, and the tolerance extended to Bunter's habit of raiding tuck-boxes confirms that this kind of theft was lightly regarded in fiction as in fact. Certainly it was not dishonourable.

Since any offence against public morality and good order ought at least to be mentioned, if only to be dismissed, in our consideration of honour, it may be as well to say that sexual behaviour and swearing simply don't count. Whatever may be said of them they are well outside the code. Schoolboys have naturally filthy minds, and are fluent in expressing them; they delight in foul language for its own sake, and have nothing to learn by the time they get to the army, or university, or prison, or wherever else disgusting abuse is common.

But if these are irrelevancies, and if stealing and bullying are minor disciplines in the study of schoolboy honour, cheating is not. Second only to lying and informing as a subject of moral controversy, it is as old as school itself and as deep-rooted. It needs to be defined.

There is dishonourable cheating, which is frequently held to be as bad as sneaking, and there is acceptable cheating, which may at worst be slightly frowned on by some, and even admired by others. Dishonourable cheating is what cads do at games, pretending a ball hasn't crossed the line when it has, or claiming a catch when the ball has touched the ground.

In Tom Brown's day, it is clear, this kind of behaviour was officially regarded as revolting, but if British sporting history is anything to go by, there may have been a considerable gap between lip-service and practice. The very existence of the phrase 'not cricket' suggests that a good deal which was 'not cricket' went on in those early Victorian years; it was a time when notions of sportsmanship were rudimentary, when gambling had such a grip that cricket matches were bought and sold, when boxing was synonymous with knavery, and football was a largely uncodified rough-house where anything went anyway. The ideals of sportsmanship, popularly associated with the good old days or various Golden Ages, undoubtedly did spread later in the Victorian years and in the present century, and public school honour had a good deal to do with promoting them; although I suspect that public school fiction, spreading through the middle classes at first, and later, with the tuppenny bloods, through the working classes, may have done more still. Even Hughes' and Reed's books did not preach a higher standard of honour in sport than the *Wizard* and the *Rover*.

In modern times – or at least in my schooldays – cheating at games wasn't done, not necessarily because of lofty principles, but because cheating spoiled the whole point of sport. It may sound pompous to say that we played for fun, but I think we did, and the very fact that I sound slightly apologetic is probably a reflection of changing attitudes today, when it is nothing out of the way to see British athletes whining, cheating, feigning injury, and even bursting into tears when they lose. I imagine that losing gracefully is still a point of honour at public schools, and that sporting standards are as high as they were a century ago.

It is important, incidentally, to draw a line, however vague, between cheating at games and what Mr Potter called gamesmanship. The latter was not, in schoolboy terms, altogether dishonourable, provided it was done with flair; if it had been, Dr Grace, whose behaviour sometimes stopped just short of downright roguery, could hardly have been a Victorian hero.

But school cheating nearly always refers, not to games, but to cribbing, copying, and dishonestly acquiring merit in class. This is universal, and obviously always has been, and whether it is regarded as dishonourable or not depends on the circumstances. Deliberately to rob a school-fellow of a prize by cribbing used to be a heinous offence, and doubtless still is; it was held to be quite as dishonourable as sneaking – indeed, it would be interesting to see if public school honour did not demand the exposure of such a cribber, if not by informing on him, at least by hounding and hammering him till he confessed his crime. But cribbing of that kind has probably always been fairly uncommon, at least in the deliberate intention; for one thing, opportunities are limited, and while it is possible to deceive an invigilator, it is extremely difficult to deceive school-fellows.

Most cribbing, however, is a matter of self-preservation, done to conceal ignorance and idleness and escape punishment, usually practised in class tests or homework, and occasionally in exams. The degree of infamy attached to it, if any, depends on the importance of the occasion, but in any event, such cribbing is not, on the whole, held to be dishonourable. Dishonest, perhaps, but that under the code of honour is something else. The general view in my time, and, so far as one can judge, right back to Tom Brown, was that such cribbing was your own business, and if you could get away with it, good luck to you. Provided it did not harm anyone else, or deprive them of reward, it was regarded with tolerance, except by swots who naturally resented seeing the idle and ignorant escaping their just deserts; they hated me, those swots. But even they would not have dreamed of complaining; the most they would do was refuse to let you crib from them, which did not improve their popularity.

I could write a long treatise about cribbing techniques, mostly from observation, for I was not a good cribber myself. The will was there, from the moment I realized that while my memory was excellent for trivia, it was defective where school-work was concerned; cribbing to me was a purely defensive response to an otherwise intolerable situation, and I attempted it with malice towards none, and no hope of reward. Unfortunately, I radiated guilt in sweating clouds. 'You're only cheating yourself, Fraser,' I would be told by sorrowing pedagogues as they confiscated my pocket dictionaries and searched my geometry set for my pathetic scraps of data; they didn't realize that they were merely reassuring me and quieting my conscience.

Masters' attitudes to cribbing were extremely interesting. Some held to the old Victorian line that it was the first step on the road to a life of crime, but even they seemed reluctant to notice it. Others viewed it almost

Privileged young men in boaters lounging beneath ancient buildings – a sight to gladden the heart of any champion of comprehensive education (Harrow 1951). And an equally familiar image, straight out of Stalky and Frank Richards – small boys in long trousers unpacking a tuck-box (Lancing 1948).

Manly little chaps indeed! Four contrasting studies of Etonian boyhood: a survivor of the Wall Game with supporters, a fag of the 1870s fetching water, a Captain of the Boats in Fourth of July costume (*far right*), and two earlier students of the College unselfconsciously attired for the Ad Montem ceremony.

Pacem volens, parens bella. The Harrow Shooting Eight (*above*), with reserves and trainer, plainly under the influence of innumerable officers' mess photographs of the time (1875).

Football at Rugby (*opposite below*) in 1870 – still with a round ball, mass charging tactics, and no nonsense about crowd control. *Above*, players of the Eton field game in 1865, and a century later, collegers on their way to the Wall Game linking arms in traditional fashion. The Oppidans arrive later in twos and threes.

Centenary service in the chapel (Lancing 1948).

The interior of a study at Charterhouse just before the First World War (*above right*).

'Reading over' at Stowe. Middle School boys hear their positions in class read out by the headmaster.

Miss Buss (*above*) and Miss Beale, Principal of Cheltenham Ladies College, both greatly influenced women's education in the nineteenth century.

While some girls' public schools date back to the seventeenth century, the great majority were founded within the past hundred years, and if they often aped the boys' schools with enthusiasm, they also evolved a style of their own. Below, young batspersons of the Junior House at Roedean learn to play forward, and (*above*) cuddly toys in a Roedean cubicle.

Boys of the Under 6th in class at Charterhouse (1909), and (*below*) a study group with a master at Westminster about twenty years later.

cynically – 'I am beating you, Fraser, not for cribbing, but for having the stupidity and bad judgement to crib from McKinnon, who knows even less than you do.' One or two quite deliberately ignored it – at least one of Kipling's masters in *Stalky and Co* regarded it as self-defeating and not worth bothering about, and he, if I remember rightly, was the school chaplain.

What was even more fascinating was the length some boys would go to in preparing cribs or perfecting techniques; there were the book-manipulators, who could transfer Mayne's *Geometry* or Kennedy from their laps to satchels beneath their seats without taking their hands from the desk-tops or even stopping writing, or those who before an exam would patiently cover their thighs with minute copying of formulae and dates – you need to be wearing a kilt for this, and I may say that any child in my day who attended an exam in tartan might as well have had 'cribber' emblazoned on his chest.

It might be thought, of these dedicated cribbers, that if they had spent as much time in honest learning as they did in outwitting examiners, they would have passed with ease. Not so: it is a matter of outlook, aptitude, and recognized ignorance, with a measure of bravado thrown in. I am not quite sure what the moral is behind the true story of the Dutch schoolboy who, rather than learn, devised a system of wires and cards which he operated by moving his body at the desk; this enabled him to consult endless prepared cribs through a hole in his desk-lid, the hole being so neatly disguised with painted gauze that it could not be detected by a master standing over him. The boy was Anthony Fokker, who became one of the greatest aerial engineers and designers of all time.

But technique is by the way, and has nothing to do with honour. So far as I could judge, none of my associates cribbed habitually; a few did so frequently, many did very occasionally, but most seldom if ever. (At West Point, where cribbing usually seems to be at the bottom of honour scandals, a cadet estimated that about one-third of his fellows cheated in exams, and the other two-thirds knew about it. That seems a pretty high figure, but accurate or not, one would think that the average of cribbing in an English public school was a good deal lower; that is not to say that English youth are any more honourable than their American counterparts, but does suggest that unwritten codes may have practical advantages.)

One last failing has to be considered in any review of schoolboy honour, and that is cowardice. This is a difficult one; public attitudes have changed, and physical bravery, while still highly admired, is probably lower in the fashionable scale of human virtues than it was a century ago. Two world wars, a wider public experience of the fine line between heroism and poltroonery, and an understanding of the strange masks that real courage can sometimes wear, have seen to that. But one suspects that schoolboy attitudes to bravery and cowardice have not changed all that much, because they were more tolerant – even in Tom Brown's day – to begin with. A whole chapter could be written comparing the public school attitude to cowardice with that of the British Army, which was once officered by public schoolboys; curiously, they are not identical. Cowardice has always been the ultimate military crime, because it has to be, but schoolboys fortunately are under no such necessity, and are usually ready to regard failure of nerve as a weakness rather than a sin, and excuse it in each other. It may not be pleasant to be called 'funk', but it is certainly less odious – and less clinging – than to be called sneak. For one thing, the funk can always redeem himself, and in schoolboy literature frequently does.

This is no accident, and it is central to the public school code, as enshrined in Victorian fact and fiction. For while cowardice may not have been the cardinal sin in the eyes of boys, there is no doubt that courage was the cardinal virtue, not only to them, but to their elders. It paid for everything. This seems remarkable, in view of the Victorian worship of truth, honesty, and other Christian virtues, but it was undoubtedly so. Our patriarch, who would rather have had a boy a thief than a liar, might well have added: 'But if he goes out and dies game, I'll forgive him anything.' We know it well – how many cads, swine and rotters have we not seen received back into grace, their bullyings, cheatings, stealings – even their lyings – forgiven and forgotten because they had had the misfortune to be disembowelled by Afghans or Zulus, or had perished nobly rescuing someone from the flames? If news had come back to Rugby that Flashman had gone down swinging before the heathen, his character would have been automatically restored, and they would have held a memorial service for him. And quite right, too.

We have chapter and verse for this in one of the great works: when Eric (or Little by Little) has fallen into disrepute – for drinking, or swearing, or calling a master 'a surly d---l' – and then risks his life for a friend, what is the headmaster's reaction? ' "Noble boy," he exclaimed, with enthusiasm; "I shall find it hard to believe any evil of him after this." '

There it is. Courage wipes the slate clean. It is not logical, perhaps, but it is probably biologically sound, even in the 1970s.

Cowardice, cheating, sneaking, bullying, lying, and the rest – it is in attitudes to these that one has to try to find some definition of honour as the public schools understood the word. At best, it can only be vague, but nonetheless true for that, and everyone understands it. A legal mind might recoil from a code that has for its principal pillars such abstracts as standing by one's friends, playing the game, not letting the side down, recognizing truth, and, in Thomas Hughes' words, 'never giving in while you can stand and see'. They are clichés, of course, but they do represent an ideal; it may not always be lived up to, it is fatally easy to sneer at – one cynic observed that the remarkable thing about the public school spirit was that it had never spread to the public schools – but it is there, and it is a good deal more fundamental than any written code or constitution; every schoolboy may not adhere to it all the time, but at least he knows it.

I like to think that it is eternal, not only in the public schools, but in all the other schools that they have influenced, and that it can survive even the present dark age, when hypocrisy has reached a pitch that makes the Victorians look frank and clean; when *suggestio falsi* and *suppressio veri*, rendered the more obnoxiously facile by being cloaked in a sub-English jargon which not even the speaker understands, are the accepted currency of the public man; when political behaviour is tolerated and even admired, that would lead to deserved ostracism in a kindergarten; when expediency and fashionable ethics have smothered fair play and truth itself; when a new generation of moral tyrants, preaching concern but cruelty personified, have consigned the poor old gods, who knew nothing of social engineering or progressive dictatorship, to the scrapheap.

Honour? Who hath it? Harry Wharton may have it still.

George MacDonald Fraser (Carlisle Grammar School and Glasgow Academy) is a former newspaperman, and is the author of several books including the Flashman novels and a history of the sixteenth-century Anglo-Scottish border, and film screenplays.

8

Secrets in the Family

DAVID PRYCE-JONES

I

English writers who treat of schools have done so with an air of amazed confidentiality. They have peeped into the inner sanctum of the tribe, of the race, and they must initiate as they have been initiated. School literature, centred on special communities of education, really kinships, is a form of national anthropology. The reader is drawn into loving or hating the revelations, to each according to his taste and personal involvement.

The cruelties of Mr Creakle's school in *David Copperfield* or Dotheboys Hall in *Nicholas Nickleby* are on a par with the Rugby in which Tom Brown could be roasted before the fire, and forced to defend himself against a bigger boy. Yet what to Dickens ought to be abolished was to Thomas Hughes the foundations of the English character. In *Coningsby* Disraeli could rhapsodize upon an Eton that makes 'grey-haired men mourn over the memory of their schooldays', but he had only a brief spell of boarding with a private tutor there upon which to base his perspective. Hard experience, for instance Trollope's at Harrow, Thackeray's at Charterhouse, would generate less romanticism.

The post-Arnoldian code, in any case, was to take the colours out of individual response. Victorian institutions were delineated in white and black; those who were In formed a bright fixed constellation, and the rest lay in outer darkness. The middle decades of the nineteenth century, when

Wellington, Haileybury, Marlborough, Rossall, Ardingly and many more were founded, were also the years when the public schools forsook their wilder raffish past, and went secret. So much so, in fact, that one motive of the 1864 Royal Commission was curiosity, to find out what was really up. The answer was of course somewhat dreary, in that the schools were consolidating after their fashion. Aristocratic impulses and standards had proved inapplicable to large numbers. If the professional classes created by the industrial revolution required respectability in order to muster alongside the gentry, and assume their station as by right, it would be suitably provided, but discreetly. Chapel twice a day, the playing-fields every afternoon, the classics ritually learnt, the sciences and modern languages resisted, elder boys as prefects with the charge of disciplining their juniors as fags – here was the steady adaptation of a certain type of education to social demands. As E.C. Mack expressed it in his authoritative *Public Schools and British Opinion, 1780–1860*, 'What the Empire needed was manly, well-adjusted, honourable boys moulded into unthinking conformity and imbued with a passionate idealistic loyalty towards authority, whether school or nation. Such boys the Public Schools have turned out by the thousands.'

Nobody much cared to admit the obvious, that the gloss of these ideals masked the reality of political power; hence the closing of ranks, the pulpit intonations, the small spurt of conspiracy, as in the taboo which surrounded 'trade', in which many fathers were indubitably engaged. Since the educational ends were so self-evidently desired, and were too estimable to be trumpeted about, the means could well be left to look after themselves – any amount of plain childhood unhappiness bubbled away down that dialectical drain. Beetle, in other words the youthful Kipling, in *Stalky and Co*, a misfit in the system and proud of it, claimed to be an authority on bullying, 'corkscrew – brush-drill – keys – head-knucklin' – arm-twisting – rocking – Ag Ags and all the rest of it'. Not only at United Services College, but everywhere, the blind eye was turned upon this, and saw something good in it, 'character-building'. How was it possible for so many adults, mostly decent and scholarly and Christian, to retire to their studies and abandon their charges blithely, silently? So that the most obvious cry for help became one of the worst offences in the code, 'sneaking', 'peaching'. Here was the licence for that most horrific but popular of scenes, the new boy, or 'bug', on his first day, breaking no custom of which he is aware, and having to stand up and fight. Codification of values, and their transmission from one intake to the next, was left in the hands of the boys themselves, who became like so many novitiate-priests of the temple; that was the source of a magic passed on by word of mouth, and displayed in school by means of waistcoat buttons left undone, or permission to carry an umbrella unrolled, or walking on patches of otherwise protected grass, not to mention the intricacies of 'the honour of the school' as reflected in athletic competitions, and personal conduct. Such lore depended for its impact upon a certain accepted secrecy among those privy to it.

Obscurers of the scene, powerful fantasists, were also at work. The tone of *Tom Brown's Schooldays* is pre-eminently cheerful, in spite of, or perhaps even because of, the resort to fists as the ultimate arbitration. The great Doctor is present in the sense that Jehovah is, though the higher interventions prompt some mawkishness. Marking a break into fiction (though based on King William's College, Isle of Man), *Eric, or Little by Little* was published only one year later, in 1858, to be followed in due course by *St Winifrid's* and *Julian Home*. Their author, Dean F.W. Farrar, also responsible for the phrase 'the great cricket-field of life', was no doubt a man of unworldly innocence, largely incapable of realizing what was actually afoot in a school – witness the unconscious homosexuality of the David-and-Jonathan friendships he describes, and, to Freudian antennae, even of his language. To him, boys were essentially free from original sin, and one good influence deserved another. Purity, however, was too easily overtaken by carelessness, in which case a boy might steal, cheat by using a crib, or turn godless. Then he was pretty well done for, clean bowled without appeal, and might lose a parent or even his own life, without preliminaries or fuss. Our Heavenly Father who kept the perpetual score-card thus had a role as a kind of super-headmaster.

In Dean Farrar's world, everything human was reconcilable, and for the best. The boy who is too stupid to learn his lessons pays the penalty by simply dying, but God is grateful to receive him, and his mother is grateful to God; nobody is too clumsy or uncoordinated to play games; the ungodly do not flourish, and the godly are tempted in ways they can overcome. It was an act of gigantic self-deception for the newly-prosperous people to whom public schools were catering to visualize Dean Farrar's pastel-shaded advertisements as value for money. Yet the novels were constantly reprinted until well into this century (for years, incidentally, the Religious Tract Society, specializing in 'pi' literature about schools, made a killing), and many boys must have been puzzled by the illusions of those aunts or godparents who had presented them with such wide-of-the-mark reading at the start of a new term. The real public school had been distorted to look like a national seminary of values fit only for mystically beauteous vapours.

Under Dean Farrar's wing hatched a whole genre of boys' novels which aimed less at depicting life than guiding morals. The white man's son's burden was thereby fastened upon the public schools. The *Boys' Own Paper* was first published in 1879, its principal writer for years being Talbot Baines Reed, a deacon in the Congregational Church. *Author, Bibliographer, Type-finder* is the title of Stanley Morison's biography of him. The outpouring of public school tales such as *The Fifth Form at St Dominic's* and *The Adventures of a Three Guinea Watch* shows how superficially Reed mistook wishes for deeds. In the former novel, for instance, the hero Oliver wins his scholarship, plays for the first fifteen, and triumphs over Loman, the aptly-named cad who had accused him of cheating, when himself in debt to the villainous local publican. The gentleman by definition always defeats the bounder.

This simple pictogram of Vice and Virtue was represented in a thousand make-believe Rodboroughs, Sherboroughs, Dunmores, St This and St That's. Endless muffs, fluffs, funks, wets, twits, cissies, ruins, are put through the mill, while up the rungs of the Shells, Removes, Fifths, Sixths, the schoolboy swells mount. Cribbing is bad, but frequent; stealing almost unknown but often suspected. 'Side', like most infractions of the code, is best treated swiftly with a kick on the shins. The house-match and 'the honour of the school' are absolute values not to be trifled with. When the captain of the school in a Reed novel asks a small boy, 'Will you be my flower?' perhaps even a Congregationalist deacon was suspending disbelief just too far, unless he was bumping against the self-imposed restrictions of the standard plot.

Horace Vachell's *The Hill*, subtitled *A Romance of Friendship* (1905), is a rare example of public school fantasy able to sustain itself on its subject matter, in large measure because it is set firmly in an identifiable school, Harrow. Its hero, John Verney, has what would have been called a 'crush' on his friend Caesar Desmond, and at a school concert sings a solo projected at him: 'Higher and higher rose the clear sexless notes till two of them met and mingled in a triumphant trill. To Desmond, that trill was the answer to the quavering, troubled cadences of the first verse; the vindication of the spirit soaring upwards unfettered by the flesh – the pure spirit, not released from the pitiful human clay without a fierce struggle. And that moment Desmond loved the singer. . . .' Scaife, known as the Demon, athlete supreme, keeps them separate; he leads Desmond into bad habits of drinking and gambling. John's friendship is therefore never quite as winged as he would wish, and in the end Desmond is killed in the Boer War. The author makes it plain that the death of Scaife would have served everyone better. More damning than Scaife's unfeeling or loose behaviour is his social origin, for his grandfather had been a navvy before making good. The implicit snobbery of other school stories is spelled out here, for the message is that the meek and humble can be as blessed as they like, but still they are not going to inherit the earth from the powerful and strong. Though this was at the centre of the secrecy that dared not speak its name, it was only Dean Farrar and Talbot Baines Reed writ large, in Edwardian script. Evidence that contemporary Harrow was not actually like that can be found in Arnold Lunn's novel *The Harrovians* (1913), a far more down-to-earth account, deprecating games, and the morbid hero-worship that went with them.

With class-magic at its heyday, F. Anstey's *Vice Versa* (1882) was almost unique as an anti-school book. Its humour depended upon exposing what in fact was generally known, but not admitted, to be the hypocrisy about school as 'the happiest time of your life'. A father like Mr Bultitude invented all manner of justifications for putting his son through trials he could not himself endure for a week. Anstey was a humorist, and pulled his punches by packing young Dick off to Harrow for a quiet life in the end. Another and more enduring comic writer, P.G. Wodehouse, began his career before the First War with the Psmith stories, in a lightly veneered Dulwich, and signally lacking in veneration, though outwardly observant in form. As so often, subversion was first sprung with the lightest of touches, and humour shifted attitudes towards such schools as not even Dickensian indignation had been able to do. Once held up to laughter and ridicule, anthropological customs of the tribe were set for extinction.

II

The closing chapter of many a public school epic had landed our hero on some frontier where the pink only just held good on the map, to be discouragingly often laid low by the fuzzy-wuzzies, but consummating his upbringing in glory. It was something quite else to have a subaltern's life-expectancy of three weeks in the trenches of the First War. Stiff-upper-lip, take-it-on-the-chin, don't-let-the-side-down attitudes vanished into mud and meaninglessness. The idea of itself and its values which a public school education had been fostering needed re-examination urgently. The moment a realistic writer came along, he would have the chance to strip off mysteries, and relate public schools more accurately to the society which had evolved them. Alec Waugh's *The Loom of Youth* (1917) did just this, and scandal was in the air. First of all, boys were shown arranging to spend half-hours alone in their study for the purposes of sex. Then the cynicism. 'The idea that the Public School boy's code of honour forces him to own up at once is entirely erroneous. Boys only own up when they are bound to be found out; they are not quixotic.' Like adults, in fact. The hero, Gordon, leaves his thinly-disguised Lancing with an unreasoning anger against the Public School system, though he can see where advantage may also lie in it. 'After all, it left him unscathed, and was in the future to bring many gifts. Others might be broken on the wheel; but he was still sufficiently egoist, sufficiently self-centred to be indifferent to them. He had come through.' As though he had gone over the top in the first of battles.

To stay on the straight old tack without veering demanded more intelligence in a traditionalist who thought *The Loom of Youth* was rotten. *Playing Fields* (1922), by Eric Parker, dwells on the life of an Eton colleger, without falsely inflated emotion, and an unusual emphasis on intellectual competition which made it seem more up-to-the-minute than it was. Warden, the colleger described, would have liked to be more proficient all round, but he accepts disappointments stoically. That he is deprived ultimately of the top scholastic and athletic successes stakes a position on the scale of decline; no nineteenth century school novel would have closed to any down-beat of that nature. As late as 1931, in *The English Public School*, Bernard Darwin could still put forward a defence such as this: 'Making due allowance for exceptions, the public school does produce a more or less typical body of men, with certain codes and manners and habits of thought and speech, as to whom it may be predicted in particular circumstances what they will do in mass.' Which of course was being more generally formulated as the accusation against them. Closed Victorian doors were held to have swung open upon a conformity as mechanical as a dye-stamp. Even in the rough old days, an individual had been accepted at a price. Before secrecy had descended, so headstrong a character as Byron had seemed to his housemaster, Drury, at Harrow, 'a wild mountain colt, who might be led with a silken string rather than with a cable'. He would never have come unscathed, or un-Scaifed, through the Harrow of Horace Vachell.

Unhesitating acceptance was over and done with, cables had snapped. In another of those historic shifts by which the public schools have so expertly brought the future to heel, gentry-values were to be ditched, and substituted by meritocracy. Citizens responsive to contemporary interpretations of progress were more assured than gentlemen of a place in the forefront of the twentieth century: general technicians, scientists, publicists, exam-passers. Criticism, once relaunched as it had not been for a hundred years, grew tidal. Using the form of a novel to write a polemic on education, H.G. Wells juggled with current theories in *Joan and Peter* (1918), and dismissed public schools rudely. As he had previously praised, in his double-edged way, Sanderson, the progressive headmaster of Oundle, his mockery smarted. *Goodbye to all That*, Robert Graves' embittered reckoning with the recent past; Richard Aldington; C.E. Montague; Aldous Huxley – it was being taken for granted that education at a public school was a root of all evil, among the contributory causes to social division, class unease, inefficiency, the lack of democracy in the country. The quickest route to the approved Marxist credentials just coming into vogue was to renounce one's educational origins, denying them, so to speak, thrice before roll-call.

Of the intellectuals who became prominent in the thirties, few who took themselves seriously would have any redeeming word for the public schools whose products they almost unanimously were. Like Alec Waugh, they had come through, and it was enough. The collective attitude is found in a book edited by Graham Greene in 1934, *The Old School*. Greene himself had been at Berkhamsted, under the headmastership of his father, and in several of his books the school represents a private damnation. 'Appalling cruelties could be practised without a second thought; one met for the first time characters, adult and adolescent, who bore about them the genuine quality of evil.' Forty years on, he is still at pains in his autobiography to score off a pair of those evil-bearing adolescents. W.H. Auden maintained that there was no more potent an engine than his Gresham's School for turning boys into neurotic innocents. 'The best reason I have for opposing Fascism is that at school I lived in a Fascist state.' Winchester, St Paul's, Malvern, Rugby, Cheltenham Ladies' College, were deftly anatomized down to the skeleton. It would have been unthinkable only a generation earlier for Anthony Powell to express gratitude that he had been sent to the very worst house at Eton, where he was left to his own devices, untroubled by games and other adversities. Running away from Wellington while a precocious teenager, Esmond Romilly launched *Out of Bounds* (also in 1934), an anti-school magazine which hit the headlines. It was not so much a type of education that was exposed in memoirs and polemics of the time, by writers as diverse as Louis MacNeice, John Betjeman and T.C. Worsley, as concentration camps in embryo.

A silken string was tugged one last time in Cyril Connolly's *Enemies of Promise* (1938). He had actually been a scholar at Eton at the very moment when Eric Parker was writing and publishing *Playing Fields*, but temperamentally he preferred to cover the nakedness of his nostalgia with the hair-shirting of guilt. True, like Auden, he spoke of the Gestapo in College, and saw himself at the age of fifteen as 'dirty, inky, miserable, untidy, a bad fag, a coward at games, lazy at work, unpopular with my masters and superiors, anxious to curry favour, and yet bully whom I dared'. All the same, the dark ages of boyhood came to a stop, he mastered the classics and was mastered by them once and for all, and he basked in the good looks, the ease and laurels, of his contemporaries. His Theory of Permanent Adolescence clearly had a good deal of truth in it, positing that 'the experiences undergone by boys at the great public schools, their glories and disappointments, are so intense as to dominate their lives, and to arrest their developments. From these it results that the greater part of the ruling class remains adolescent, school-minded, self-conscious, cowardly, sentimental, and in the last analysis, homosexual.' What were the inky fag and the self-conscious, half-queer member of the ruling class but Dean Farrar prototypes enlarged and modernized into travesties? As with the figure of the mother, so with the *alma mater*, too much affection carried the psychological reaction of breeding hatred. Hundreds of defectors existed already, but with *Enemies of Promise* the public school was betrayed from within.

Novelists, always prone to be harking backwards, continued to go through the motions of aggression even after the Second World War, when the debate in politics was about abolishing the public school altogether, and governing bodies and headmasters were trying to salvage academic standards primarily out of the ruins of the old code. Unlike old soldiers, ancient grievances do not even fade away. *George Brown's Schooldays* (1946), Bruce Marshall's attack on a school like Glenalmond, for example, was actually set in a historic past, where the name of Brown itself was bound to have special resonance. The entire range of bullying and pettiness, bad manners, and the desire to excel at games, was on display as though it were all still being hushed-up. The times might never have changed. Even David Benedictus' *The Fourth of June*, as recently as 1962, was only *Tom Brown's Schooldays* spun with weary sophistication instead of energy. Its scenario of a boy victimized by older brutes, beaten so hard that he is paralysed, was no doubt intended as social protest, but was only bringing tradition up to date in hallowed style. And when one of the nastiest boys says sarcastically of a sermon, 'Bloody funny bishop, that!' a whole cycle has been completed since Squire Brown first led Tom off to Rugby to turn him into 'a brave, helpful, truth-telling Englishman, and a gentleman, and a Christian'.

III

Yet the reversals of public school influences were not quite what they seemed. George Orwell, Connolly's friend in College at Eton, where he was happier than he later cared to admit in public, was the first to sniff out the extraordinary fact that the fantasists of the public schools had succeeded in bewitching large parts of the population whom they had not really been addressing in the first place. His justly famous essay, *Boys' Weeklies*, written in 1939, drew attention to the school story as a thing peculiar to England. 'The reason, obviously, is that in England education is mainly a matter of status . . . It is quite clear that there are tens and scores of thousands of people to whom every detail of life at a "posh" school is wildly thrilling and romantic. They happen to be outside that mystic world of quadrangle and house-colours but they yearn after it, day-dream about it, live mentally in it for hours at a stretch.'

The instruments of day-dream were comics like *Gem* and *Magnet*, or the *Boys' Own Paper*. Orwell went on to analyse Billy Bunter and his chums at Greyfriars in terms of class attitudes, and he now sounds a little dated, but in the main he had pointed to a social truth: that all sorts of boys were identifying with a model not theirs; a model, moreover, which was not an approximation of reality, but its parody, and in so far as they knew this, they did not care. No public school had ever been like Greyfriars and the rest. The vulgarized model had descended from myth-makers in the past, the Dean Farrars and Talbot Baines Reeds, and lesser but prolific fry like Frank Richards and Gunby Hadath. A superior shrine had been erected, and its purity cherished with the theological complexities of school lore. The sons of gentlemen knew better, but nobody else did. The public schools had stayed secret long enough to have evolved the lurid, specious attractions of Never-Never lands where privilege and pleasure reigned supreme and constant. Admission, for the masses, was by proxy only. If the living conditions had been properly perceived, the cold, the food, the learning by rote, the beatings and discipline and cult of athleticism, then the subject-matter of the comics would have collapsed of its own accord.

Orwell wanted a wider social outlook in boys' stories and comics, in which he was failing to understand quite what an act of imagination they already represented to the majority of their readers. He could not know that the form of the public school was about to be pulverized by the Second War and its aftermath, that the gentry-spirit was on the point of expiring, and a generation brought up to television and technocracy would find nothing to chortle at in Billy Bunter and his chums. Secrecy, or anything like it, was over and done with, when the one criterion of education was to be a success in a formal academic sense.

Nor did Orwell follow through to the conclusion implicit in his essay, that although the conventional public school code may have ceased to be quite credible to those in whom it was immediately being implanted, the general public had nevertheless been captured by it in many ways, of which the widely read boys' weeklies were only one instance. At the point when the ruling magic was blown, it had acquired currency. Nathanial Woodard, the proselytizing founder of Lancing and Hurstpierpoint and other schools, had presented the challenge: 'Somehow or other, we must get possession of the Middle Classes, especially the lower section, and how can we so well do this as through Public Schools?' The middle classes, especially the lower section, widening with prosperity and confidence, did indeed take possession of the public schools, to find themselves possessed in turn by their capture – just as Rome is held to have conquered Athens but to have been in the thrall of Hellenistic culture as a result.

Everything which had made the public school what it was had worked its way outwards and downwards into society at large. Here was a transfusion of morality, and even of organisms. It is ironical that during the final period of this fertilizing process the educational establishments themselves appeared exhausted and diffident. In his book, *The Prefects* (1964), Rupert Wilkinson has many sharp *aperçus* into the colonization of our institutions by public schools. To him 'there is a marked parallel between the values and mechanisms of public school society and those of British government' – for instance in the components of the gentleman-ideal, in the status-symbol of leisure, the attitude to privilege and duty, and community service. 'The Civil Service maintained a public-school type tradition of emotional detachment and deference to senior office [because] reliance on traditional wisdom is a deep-rooted element in the British social character.' One thinks of the wearisome promotional grind, examination-based, of the entire bureaucracy, with its removes upwards to clerk, assistant, principal, deputy, under-secretary, through the classrooms of power, appropriately furnished with graduated decorations, not just the better carpets and pictures of the senior men's studies, but their very 'caps', their CBEs and KCMGs. And is the social organization of business and industry any different?

The educational system of the ruling class, as Rupert Wilkinson argues, has found its reflection and transmission in the British political character.

Public life is in effect an enormous Public School; though whether the demands of government or the supply of the schools came first is a perfect chicken-and-egg discussion. The comparison holds even in details – was it not fagging which provided the inspiration whereby otherwise fully grown-up people have to stick weekly insurance stamps into little books? And is not a parking-warden the model of a monitor, and the ensuing fine (not to mention breathalyser tests) the illustration of a headmaster's directive on the notice-board?

Take organized games, one of the main props of the public schools. The Football League was founded in 1888 by a dozen private clubs on a subscription basis. Within forty years, a complete replica of public school football had been established nationally: the clubs in knock-out contests, with silver cups to the winner as though in a glorified house-match; scarves, blazers, coloured shirts, and admirers who are under obligation to cheer on their teams in a highly competitive spirit, with a kick on the shins for slackers; Wednesday and Saturday afternoons for all the world like a half-holiday. Even the curious school distinction between soccer and rugger has been carried through. What once was an enclosed public school ethic and language around ball games has become the national heritage.

The one intangible asset, so beloved of many a myth-maker, was supposed to be the Old School Tie, that nexus of adolescent 'honour' supposedly grown into adult favouritism. A far cry from the public schools, its actual embodiment has come to rest in the Trade Union movement, which insists upon loyalties defined by exclusive membership; not only is entry restricted in some unions (with the sanction of law), but family ties are taken into consideration; certain jobs may be filled only by those of the right sort; good fellowship is required above qualifications. Fantasies are infectious, and it has its poetic justice that the lyricists of public school superiority should have been heard so attentively and emulated, sedulous apes that they were. In the countryside, the public school may lie a-mouldering, its prime function to tot up university entrances, but elsewhere its soul goes marching on.

David Pryce-Jones (Kent College for Girls and Eton) has published six novels, as well as works of non-fiction, the latest of which is a biography of Unity Mitford.

9
The Shadow of *Tom Brown*
RICHARD USBORNE

If you started hitting in the face, it meant that you had lost your temper. You could scuffle and wrestle, pummel and punch anywhere above the belt and below the throat. But once you hit in the face, it was serious and spelt danger. Someone probably slid away and told a prefect, or a master, or the matron. Others certainly wanted the affray stopped before authority intervened: but they wanted it then to be continued as a set piece in the lavatories yard, behind the Chapel and in front of the boot-cleaner's shed. There were always boys enthusiastic to organize a proper fight between two other boys. And we all knew the drill . . . about sponges and towels and two-minute rounds and umpires (not referees: why?) and seconds. We knew that one of the seconds knelt on one knee and provided the other knee as a stool for his combatant between rounds.

I have gone back fifty and more years in time and to a hundred other little prep-school groupies, moralists, voyeurs and sadists. And we knew our fighting stuff because most of us had already read *Tom Brown's Schooldays* (with illustrations), our school library was full of public school novels (with illustrations) that *Tom Brown* had spawned in the last seventy years, and the *Boy's Own Paper* and *Chums* had more public school stories (with illustrations) full of cricket and fights, football and fights, sports and fights.

I am advancing four propositions. First, that public school fiction was, in those paulo-post-World-War-I days, read mostly by boys of prep-school age. Second, that *Tom Brown's Schooldays*, read too early, frightened us badly about boarding schools in general. Third, that *Tom Brown's Schooldays*, read too early, left a nasty and unacknowledged residue. It made us prep-schoolboys think that, if we came near the end of our prep-school years without taking part in a fist fight, hitting in the face, we had not proved ourselves men, manly, manful or whatever the pulpit/'If' jargon word of our boyhood was. This thought on its own sometimes generated fights, sometimes (less often, probably) bullying.

My fourth proposition is this: that *Tom Brown's Schooldays* has been a front-runner in imprinting on the English ruling classes two irrational beliefs: (a) that corporal punishment should be, by the male, bravely received (bullying, caning, boxing, school fights, 'going hard' at games, biting and gouging in the scrum, breaking your neck in the huntin' field, wounds or death in battle for your country), and (b) that corporal punishment should be bravely inflicted when sanctioned by authority and sometimes when not so sanctioned (beating small boys when you are a prefect, housemaster, headmaster or father, biting and gouging in the scrum – if not seen by the ref – capital punishment if you are a judge or hangman, casualties by the thousand, preferably on the enemy but, where necessary, on your own men if you are a warlord, in uniform or civilian).

I cannot prove any of those propositions, but I advance them confidently.

I am thankful to say that I came through a decade of boarding schools without having to fight anybody. But in my last year at prep school I twice picked hit-in-the-face affrays with smaller boys (naturally) for no reason that I can retrospectively claim other than that I had *to have had* a fight. Sorry, Stubbs. Sorry, Scott-Ellis. That's all it was, and I am still ashamed of myself and still a great hater of *Tom Brown's Schooldays*.

P.G. Wodehouse, in his stripling years as a City bank clerk trying to write his way out to freedom and fame, teased *Tom Brown* in print in the *Public School Magazine* as early as 1902. But not for the fighting ethic . . . he was to make full use of that later in his own excellent and unfrightening public school novels. Wodehouse went for *Tom Brown* on the grounds of its style and structure. He said it was a broken-backed story and its two dissimilar parts must have been written by different authors. (He gave the book a bit of the treatment he had learnt, for exams, to give Homer in the Sixth at Dulwich.) Could, he asked, the same author have created East and Arthur? Could the same man have written the football match at the beginning and the cricket match at the end? Wodehouse credited Hughes with the first part of the book and with the Slogger Williams/Tom Brown fight (except for the gross interference of Arthur before its rightful end) in the second half. But the rest he attributed to a committee of the Secret Society for Putting Wholesome Literature Within the Reach of Every Boy and Seeing That He Gets It – the SSPWLWREBSTHGI. Would, asked young Wodehouse (P.G.), Hughes's Tom Brown, now captain of Rugby cricket, having won the toss, have put the MCC in on a plumb wicket? Would Hughes's Tom have allowed comic songs and speeches during the lunch interval of an important one-day school match? Would Hughes's Tom have blatantly given his soppy chum Arthur an undeserved place in the school team simply because he thought it would do Arthur a lot of good?

You can find this Wodehouse essay at the end of his *Tales of St Austin's* (1903, but recently re-published by Souvenir Press). My own quarrel with *Tom Brown* is angrier. My mother, probably at my absent-in-India father's casual suggestion and without reading it herself, gave me *Tom Brown* (with illustrations) to read before I went to my prep school, at the age of seven. It put the wind up me vertically. I didn't know the difference between public and private schools, nor between *Tom Brown*'s coy '183–' and my 1918. But I did learn from it that school would mean my being boxed on the ear, caned, flogged, fagged, bullied, tossed in blankets, roasted in front of fires, made to sing songs solo, made to fall on footballs and faint under the tons of beefy enthusiasts who would fall on top of me, and be constantly involved in fist fights with bigger boys, velveteens and louts. I would have to endure these things bravely and without peaching (is that a Rugby word?) so that I 'might never bring shame or sorrow to the dear folk at home'.

All that violence, and I a coward! I knew I was a coward. I yelled at the dentist's, wouldn't climb trees, fled from wasps, feared the dark. And Hughes extolled manliness from the start: 'The Browns are a fighting family. One may question their wisdom, or wit, or beauty, but about their fight there can be no question. Wherever hard knocks of any kind . . . are going, there the Brown who is nearest must shove in his carcase . . .' Chuckle, chuckle. Then a chuckling description of the 'noble old game of back-sword' in the Vale (crack your stick on his head and draw blood before he does it to you, and you're the winner!), and new-boy Tom's coach-ride through the night to Rugby. The cold numbed Tom's legs in the first half hour. 'But it had its pleasures, the old dark ride. For there was the consciousness of silent endurance, so dear to every Englishman – of standing out against something, and not giving in . . .' Thence to the ardours and endurances of Rugby under the beneficent rule of the great Dr Arnold.

Do you remember that the Slogger Williams/Tom Brown fight was sparked off by Arthur, blubbing over the pathos of a passage of the *Iliad* that he was construing in class? And it was Arthur who got the fight stopped just when his champion was winning. And do you remember the last three sermonizing paragraphs of that chapter . . . ?

Boys will quarrel, and when they quarrel will sometimes fight. Fighting with fists is the natural and English way for English boys to settle their quarrels. What substitute for it is there, or ever was there, amongst any nation under the sun? What would you like to see take its place?

Learn to box, then, as you learn to play cricket and football. Not one of you will be the worse, but very much the better for learning to box well. Should you never have to use it in earnest, there's no exercise in the world so good for the temper, and for the muscles of the back and legs.

As to fighting, keep out of it if you can, by all means. When the time comes, if it ever should, that you have to say 'Yes' or 'No' to a challenge to fight, say 'No' if you can – only take care you make it clear to yourselves why you say 'No'. It's a proof of the highest courage, if done from true Christian motives. It's quite right and justifiable if done from a simple aversion to physical pain and danger. But don't say 'No' because you fear a licking, and say or think it is because you fear God, for that's neither Christian nor honest. And if you do fight, fight it out; and don't give in while you can stand and see.

In the *Inside Linda Lovelace* trial at the Old Bailey, a witness for the defence said that there was kinky sex in, amongst other classics, *Tom Brown's Schooldays*. The judge didn't ask where, and I can't remember any. The author's love for Dr Arnold? Tom's love for Arthur's mother? But perhaps the witness (a lady) meant that the whole violence ethic of the book was sexual or homosexual.

The point hadn't occurred to me. But add the three paragraphs quoted above to the Arnold-of-Rugby doctrine of giving responsibility to the top boys, plus power (to beat bad boys) and privileges (having fags and wearing egregious clothes). Hughes's hagiographic fiction, plus Arnold's disciples – junior masters and devoted prefects – carrying the Old Man's principles and spreading his doctrines into other boarding schools – these were two strong factors for keeping honour bright in the privileged English boarding school for the tradition of the cane, wielded by master on boy or by big boy on smaller boy, and for the tradition of the mandatory suppression of the newcomer of this year by the newcomer of last.

In the course of a single month of undisciplined book-borrowing from my local library, I have recently read three examples of upper-class English boarding school beatings which shivered my old timbers. Frances Donaldson quotes, in her *Edward VIII*, her subject's own account of a beating at Osborne Naval College during his first term as a boarder there (or anywhere). The Head of Osborne then was a Captain Alexander-Sinclair, R.N., and his own son was a first-termer with the Prince of Wales. Young Alexander-Sinclair was constantly being reported to his father for this and that misdemeanour, and

> . . . his father presently sentenced him to 'six official cuts' with a bamboo cane. For this rare and extreme punishment, the Duke [of Windsor] tells us, the boy was strapped to a gymnasium horse, and a naval doctor had to be present. The cuts were then administered by a physical training petty officer. What turned the scene of this punishment, horrible enough in itself, into one of organized cruelty was the presence of other cadets drawn up in two lines to watch it. Every boy must have noticed with some degree of disturbance that it was the boy's father who inflicted this punishment on him and ordained that it should be watched. To the Prince, who was so nervous of his own father, the effect must surely have been traumatic.

I then read, in John Watney's life of Mervyn Peake, the author and artist, that young Mervyn, newly arrived to join his elder brother at Eltham College (for the sons of missionaries) in Kent, was, on his first night, copped talking in his dormitory after lights out. And the prefect who copped him and had, however unwillingly, to cane him, was his elder brother Leslie. The brothers were, and happily remained, very good friends: which says something for the Peake family, but nothing for Eltham College.

Last, Kenneth Clark at Winchester, from his autobiography *Another Part of the Wood.* Travelling from London for the first term in the school train, young Clark chattered to other boys, individually and in groups. He found them all cold and unresponsive. On his arrival at his House, he was told to go and see the head boy, who turned out to be one of the individuals he had tried to talk to on the train.

> 'Sport an arse,' he said (which in Wykehamist language means 'bend over'): and he gave me three or four very painful strokes with a stick, known as a ground ash. 'That will teach you to speak to your seniors,' he said. It did. In the twinkling of an eye the jolly boy from Wixenford [preparatory school] became a silent, solitary, inward-turning but still imperfect Wykehamist.

On his second night at Winchester young Clark was luckier:

> . . . one of the prefects, who was himself an amateur artist, said, 'Bloody little new man. Think you know all about art. Sport an arse.' Fortunately he was short-sighted and clumsy, as was apparent from his water-colours, and his blows were much less painful than those of the night before.

To be beaten on your first *and* second nights at your public school must have been fairly rare even in those days, I imagine.

Caning, beating, swishing, cocking up, sporting an arse, tanning – the jargon words differed from school to school. There is a malady, fundamentally agonizing if, mercifully, of short duration, which doctors refer to as *proctalgia fugax* but don't, apparently, know how to prevent, predict or cure. It is thought to be a stress warning. The public school version in the period covered by my schooldays, Edward VIII's, Kenneth Clark's and Mervyn Peake's, was said to have made men of its recipients. I was not a recipient. I had had enough of the cane at my prep school. I lied my way out of culpable situations all my time at public school.

* * *

It came as no surprise to me to find that Hughes wrote a book entitled *The Manliness of Christ*. But, having read that weird cricket match at the end of the book, I was certainly surprised to learn that Hughes had played in the Varsity cricket match as a freshman at Oxford. He was, for good measure, a QC, a Member of Parliament for ten years and a County Court Judge for fourteen. And he lost his shirt investing in a large estate, named 'Rugby', in Tennessee for the establishment of a model community of settlers.

The *Dictionary of National Biography*, in a long piece on Hughes, says:

> His object in writing it [*Tom Brown's Schooldays*: it appeared anonymously, 'By an Old Boy'] was to do good . . . The book was written expressly for boys, and it would be difficult to measure the good influence which it has exerted on innumerable boys by its power to enter into their ways and prejudices, and to appeal to their better instincts.

It was Charles (*The Water Babies*) Kingsley who recommended the ms. of *Tom Brown* to Daniel Macmillan, the publisher. 'As sure as eggs are eggs,' Kingsley wrote, 'the book will pay both of you well.' It did and, as a grace note, I may record that a son of Thomas Hughes was one of the first pupils at that prep school of mine and that the publishing Macmillans, including a recent Prime Minister, have been boys there for four generations.

It was only decades later that I worked out that the two blood-letting quarrels that I picked, with smaller foes, at my prep school were generated by the violence ethic of that seminal classic, *Tom Brown*. And the two other fights that I remember – I'm sure they were attributable to *Tom Brown* (with illustrations) too. The Taylor/Bannister fight in the lavatories yard . . . they were two peaceful, apple-cheeked twelve-year-olds, but somehow . . . O, Taylor had bagged Bannister's conker, or Bannister had read some letters to Taylor from his mother and discovered his Christian name . . . it had to be fought out. And a pushful, pummelling, messy, inexpert, nose-bleeding and inconclusive mill it was. And the Spencer/Cochran fight in my last term. What was that about? I don't know. I was a prefect and I kept out of the way. But the fight produced a lot of blood on their stiff Sunday Eton collars and a genuine black eye (of which the silly ass was proud) for Cochran for a fortnight afterwards. They were heroes to the rest of us. They had justified their manliness. They had Done The Right Thing. They had faced a fist-fight, 'hitting in the face allowed'. Aged eleven or twelve.

The Shadow of Tom Brown

In ancient shadows and twilights
where childhood had strayed,
the world's great sorrows were born
and its heroes were made.
In the lost boyhood of Judas
Christ was betrayed.

A major strand in the plot of *Tom Brown* is the slow salvation ('growing in manfulness and thoughtfulness') of Tom as a result of having young mammy-sick Arthur foisted on him as a protégé ... a clandestine but typical ruse of the great Doctor's. The elder boy/younger boy, or tough boy/weedy boy friendship theme was common in public school stories for half a century after *Tom Brown*, and I suppose it needed a few late-Victorian scandals and Alec Waugh's later *Loom of Youth* to put the theme finally in baulk for the author who hoped for *B.O.P.* or *Chums* serialization. The Rev. Colin Stephenson, in his autobiographical book, *Merrily on High*, referred to his schooldays at Cranleigh, when the Chaplain preached from the text 'See that you love one another'. 'This caused a great stir among the housemasters, who spent a lot of their time and energy in trying to ensure that we did no such thing.' Which leads me, with, again, some help from the young P.G. Wodehouse, to a very odd book, published in 1895, called *Gerald Eversley's Friendship*. As a public school novel it is bad to the point of absurdity, and you will probably have difficulty in even finding a copy. I was first aware of it from a glancing review Wodehouse gave it in *The Public School Magazine* in 1902, and I later found an essay, mocking it, by E.F. Benson. Neither Wodehouse nor Benson gave the name of its author. One wonders why. The author's name was writ large in it.

Gerald Eversley's Friendship was, astonishingly, written by the then headmaster of Harrow, J.E.C. Welldon. It is conceivable that Wodehouse let Welldon off without mentioning his name because Welldon had been, briefly and some years before Wodehouse's own schooldays there, headmaster of Dulwich. His two years there had been sufficient for him to have composed, and imposed, the school song, *Pueri Alleynienses* ('*quotquot annos, quotquot menses* ...'). That young Wodehouse had had to sing it may have given him a revenge motive for attacking the lyricist's novel though sparing the lyricist.

Benson, son of the Archbishop of Canterbury, may have let Welldon off with anonymity because Welldon was, as Benson's father had been, on the ladder set for well-connected schoolmasters in holy orders . . . a headmastership or two, a mitre and, who knows? . . . eventually Canterbury. You may remember the first Wodehouse Buck-U-Uppo story, in which the Rev. Trevor Entwistle, headmaster of Harchester, and his old school crony, now Bishop of Stortford, drink the tonic Buck-U-Uppo in jumbo strength, and go out at midnight and paint pink a benefactor's statue in the school close. The bishop, in his exuberance, leaves his shovel hat, with his name in it, on the statue's head, and the next day things begin to look very black for the culprits. 'If this is found out,' wails the headmaster, 'bim go my chances of becoming a bishop!' But all ends well. They are saved by the subsidized intervention and confession of a young Mulliner, a boy at the school whose elder brother is the bishop's chaplain. The headmaster gives young Mulliner a very light imposition for his high-spirited prank. And the bishop, who had been writing, for a Church magazine, a rather sceptical article on Miracles, revises his views and comes out as a firm believer in miracles, ancient and modern. He will also reward his chaplain with a vicarage as soon as he has one in his gift.

You can find Benson's mockery of *Gerald Eversley's Friendship* in his book, *The Babe B.A.* (1897). But read the novel before reading what these two critics say about it. It is the story of a blessed friendship at a public school (St Anselm's) between a poor clergyman's weedy, bespectacled scholar son (Gerald) and a rich lord's handsome, lithe, sunburnt, popular son (Harry Venniker). Two new boys, they are to share a study-bedroom. The housemaster likes to couple boys of different backgrounds, so that they can 'rub off angles' from and on each other. (There are a number of other echoes of *Tom Brown* in *Gerald Eversley's Friendship*, though Welldon would have been surprised and hurt if you had suggested cribbing.) Harry has come with a fiver from his father in his pocket: Gerald with a mere half sovereign from his in his. Harry, for a start, unpacks a royal stag's head, shot by his father, from his playbox to decorate their room: Gerald has a horror of blood sports. Harry puts up a photograph of his beautiful only sister and finds that Gerald has eight half-sisters. Such a lot of angles to be rubbed off!

Gerald hasn't been away from home before . . . his father had tutored him up to his scholarship at St Anselm's. He blubs into his pillow on his first night. Harry comforts him with a hand upon his shoulder. 'He was breaking a rule of the house in getting out of bed after the lights had been extinguished; but it may be that a Higher Authority than Mr Brandiston [the housemaster] would have acquitted him.' One assumes, from the capital letters, that the Higher Authority was God, not the headmaster.

So Gerald 'laid his head anew on the pillow, and was at peace'. But only till the next night.

> It was the humane and merciful rule of Mr Brandiston's house that a new boy might not be molested or persecuted by impertinent interrogations until twenty-four hours after his entering the house. The reason of it was that on the evening of the second day of the term all the boys liable to fagging (including, of course, all the new boys) were divided by a long established principle of selection among the Sixth Form, and after that time, but not before, a new boy was felt to possess a natural patron or protector, and therefore to be a legitimate victim for the shafts of his natural enemies.
>
> The ceremony of choosing the fags, or, as it was technically designated, 'fag-spotting', deserves something more than a passing notice. It was a strange and almost barbarous ceremony. In some respects the nearest parallel to it may be said to have been the sale of slave girls in the market at Constantinople.

Well, Harry gets picked, one of the first, by the Captain of the Eleven. And poor Gerald, alone and last, is grudgingly accepted by an insignificant Sixth Former.

The fag-spotting ceremony over, the 'trying of voices' begins, and now poor Gerald has to sing, solo, a verse and chorus of a song which has the word 'd . . .' in it.

> . . . a word . . . which his scrupulous conscience felt to be wicked. It was not a word that he had known to be used, except once, on a very hot day, by a labourer at Kestercham [the village of which his father was vicar]. But he conceived it to be an offence against God. He had heard his father speak of its solemn and terrible meaning in preaching upon the text 'He that believeth not shall be damned'. It was one of the words he had promised never to use . . .

So, when Gerald's turn to sing it comes, he breaks down, hides his face in his hands and rushes from the Hall.

What's to be done with young Eversley (G.)?

Some boys . . . urged that Gerald ought to be brought back at once perforce, and made to sing, being subjected to corporal chastisement if he refused; others that his behaviour, as being an unprecedented violation of the rules and customs of the house, should be referred to the Sixth Form; others, again, that he should be sent to Coventry for a month; others that he should incur a double measure of fagging.

But Gerald's friendship with the Hon. Harry protects him from the 'considerable trouble' that the other boys would have inflicted on him normally. As it was they

did nothing worse than leave him very much to himself; they would look at one another in a knowing way, and perhaps shrug their shoulders, when he passed, or one of them would nudge his arm at dinner to prevent him eating with absolute equanimity, or ask him the Latin for a saint, or inquire if his mother or sisters knew that he was out; once or twice he found his boots filled with water in the morning, or a blot of ink upon his carefully written exercise; or his hat was hidden away, to make him late for chapel . . .

(You get the feeling here that the Headmaster of Harrow, who describes himself as such on the title page of the novel, writes this with a slight chuckle . . . 'Boys will be boys. Young scamps!')

And so the terms pass. Harry, good at games, 'a splendid animal, healthy, vigorous, proud, elate, with no low tastes', becomes more and more popular. Gerald, let off games because of his eyesight, works at his books, plays the organ (Handel) to himself in Chapel and finds a churchyard near the school where he can go and brood and read poetry. He is a great churchyard-fancier. At home he likes to read poetry above his mother's grave, and at the end of the book he is going to have two more graves, side by side, in another churchyard to visit.

But twice he is accused of grave schoolboy sins and he is in dire trouble. The House bully and his cronies organize Sunday afternoon boxing matches (between other boys) in the House: safe, because Mr Brandiston is always occupied with tea and visitors upstairs then. But one Sunday Mr B comes storming in and there is trouble for all, especially for Gerald because the other boys suspect that it was he who had tipped Mr B off to this desecration of the sabbath. (It wasn't Gerald.) A few terms later Mr B suspects Gerald of having stolen an exam paper from his desk and thus done brilliant answers in the exam next day. (It wasn't Gerald.) The headmaster grills Gerald, who denies it with hot flushes, and the headmaster accepts his denial eventually.

The author of the book never tells us who *did* bring Mr Brandiston down to break up the Sunday boxing, nor how the charred fragment of the missing exam paper got into the grate in Gerald's room. The fact is that the Rev. J.E.C. Welldon may have been a fine translator and editor of Aristotle, a superb player of Eton fives, a great headmaster. But he was a terribly bad novelist: he just didn't know how to put it together. The young Wodehouse had seen that. You mustn't steam the reader up with the mystery of the housemaster discovering the boxers, and then not say *how* he found out. You mustn't have the great mystery of the missing exam paper (and Gerald's subsequent brilliant rendering of Cicero's *quodcumque in solum venit* as 'whatever is on the *tapis*') without solving it for the reader. And when Gerald, having won the scholarship to Balliol, begins to lose his Christian faith, you mustn't produce, as a whole chapter of a school novel, an essay in metaphysics and theology. Not in a school novel, Welldon. As a paper for episcopal examiners if you're trying for a mitre, yes. As a sermon for leaving Sixth Formers, perhaps. But not in a school novel, Welldon.

Quickly . . . how did the story end? Well, love came to Gerald . . . love of a lovely girl. Harry's sister, Ethel, no less. You see, Harry scored the last minute winning goal in the final of the House matches and almost immediately went down, or up to the sickroom, with inflammation of the lung. His father came down to the school. Sir William D——, the great London specialist, came down. Eight days of delirium, calling for his mother: prayers in the house: corner turned: recovery: sister Ethel came down to stay with the Brandistons, to relieve her father, to smooth Harry's pillow and to meet Harry's faithful friend, Gerald.

Gerald goes often now to stay with Harry at home. Lady Venniker invites him again, and this time he writes back:

> 'Sorry, dear Lady Venniker, I can't. I mustn't. I'm in love with your daughter . . . But it would not, I think, be honourable to see more of Miss Venniker without informing yourself and Lord Venniker of my feeling, and I cannot now trust myself to meet her again and not let her know what I feel . . .'

Lord and Lady V. reply that they will put no bar in the way of Gerald telling their daughter of his love. 'You must come and ask her. Come for

Harry's birthday.' So . . . Ethel says Yes. Gerald tells his father and mother and all seems set for happiness. Gerald wins a Fellowship at Balliol (it says Balliol, but somewhere inside the College there is a stream with a bridge over it. That doesn't sound like Balliol) and kisses Ethel for the first time in his excitement at the news. Gerald's snobbish stepmother invites Ethel to stay at the vicarage and makes ready for her to bring two ladies' maids. But Ethel comes 'alone, simply and quietly'. She finds no fault with the food. She goes to the nursery and plays with the children. She begs to be allowed to accompany Gerald's father on his visits to his sick people and, in spite of his protests, she 'carries a basin of soup to a poor woman who has just been confined'. She sings in the church choir and the villagers think they are hearing 'a voice from a better world'. She brings the now re-faithful Gerald to first-Sunday-of-the-year Communion, to the delight of his father. She comes to a tea-party Gerald's stepmother gives for the village mothers and sings to them at the piano, ending with 'Home Sweet Home'. 'It was somehow like being in heaven,' says one of the lucky village mothers.

Then, a few days before the wedding date, Gerald gets a telegram, 'Come at once.' Too late. Ethel is dead, of acute diphtheria, probably caught while selflessly visiting a tenant's cottage with faulty drains on her father's estates. 'Her act of charity had been fatal to her. O God!' Gerald decides to commit suicide, but leaves a note for Harry saying when and where and good-bye. Harry saves him. Ethel has left Gerald some verses and a crucifix. Ethel's mother dies, in Mentone, and is brought back to be buried next to Ethel. Every year during Passion Week a man dressed in black is seen to come late at night to the graveyard and lay beautiful flowers on the two graves. Gerald (for it is he: had you guessed?) never marries. He carries a locket with the picture of a beautiful young girl in it, and a single name ETHEL.

Benson mocked the novel in general because on its title page the author described it as A STUDY IN REAL LIFE. 'If this is real life,' says Benson, 'give me fiction.' Young Wodehouse felt much the same, and said so rather more pithily.

* * *

In its long obituary of Welldon, *The Times* made no mention of *Gerald*

Eversley's Friendship, his only novel. Nor, in a long entry, does the *Dictionary of National Biography*. I like to let my imagination boggle on the question: if I had been an ambitious junior master at Harrow in 1895 and had read in the holidays the absurd new novel *Gerald Eversley's Friendship*, what would I say to the headmaster when I greeted him in Common Room next term? Would I pretend I hadn't read it yet? Or would I bring my copy to the Old Man for signing? I was interested to find that *Gerald Eversley's Friendship* is not required reading at Harrow these days. A friend of mine who was on the point of retirement as a Harrow 'Mr. Chips', said he had never heard of the novel. There is a copy in the Vaughan Library, but it is not taken out much, by boys or masters.

Welldon, son of a schoolmaster and nephew of a headmaster, was elected to be headmaster of Harrow without standing as a candidate. He had gone straight from a Fellowship at Cambridge to be Head of Dulwich and now Dulwich's loss, after a mere two years, was Harrow's gain. He had been at Eton as a boy, an outstanding games-player and fine classical scholar. And he had won most of the Cambridge classical prizes at King's. He left his beloved Harrow, after thirteen years, to become Bishop of Calcutta and Metropolitan of India. Here his avowed intention of converting the Indians to Christianity annoyed his old friend George Curzon, the Viceroy. Welldon resigned from India on 'medical' grounds. He was not the only old friend with whom Curzon had a sundering quarrel. Back from India, and without rancour, Welldon became a Canon of Westminster, Dean of Manchester and Dean of Durham. He was very fat and a lifelong bachelor. Someone who met him as Dean of Durham said 'I have never understood till now the meaning of "a pig in clover".' Welldon had a servant, Edward Perkins, his butler and factotum for nearly fifty years. Perkins died a short while before his master did. If it had been the other way round, Perkins would, by Welldon's will, have inherited his all.

A good man, doubtless, Welldon. And doubtless he, like Hughes before him, wrote his novel with the idea of doing good. It may have done good by convincing its author that he was no novelist and that he had better stick to sermons and schoolmastering. If the book did anybody any harm, it can only be through its author's obvious admiration of aristocracy and by frightening the weedy, spectacled, stooping, poor-scholar type of boy who, coming to St Anselm's, or Harrow, would expect to get sent to

Coventry, with his boots full of water, if he didn't swear, play games or box.

Tom Brown's Schooldays is another matter altogether. In *The Victorian Public School*, a symposium edited by Brian Simon and Ian Bradley, and published by Gill and Macmillan, there is a chapter, by Patrick Scott, analysing *Tom Brown's Schooldays*. Scott is more scholarly, and much more respectful, than I have been. He quotes P.G. Wodehouse's essay, as I have done. It is sad, and interesting, to learn that Hughes did write his novel in two moods: the pietistic second half (but not the Slogger Williams/Tom Brown fight: that had been written earlier) following the death of his eldest daughter with scarlet fever.

Hughes said that his whole object in writing the book at all was to get a chance of preaching, and he advances a swingeing literary doctrine: 'I can't see that a man has any business to write unless he has something which he thoroughly believes and wants to preach.' But, remembering the terrors that *Tom Brown's Schooldays* gave me at the age of seven, I am all the more sorry for Hughes's son, aged eight (not the one who went to my prep-school as a new boy in 1864), when Scott tells me that Hughes wrote, much later, 'Thinking what I should like to say to him [the son] before he went to school, I took to writing a story, as the easiest way of bringing out what I wanted.' I wonder what the son made of it.

The Times at the time gave *Tom Brown's Schooldays* a pat on the head . . . a book 'which an English father might well wish to see in the hands of his son'. The *Christian Observer*, however, said 'This book is better out of a boy's hands than in them.' Perhaps we can leave *The British Quarterly Review* with the ghoulish last word: 'A capital book, brimful of the blithesomeness, fun and frolic of boyhood, tempered with excellent sense and wisdom . . . a spirited record of genuine schoolboy life.'

No. Let *me* have the last word. As spokesman for generations of weedy, spectacled, stooping, poor-scholar, six-stone weaklings on the brink of boarding school, I say 'Ouch!'

Richard Usborne (Summer Fields and Charterhouse) is the author of *Clubland Heroes* (a study of the fiction of Buchan, Sapper and Dornford Yates) and of *Wodehouse at Work to the End*. In 1964, for the centenary of his preparatory school, he edited a book of reminiscences of Old Boys and masters.

10

Breathless Hush in the Close

GORDON ROSS

If you happen to come across a faded photograph of a public schoolboy, treasured and preserved from Victorian days, it is unlikely that he will be wearing a normal school habit, which possibly included a stiff collar – the *bête noire* of generations of uncomfortable choirboys. He will almost certainly be attired in cricketing clothes, or wearing rugby kit and blazer, with a tasselled cap signifying that he has won his colours. Why a tasselled cap became associated with prowess in sport in the first place remains something of a mystery because to the uninitiated it might appear more appropriate in a piece of Gilbert and Sullivan opera. The blazer would have an emblem enshrined upon it which represented the highest honours in one sport or another. The facial expression of our subject would radiate a far greater pride than some academic accomplishment could possibly have stimulated, because at the public schools, the sport a boy has played lives after him; what he has learned about Pythagoras's theorem, or Milton's *Paradise Lost*, is usually interred with his bones. Biographical details of individuals recorded for posterity define this trend very forcibly. Here is one, picked at random:

Muttlebury, Stanley Duff. Born 1866. Eton 1880–1885 (Rev. H. Daman's House) and Trinity, Cambridge, 1885–1890. At Eton won Lower Boy Pulling 1881, Junior Sculling 1882, School Pulling 1883, and School Sculling 1884. In Henley Eight 1884 and 1885, 2nd Captain of Boats 1885. Oppidan and Mixed

Wall 1884; won Hurdles 1884, and Weights 1885; Swimming 1883 and 1885. Stock Exchange. Sport: rowing. Clubs: Oxford and Cambridge, New University. Address: 3 Westbourne Crescent, W.2.

Stanley Duff Muttlebury is just one of hundreds of thousands of public schoolboys who have come under the immeasurable influence of sport at school. For generation upon generation sport and the public schools have been synonymous, and they have had a tremendous influence upon sport in all walks of life. In some cases the schools have been the prime architects in inventing and then developing a game; in many others they have been the hatcheries for supplying a never ending stream of participants of a very high quality. I suppose the most famous sporting schoolboy of all time was a pupil at Rugby School and, strangely, there is no reference to him anywhere which refers to him possessing any particular skill. What the boy, William Webb Ellis, did was to pick up the ball and run with it when he was playing football, in the year 1823; in doing so he invented the game of Rugby Football, and is now immortalized. Rugby has never had such a distinguished boy, before or since, and is never likely to!

So in 1823, Rugby had its own brand of football, but even then it was not the first public school to organize some kind of recreation or to invent rules – mostly unwritten (which could be bent a little according to the occasion!) for its football. But the Rugbeians were delighted at the game they had found by accident and would not allow their rules to be watered down or altered. They found staunch allies in Marlborough, so Rugby Football grew in stature and flourished. The valleys of Wales, where the game is now the principal religion, are a far, far cry from the playing-fields of Rugby, although the players of Abertillery and Ebbw Vale do not refer to it as 'Rugger', a term of endearment which remains the prerogative of the products of the English schools. It is fitting, in this instance, to refer to the schools as a whole, because the grammar schools have shared this love of sport, and they have produced some fine sportsmen but, for a variety of reasons, on nothing like the same scale as the public schools. On average, the facilities are better, the public schools attract more university sporting blues as masters, who prove to be admirable coaches, and the boarders at a public school have more time at their disposal for sporting pursuits – and so have the masters. Both denominations, however, have opted to a greater extent for rugby in preference to association football; there has always been a little bit of a 'snob' complex about it, none more than the early definition of the two games, that rugby is a rough game played by gentlemen, and soccer is a gentleman's game played by roughs! This, of course, is a contradiction in terms, because when Rugby conceived their game and developed it, the stronghold of association football was at Eton, who later were to play a major role in the Football Association Cup. Old Etonians appeared in six Cup Finals, winning twice, in 1879 and 1882. In 1881 the Old Boys of Eton and the Old Boys of Charterhouse contested the Final, and the Carthusians won. Soccer has continued to prosper in certain public schools. In 1951, Pegasus, a team composed of players from the Universities of Oxford and Cambridge, won the Amateur Cup, and their team included Old Boys from Shrewsbury, Charterhouse and Repton.

In shaping the destiny of the game of cricket, it could be argued that the public schools have exerted their greatest influence, and that this so very English game epitomizes the spirit of public school sport more than any other. The expression 'It isn't cricket' is intended to embody any piece of behaviour which falls short of the very highest sporting principles, the very principles which public school sport has fostered as an essential subject in the curriculum. If it were possible to select one man as the whole manifestation of these ideals while at school, at university, and in later life, it would surely be C.B. Fry, a Reptonian. Fry was the most outstanding athlete of his, or any other generation, as well as being a brilliant scholar. At Oxford, he won first-class Honours in Classical Moderations at Wadham, and it is a tribute to his calibre as a scholar and to his personal force that most of the obituary articles written after the death of Viscount Simon named Fry in a Wadham trinity with him and Birkenhead. Fry captained England at cricket, and England were never beaten under his captaincy; he played association football for England against Ireland in 1901; he was at full-back for Southampton in the F.A. Cup Final of 1902, and he put up a world's long jump record of 23 feet 5 inches in 1892 which stood for twenty-one years. Fry was the last of the old English tradition of the genuine amateur; he was the supreme connoisseur, and yet in the most delightful sense of the word, the dilettante. Sir Neville Cardus wrote of him: 'The cricket field has seen no sight more Grecian than the one presented by C.B. Fry in the pride and handsomeness of his young manhood.

With all his versatility of mind and sinew Fry himself wished that he might be remembered, as much as for anything else, by his work in command of the training-ship *Mercury*. For forty years he and his wife directed the *Mercury* at Hamble, educating youth with a classical sense of values.'

In the days when only an amateur could captain England at cricket, the public schools provided England with a wide choice of candidates for the captaincy in the golden age of cricket. The gaily coloured caps worn by the amateurs were usually a symbol of flamboyancy, flourish and aggression, and gracious living. They played the game for the sheer joy of playing it, but they played it hard and uncompromisingly. No one dared let the side down under their leadership; it would have been a worse crime than assault and battery, or even murder! They commanded unstinting respect because they set high standards in their own performances.

Another sport to benefit considerably from public school teaching is rowing. In the first University Boat Race at Henley in 1829, Westminster had three representatives in the victorious Oxford boat, Harrow and Shrewsbury had two each, and Eton and Winchester, one. Cambridge included in their crew three from Eton, one each from Charterhouse, Harrow and Rugby, and three from other schools. In fact, it was a public school influence which resulted in Cambridge adopting the colour of Light Blue, for just as the crew was about to push off for the second Boat Race in 1836, it was realized that no colour was displayed in the bow of the boat, so a Mr R.N. Phillips ran to a nearby haberdasher and bought a piece of light blue ribbon which was hoisted as a flag in the bows. Why a piece of light blue ribbon? Probably because Mr Phillips was an Etonian, and this was the Eton Blue.

The discipline in a rowing eight is surely the most severe in any sport, because unless all eight row as one man, in perfect unison, the boat cannot be adequately propelled. Guy Nickalls, a famous Etonian oarsman, wrote of his first University Boat Race in 1887:

> Good chap as Frank Wethered was, as President of Oxford University Boat Club, he was a terrible martinet to the new boys. No new Blue was allowed to speak to an old Blue unless first addressed. We were never left alone, we were harried from pillar to post; our rations of drink were terribly limited; we were marched like a lot of schoolboys twice to church every Sunday, no matter what

our religion. No matter how uncomfortable you were in a boat, how infernally badly you were rigged, no matter how deeply your oar dived, you were not allowed to make a complaint. If you complained you never rowed again!

Wethered was an Etonian, as were five others in the boat; whether his exacting standards were the result of Eton's disciplinary teaching, or just the foibles of one man, can only remain as speculation, but Eton's domination of University rowing is beyond all doubt. At the time of the one hundredth Boat Race in 1954, Eton had provided Oxford with 186 Blues and Cambridge with 121. The second highest contribution was by Shrewsbury with 28 and 29.

Eton is singularly fortunate in the width of the river at the school, which enables several boats to race abreast, an ideal situation for rowing training, but Eton's sporting traditions are founded on something far more deep-seated than this, for its energies in the sporting field are widely diffused and even include their own brands of football, the Wall and the Field. The Eton Wall game presents, to every non-Etonian (and many Etonians, too!), the strangest sporting encounter anywhere in the world. Yet for those who play it, it is part of a great heritage, cherished and revered in the words of 'J.K.S.', the Eton poet:

> There's another wall, with a field beside it,
> A wall not wholly unknown to fame;
> For a game's played there which most who've tried it
> Declare is a truly noble game.

The poet is freshly remembered every St Andrew's Day, when the Keeper of College Wall, and after him each member of his team, stands up in Hall in front of the big fireplace and drinks '*In piam memoriam J.K.S.*'. Not all Etonians would agree that it is a noble game, but in the breasts of some of them it has kindled a fire of passion which glows in the following account:

> There are truly heroic moments when one side, having got the lead, sets out to 'hold'; that is to say, to keep the ball right in the bully and not let it out at any cost. Then you may dimly discern some splendid 'second', propped up by his own bully, bent double over the ball and keeping it into the Wall while his enemies hurl themselves in fruitless waves against him, and the outside jostle one another furiously, and a thick cloud of steam rises up into the air. Collegers will always read with a thrill how in 1887, R.A.S. Benson crawled into the bully

and, assuming the attitude of a frog, planted himself immovably on the ball. The game may be only a quaint survival, kept alive for sentimental reasons, yet it is also a fine test of courage and spirit, and it grips the heart of every one who is proud to have been a Colleger. *Floreat Etona et hic noster ludus muralis esto perpetuus.*

The whole fabric of sporting teaching at the public schools is based almost entirely on the team game as a character builder; it breeds unselfishness, all pulling together in the common cause, an absolute dedication in a determination not to let your team-mates down, a trinity of virtues which, if carried through life, make for the better man. These sentiments are expressed in this verse, which Harrovians will remember:

> Oh, the great days in the distance enchanted,
> Days of fresh air and the rain and the sun,
> How we rejoiced as we struggled and panted,
> Hardly believable forty years on.
> How we discoursed of them, one with another,
> Auguring triumph or balancing fate,
> Loved the ally with the heart of a brother
> Hated the foe with a playing at hate.
> Follow up! Follow up!

Loving the ally with the heart of a brother, and hating the foe with a playing at hate, and accepting defeat with the same graciousness as victory, auguring triumph or balancing fate, are all the essential characteristics in the moulding of an attitude to life which the public schools were absolutely sure was the right one. They knew of no better way of achieving it than through team games. Games which are primarily individual have not been eliminated from the sporting activities of most public schools, but they are practised to a much lesser degree, and with far less distinction in terms of their influence on the particular sport. E.B. Noel once wrote of golf at Winchester: 'Winchester is one of the few schools where golf is permitted, but it is not in any sense a School game. It has never been allowed to interfere with the ordinary school games in any way, and it is not played at all in cloister time. No cap is given for it.' This is not to deny that many fine golfers have come from the public schools, but they have produced themselves rather than having been produced by the school.

Repton taught Harold Abrahams, who won a gold medal in the 1924

Olympics; Roger Bannister, who was at University College School, Hampstead, made athletics history on 6 May 1954 when he ran the first four-minute mile, and running with him on that memorable occasion were Christopher Chataway (Sherborne) and Christopher Brasher (Rugby); the latter, deciding to have a go for the steeplechase in the 1956 Olympics in Melbourne, surprised the world, and perhaps, even himself, by carrying off the gold medal. These, however, have been rather more isolated cases than representatives of a continuity of considerable athletic prowess stemming from the public schools.

Tennis has attracted even less attention at the schools, principally because six tennis courts can accommodate twenty-four boys at a time playing doubles, or twelve engaged in singles, whereas six cricket pitches can provide activity for one hundred and thirty-two competitors, and cricket would always be encouraged by the school in preference to tennis because it is a team game. It has sometimes been suggested – and not without a grain of truth – that the mediocrity of British tennis at the highest level is due to the fact that it is not played extensively in the schools, although some schools, particularly Millfield, are making efforts to remedy this deficiency.

Although the schools have shown their love of team games they have still fostered some pastimes for the individual – none more, perhaps, than rackets. It is believed that Harrow was the first school to introduce the game as long ago as 1822 and it was well established there by 1826. The game was first played in the school yard against the school buildings, but two walled-in courts were built in 1851. The Public Schools Championship was inaugurated in the spring of 1868 at the famous Match Court of Old Prince's Club in Hans Place. Rackets has flourished in the public schools because, like squash and fives, it provides excellent training for quickness of movement, both foot and hand, quick reflexes, and the ability to think swiftly in outwitting an adversary. In fact, the whole ethos of sport in endeavouring to outwit an adversary makes it the first substitute for war, and the two are inextricably close together. Both represent an attempt by an individual or set of individuals to dominate another, and to strain every nerve and sinew, displaying exemplary courage in striving for victory. Thus the sporting training at the schools has produced exceptional deeds of heroism on the battle-fields of the world. Over a century ago twenty boys from Clifton College alighted from the Bristol train at Swindon, boarded a stage coach, and set out over the Downs to do battle at rugby football with Mr Bradley's academy at Marlborough. One side played the hacking rule, and the other, with upper lips horizontal and shins dripping with blood, did not; when appeal was made to the watching master of Marlborough to end the slaughter, he told his men to 'Win the game first and adjust the laws afterwards'.

This, for the competitors, represented the basic fundamental of warfare, that despite injury and suffering and being at a marked disadvantage you battle on with a total disregard for self, thinking only of the team and victory, even if that victory has already begun to recede over the far distant horizon, and bruised and aching bodies, desperately short of breath, have precious little chance of retrieving it. Whether it be on the playing-fields of Eton, at Waterloo, the Somme, or Dunkirk, you never surrender!

It may seem invidious to select just one public school sportsman who achieved distinction in battle when there are many who won the Victoria Cross in two wars, but just as we picked out Stanley Duff Muttlebury to illustrate a point, we can do so again in this context. Douglas Bader was at school at St Edward's, Oxford, where he was an exceptional games player, and continued to display his sporting talents at the Royal Air Force College at Cranwell; there was every possibility that he would play rugby football for England, but he lost both legs in a flying accident in December 1931 and was invalided out of the service in 1933. Bader was accepted back into the Air Force at the outbreak of war in 1939, and despite the enormous physical handicap of having no legs, persuaded the authorities to let him fly again. By 1941 he was a Wing Commander leading the first Royal Canadian Air Force Fighter Squadron, but after colliding with an enemy aircraft over Bethune in August 1941, he was taken prisoner. It is the duty of every officer to escape and despite his immense disadvantages Bader became a known escaper and was finally transferred to Colditz, that impregnable fortress built on a cliff-edge, moated, wired and floodlit, with more guards than prisoners. Bader was not released until the end of hostilities in April 1945. The knighthood conferred upon him in 1976 was not for his war services; it was for his untiring devotion to the welfare of the handicapped, to whom he was the inspiration. 'If I can play golf without legs,' he would say, 'so can you,' and hundreds believed him and took up the challenge to overcome their handicap, just as he had triumphed over far greater adversity.

Bader's whole life was the epitome of every single virtue that his sporting training at school had taught him. He was a great leader because he led by personal example, the principal requisite of leadership practised on the playing fields at the schools. Leadership, it is said, is inborn, it cannot be taught, but even if this is so, it can still be fostered and developed.

The Captain of Cricket, the Captain of Rugby, or the Captain of Boats is a revered figure at school in the eyes of the other boys. For the Captain himself, his position is the apogee of his ambition – he has striven and reached the top, and he has been taught to carry his authority with firmness but with dignity and understanding. To the new boy, the Captain is the subject of a form of hero worship, as all the time, in his mind's eye, the small boy sees himself one day in that supreme position. Here is the goal for which he can strive throughout his schooldays, a goal which, for him, carries far richer rewards than an 'A' in chemistry, and during the years ahead where else could he find himself faced, outside of mortal conflict, with so many vivid situations to test and develop his fibre? His behaviour under extreme pressure will show him in his true light. He knows that should he catch a crab while rowing in a vital race six months' training can be undone by him in fifteen seconds; that his penalty kick, in blinding rain in the dying moments of a crucial match, will decide victory or defeat; that if he muffs a baton hand-over all the advantage won by his team-mates in the relay race will be thrown away. The final test of the mettle of an individual can be psychological; some crack under the strain, but the philosophy of the teaching of sport at the public schools is to face any situation with courage and calmness. The boys are taught to come to terms with the facts of life. They are taught to remember Disraeli's words: 'Nurture your mind with great thoughts. To believe in the heroic makes heroes.'

The public schools are thinking of more concrete benefits than aesthetic judgements when they teach the young to play games, and they regard games teaching as an integral part of an overall education which the schools are committed to provide. Boys are not excused games until they have tried their hand, so that the proof of the pudding is in the eating, and they then have to produce a genuine reason for their total dislike of all sport; this percentage of the total is very small, and will probably vary between 5 and 10%. One boy, sincere in his beliefs, confessed that he could see no end product in playing games, so he was allowed to do forestry in games periods and seemed happy in the knowledge that when he plants a tree he will see the tangible results of his labours. Usually the boy who detests games is the brilliantly academic, or in his physical structure totally lacks co-ordination. The type of game a boy chooses can be a reflection of his make-up; the introspective, temperamentally tied up with himself, or the highly-strung, or the *prima donna*, are all likely to go for individual games where they are expressing themselves and their fate is entirely in their own hands. This type of boy would be well suited to rackets, but would never make an oarsman. But quite irrespective of the combined character-building qualities in playing games, physical fitness is an absolute essential, and physical fitness is often the corner-stone of mental fitness – a sharpness of mind as well as of body.

Sport, most of all, should conjure up visions of happiness. There are those who, in their choice of pastime, find pleasure in things essentially painful, like the marathon runner; others, much more numerous, were first attracted to the sport at which they afterwards won fame by the physical pleasure derived from playing it. Mr Jorrocks once suggested that all connected with hunting enjoy the sport, even including the fox; the majority of boys enjoy their sport, for there is a great deal of satisfaction to be derived from exercising to the full the strength and stamina of a trained body. The pleasure of hitting a cricket ball over the school pavilion for six, or a spirited dash down the touch-line outstripping all pursuers to score a match-winning try, or thumping a golf-ball an enormous distance down the fairway as straight as a die, is an elation which sportsmen the world over appreciate to the full. It is the fulfilment of smouldering ambitions, a sense of something worthwhile achieved, to be seen and admired by friend and foe alike. It is moments like these which have magnetic powers for the aspiring schoolboy sportsman. He looks forward all the week to the excitement of assembling in mid-morning to travel to an away match. The players in those teams experience their moments of extreme but fleeting responsibility, when everything depends on one action. This kind of self-knowledge is as revealing as any other in school life. The manner in which games are played, the courtesies and the self-control, is regarded as a matter of considerable concern in a public school education. Many boys who enjoy a lifetime of sporting activity recall with gratitude the dependence of a junior team upon an enthusiastic young master, or the delight of the rare days when everything went right, and even the clowns played like princes.

The notion that competitive games play a vital part in education is far older than Aristotle. Agias, great hero of the Pythian games, would have inspired the Greeks as generations of great sportsmen have inspired their countrymen since. By tradition, Great Britain's heritage and the whole fabric of its civilization has been interwoven with an unshakeable love of sport, which stretches back into the mists of antiquity. The Bodleian Library contains a picture of a monk bowling a ball to another monk, who is about to strike it with a cricce. In the field are other monks, and the art of the game was either to get the ball into a hole guarded by the monk with the cricce, or catch it. The monks depicted in this picture are thought to have lived in the fourteenth century. So sport is inbred, it is instinctive, full of natural impulses and the opportunity for self-expression. Is it any wonder that at least ninety boys out of every hundred are champing at the bit to become involved? Only 5 or 10% have to be dragged there by hook or by crook, and would prefer planting trees or putting heart and soul into a history essay; admirable though both intentions may be, neither contains any of the basic requirements for shaping character and attitudes to life.

In his Memoirs, Field-Marshal Viscount Montgomery of Alamein wrote of his days at St Paul's School:

I hurled myself into sport and in little over three years became Captain of the Rugby XV, and in the Cricket XI. The same results were not apparent on the scholastic side. In English I was described as follows:

1902 essays very weak
1903 feeble
1904 very weak; can't write essays
1905 tolerable; his essays are sensible but he has no notion of style
1906 pretty fair

My time at St Paul's was most valuable as my first experience of life in a larger community than was possible in the home. The imprint of a school should be on a boy's character, his habits and qualities, rather than on his capabilities whether they be intellectual or athletic. By the time I left school a very important principle had just begun to penetrate my brain. That was that life is a stern struggle, and a boy has to be able to stand up to the buffeting and set-backs.

It is to provide a boy with the necessary machinery to withstand life's buffeting and set-backs that the public schools have always regarded sporting endeavour as being their most effective instrument. Cricket is not just flannelled foolishness; nor is the Eton Wall game, archaic as it may seem, an utter waste of a boy's time; Rugby Football is given preference over soccer in most public schools, not only because it provides fifteen players with a game instead of eleven, not only because it might be preferred purely for its merits as a game, but largely because it subjects a boy to harder knocks and a much closer physical contact, in which he can be constantly provoked, but must never retaliate in temper or show any of the tantrums common to some aspects of 'the other game'.

Some of these values are in mortal danger with the commercialism and professionalism of contemporary sport, where winning at all cost is replacing the Olympic ideal of the honour of taking part, but in equipping the young for the buffeting of life the public schools will be wise not to deviate from centuries of tradition and a policy in which they have believed devoutly. Frank Wethered's inflexible attitude to the new Blues in the Oxford boat of 1887 would not be tolerated in the changing times in which we live, but even so a strict sense of discipline is a valuable quality which has shown its true worth in peace and in war. The team-work before self, the good chaps together, working as one for a common goal which means everything to them as they strive, has been impressive teaching. The Hon. Robert Grimston, a great Harrovian, crystallized the public schools' mandate when he said at the Tercentenary Festival:

> I claim for our cricket ground and football field a share, and a very considerable share too, in the formation of the character of an English gentleman. Our games require patience, good temper, perseverance, good pluck and, above all, implicit obedience. It is no bad training for the battle of life for a boy to be skinned at football, or given out wrongly at cricket, and to be able to take the affliction quietly, with good temper, and in a gentlemanlike spirit.

The principle of self-sacrifice, of sinking the personal advantage of the individual in the welfare of the school or the Eleven, is the very essence of public school tradition, and under two portraits in the Harrow pavilion is the following inscription:

> The Hon. Robert Grimston and Frederick Ponsonby, Earl of Bessborough, famous Cricketers, loyal Harrovians, blameless gentlemen whose friendship, begun in school days and cemented on fields of English sport, rendered more conspicuous the love they bore to Harrow, where, through fifty summers, while teaching skill in cricket, they taught manliness and honour.

Gordon Ross (Fairfield House and Colfe's) is a director and executive editor of *The Cricketer*, and is a sports consultant. He has written six books on sport, and has contributed on cricket and rugby to *The Times* and the *Sunday Times.*

II

Manners Makyth Man?

TIM BROOKE-TAYLOR

In January 1954, as a thirteen-year-old struggling to keep down a Knickerbocker Glory, an effective last minute bribe on the part of my mother, I entered what was for me a completely alien world. Coming from a family with no previous connections with Winchester College, and from a small Derbyshire prep school which itself had rarely sent anyone south of the river Trent, I had not the slightest idea what to expect. My second shock – the first was an immediate and simultaneous loss of face and Knickerbocker Glory – was to discover that the school had a language all of its own. One of the first sentences I overheard could just as well have been Martian, 'That spree sweater is lobbing because I have jockeyed his suction,' or, as I now understand it, 'That cheeky fag is crying because I have confiscated his sweets.' I wanted to go home.

The first two weeks were similar, I would imagine, to the initial period of military service, the difference being that my mother was actually paying for it. Each 'new man' (there were two of us that term) were for this two week period dubbed 'Protégés' and put in the care of our 'Tégés'. My Tégé had arrived a term before me and it was his job to see that I knew everything. He was a nice man, which made it rather worse if anything for if I failed my 'notions' exam at the end of the fourteen days, it would be he who was beaten for it.

Also hanging over our heads at this time was the 'run up Hills'.

Traditionally on the second Sunday of term any 'new men' were marched, in their games clothes, to the foot of St Catherine's Hill. The first task was to run up the steepest route to the top. In theory it could be done in our own time, but as all the other juniors were lined up the hill ready to hit us with small branches, more speed meant less pain. At the top we were blindfolded and led to a maze, really a series of ditches, and told to get to the middle. The branches were once more put into operation, but I think it was the humiliation that was more painful than anything else. We next had to find a special stone, which, it turned out, someone had been sitting on. Oh, that did make everybody laugh. The final agony was a run down the hill with the threat that the last one back would have to do the whole thing over again. My partner and I managed to contrive a dead heat, but even then we wondered if this would be construed as equal first or equal last.

To be charitable, I honestly don't think the other 'men' were aware of the real misery they were causing us. A mind can change a lot in a few months and when the following term this practice was abolished by our housemaster, I remember a strong feeling of resentment. After all, I'd lived through it and 'it was only a bit of fun wasn't it?' I'm appalled now that I could have got around to thinking like that after such a short time. I had fallen for the old public school line of 'A little of what you don't fancy does you good.'

I am deliberately painting the picture all black at this stage because this is how I saw it. There was light at the end of the tunnel, but I couldn't see it then. I wasn't expecting comfort. I wasn't used to luxury, but I was expecting baths, and all we had were metal washtubs. No soap was allowed in these and so any decent bathing had to be done standing with one foot in a basin and the other on a slippery floor. Strangely enough, the dormitories (galleries) had a luxury that I never quite got used to. Each bed had its own washstand which was filled and emptied by the 'sweater' whose turn it was. During cold spells we had to break the ice in the washbasins that had been left overnight. A 'sweater' incidentally was basically a fag, but not allocated to anyone in particular. It was quite a sensible system; we were really all part-time parlour maids. The chores had to be done and the responsibility for them might as well be got over with in the first two years before getting on to rather more serious academic work. However it did seem ironical at the time, as we washed the dishes and scrubbed the floors, that we were being dubbed 'the privileged few who went to Public Schools'.

I probably hated the lavatories (foricas) most. They were all in one room and none of them had doors. This was, presumably, to stop any mutual or indeed personal satisfaction, but I have always felt that an Englishman's lavatory is his castle, and these particular castles had no drawbridges – moats all round you, yes, but no drawbridges. It is an undignified, crouched position at the best of times and I defy anyone to be totally relaxed with their trousers round their ankles, within sight of what seems to be the whole world. It was here though that I received the most useful piece of teaching of my entire school career. Always place a piece of lavatory paper (foricas bumf) in the bowl, thereby ensuring, before it's too late, that there is a plentiful supply, and with the added bonus of no subsequent 'splashback'.

I started with an unfair disadvantage in that my mother had been sent an out-of-date clothing list (the new supply had run out). Consequently I was the only boy in the House with collar-detached shirts and sock suspenders. At the time I could see no possible purpose for sock suspenders. Now I know better, for when used upside down they provide the nightshirt wearer with protection from 99% of all known household draughts. But then, with a collar clamped round my neck, sock suspenders round my ankles and a bright red face – partly through the tightness of the collar and partly through the horror of the dreaded trailing sock suspenders – I was ready to face absolutely nothing.

Winchester has always been an admired school. It doesn't quite have the social cachet of Eton or Harrow, but if there is to be a trio of public schools placed at 'the top', then Winchester is always there. There is a story which I am not sure whether I subscribe to or not. There were once an Etonian, a Wykehamist and an Harrovian. All three were competing for a stunningly beautiful girl. The Etonian noticed that she had no chair. The Wykehamist went to fetch her one. And the Harrovian sat on it. When at school I always thought the Etonian came out of this best. Now I tend towards the Harrovian.

Generalizations about schools are dangerous. They change with headmaster, housemasters, financial climates, everything. But one constant factor always remains with Winchester and that is its academic standard. The teachers and the pupils were of an almost frighteningly high calibre and I speak as one who squeezed into the bottom form at a second attempt. There was no question of moving up the school at the end of each year. You moved up in terms depending on your capabilities. The top scholar was automatically placed in a high form, a form that was to take me nearly two and a half years to reach. My problem was an uncontrollable fear of Latin. I panicked when it came into sight. I could deal with the early days of learning by rote:

Amo, amas, amat,
I had a little cat
Amamus, amatis, amant,
I gave it to me Ant.

(Ant=Aunt. You could tell that I came from a northern school.)

However, the application of Latin grammar into Latin sentences paralysed my brain. For every other subject, thanks to the magnificent teaching and the general air of 'learning is a good thing', I am extremely grateful to Winchester. The school pushed me hard and I benefited considerably. But only those who have a complete mental block for a subject (I believe Maths is quite common) can appreciate the horror of facing a blackboard filled with nice cosy English words, only to be asked to translate them into the most pedantic language I have ever come across. Many arguments are put forward in favour of Latin. To me they appear, not so much as arguments, but more as rather feeble excuses. The reason I harp on Latin so much is that it was this, more than anything else, that made my first three years at Winchester a relatively unhappy experience. I just happened to be bad at the one subject that really mattered. However well I did in the other subjects, and I did do rather well, I was not allowed to move up the school because of my Latin. 'Caesar, but that not . . .' – it still fills me with horror. Once freed from this dreaded language, I was able to spread my wings and by the end was quite happily ensconced in the top form of the school. I do sincerely hope that this over-weighting in favour of one subject has changed.

The 'dons' (masters) were on the whole humane and helpful. But there was one, a cleric, who instinctively knew my blind spot and sadistically picked away at it. He was a stickler for tradition and insisted that everything was done by the letter of the law. I led a small, underground movement which proved totally ineffective and probably made our lives a great deal more uncomfortable. But one day, I wish I could remember the date, for I would like to rename my street after it, the revolutionaries had a glorious hour. Hidden away in some subsection of the Winchester traditions was a ruling that all masters, when teaching, must wear gowns. If any master offended on this, then he was liable to have a Latin Dictionary thrown at him. Of course we would never do this, nor be so petty minded – but if the master happened to live by these rules, and the same master was making several lives a misery, then, perhaps . . . It all happened so quickly. 'He's coming,' 'He's got no gown,' 'Here, Taylor, take this dictionary,' 'Well go on.' I had no intention of actually throwing it. I was just going to threaten him, but once his beaming self-satisfied face appeared at the door, something went snap in my mind. That dictionary didn't just fly, it rocketed. Any baseball team in the world would have signed me on immediately as their number one pitcher. It caught him plum on the forehead from right across the room. The dictionary seemed to explode into a thousand tiny pieces. I don't think it hurt him physically, but mentally, that was a different story. The complexity of reactions that crossed his face was a marvel. With total silence in the classroom he went from surprise, to anger, to extreme anger and then the excruciatingly painful realization that he'd been caught at his own game. He controlled himself superbly and started to put his gown on, looking down as he did so. At this moment his control went altogether. Why now, I thought? It was then that someone whispered to me, 'It was *his* Latin Dictionary you threw.'

From this you might have gathered that I was a bit of a firebrand. Actually I was very conformist. I worked and played as hard as I could and was quite 'priggish' about 'men' who strayed from the straight and narrow. The Corps, however, provided a marvellous opportunity for being really rather silly. The cadet force was technically voluntary, but was in practice compulsory. Nothing could have appeared more absurd than a group of small boys landed in the middle of Salisbury Plain, trousers fitting snugly under the armpits and berets pulled down tight over their eyes. The masters were roped in on this. Some of them were quite clearly embarrassed and others took a rather pathetic delight in commanding 'their troops'. They used to take it so very seriously. 'Now men, if you're shot, then you must remove your berets. Taylor, put your beret back on at once. What do you mean, you're committing suicide?' One particular Field Day I remember with affection was held 'against' Charterhouse. In the morning they had the tank and in the afternoon we had it – three hundred boys moving with this armoured contraption, driving three hundred others before them. Then after lunch the whole procession was reversed. I had the plum job of being in charge of my platoon's 'mortar'. This was a wooden box out of which I was to fire a rocket – a tiny November-5th-type rocket. I still get a feeling of toe-clenching joy when I remember the moment I was ordered to fire at the tank. 'Mortar.' 'Sir.' 'Fire.' The tank was a hundred yards away, my rocket rose thirty feet in the air and landed right in the middle of my platoon about twenty yards in front of me. To a man, with perfect precision, they all removed their berets and sat down to eat their apples and 'Penguins'.

The same 'officer' who had objected to my 'suicide' was also cursed with having to teach science to me and others from the 'Arts' stream. Once a week, for an hour, he would have to get over this colossal subject to a form of very uninterested pupils. This was pure prejudice on our part and I now very much regret it. In those days the science side of the school was fairly small, and treated rather as the RAF had been in its early days – not quite O.K. We knew we were wasting our time and he knew we were wasting our time. In one last effort to gain our interest we were asked to write poems on any scientific subject we cared to choose. He was right in one way – I spent a great deal of trouble over this and my prize entry ran like this:

'Did Newton ever go to Bengal?
No he went to a fancy dress ball.
He thought he would risk it
And go as a biscuit,
But a dog ate him up in the observatory.'

All I got, in red ink, was, 'Doesn't rhyme. 0/5.'

Winchester was geared to produce successful scholarship candidates for Oxford and Cambridge. If the worst came to the worst an Exhibition would do. Those of us who were aiming for humdrum 'A' Levels and ordinary University entrance had to fend for ourselves. If 'set books' were required for a particular exam, then we had to cover them in our own time. Everyone took 'A' Levels, but the scholars treated them rather as Upper Class Twits might treat a transport café – 'So this is what the workers do.' 'Isn't it fun?' 'They don't even serve wine.'

I didn't realize quite how unimportant these exams were considered until I actually had to take them. My first 'A' Level was a three-hour history exam in the morning. In the afternoon I was expected to play for my House at cricket. Actually I was a hero that afternoon – I batted for an hour at the end of the game without losing my wicket. I hadn't actually scored a single run, but the draw I had helped to produce destroyed the cup chances of our opponents. I was a proud man and glowed in the congratulations of all those around until I realized that within half an hour I would have to run three-quarters of a mile, change, have tea and run the same distance back just in time for a 6.30 start to a three-hour 'A' Level English Literature exam. All I can remember was the paper spinning before my eyes and a hastily scribbled essay comparing one of Shakespeare's love sonnets with a game of cricket. Shakespeare lost.

Sport, as well as academic work, was very important at Winchester. The 'Athlocrats' of the school held enormous prestige. I was no great athletic star, but I loved games, which was just as well. We had to take exercise every day, except Sunday, and twice a day on the three half holidays. At the end of the week our 'Ekker' rolls were examined by the prefects. Woe betide anyone who hadn't taken a 'Toll' (a long distance run) that week or played 'fives' at least once. If there was any doubt, witnesses were required. I imagine some of these sporting activities must have been viewed with as much terror by some boys as my horror for Latin.

My tiny sporting triumphs at school still loom large in my book of achievements. They were all-important then, and even now they have a significance out of all proportion. I was the only qualifier in the Junior Long Jump and had three jumps against myself in front of the whole school on Finals Day. I won. Mind you, it was touch and go – I had to hit the pit. The race of my life was in the Interhouse Relay competition when we broke the school record. The eighty yard shot – I swear it must have been as much as that – to win the soccer cup is a moment that will live with me for ever. Oh, I am enjoying writing this! But perhaps my greatest triumph was to walk out as the O.T.H. six 'hot-watch'. A 'hot-watch' was a type of scrum half in Winchester's own brand of football. This was a particularly rough game and indefensible on all levels. In my last year a master computed from sporting records that Winchester Football was exactly due for another death. I'm happy to say it never arrived. Despite all this I can honestly say that this particular type of football is the most enjoyable game I have ever played.

In assessing my schooldays I keep coming across the same problem. It wasn't the school that mattered or the headmaster, it was 'the House' and, above all, the housemaster. Winchester was divided into eleven Houses and each one was a self-contained unit. The power and influence of a housemaster were therefore paramount. A House could change radically for better or worse within two or three terms of a new appointment.

My housemaster was a middle-aged, almost elderly bachelor called 'Sponge' Walker. His life was devoted to 'the House' and we rested in the knowledge that everything he did was done for what he considered to be our best interests. In retrospect I realize that I never really knew the man, which is strange as he certainly knew me. In fact he knew everyone and was very much aware of everything that went on around him. Once a tough, rather emotional boy had run riot in the House and had stabbed another in the leg. 'Sponge' recognized this 'cri de coeur' for what it was. He had the supreme teacher's gift of taking you into his confidence. He called me into his study, explained that he thought the boy was unhappy and wondered if I felt anything might be gained by the two of us being moved into the same class. Of course I fell over myself in an effort to befriend the 'stabber'. It proved surprisingly easy. No one had ever really tried to get through the noisy exterior before. He proved to be a very nice, interesting man and we soon became close friends. There were no more stabbings.

This cosy little story illustrates, I think, the crucial importance of a good housemaster. He is of course the one adult in a small, tightly-knit community of about forty-five adolescent boys, where a wrong decision, punishment for example, could have been catastrophic. He appreciated the physical and mental problems of an adolescent and was able to help. A friend of mine at Harrow at the same time had a rather different experience. At the age of eighteen, when he was about to leave, his housemaster felt that it was time for him to face up to the facts of life. His housemaster began, hesitantly, 'I don't know if you've ever noticed, but between your legs . . .' The fact that it was Harrow is irrelevant. He was a bad housemaster, that is all, and we had our share at Winchester.

In retrospect I'm amazed that I came across no homosexuality in the school. There were stories from other Houses that each night, 'half the beds are empty'. I say I'm amazed because the frustrations through lack of female company were extreme. I corresponded with a girl at another boarding school and if her scented letters didn't arrive on time every week, I was quite ready to smash the windows and howl at the moon. Once I was asked to a local girls' school dance but was refused permission to go on the grounds that, 'You get quite enough of that sort of thing during the holidays!' I never quite knew what 'that sort of thing' was, but I certainly never got enough of it during the holidays.

The other clichés of a public school education were present, but could easily be magnified out of all proportion. Cold baths, or in our case cold tubs, were on the menu, but most of us only subscribed when it was part of a punishment. There was caning, but there always seemed to be a remarkable reluctance to use this ultimate deterrent. When I eventually became a prefect and it was 'necessary' for someone to be beaten, the cane was passed around like a hot potato.

There was also remarkably little snobbery. As non-scholars who were not prefects we were technically known as Inferior Commoners. You could even be a Junior Inferior Commoner. This was hardly the stuff of which elitism is made. The only real snobbery I came into contact with was at Cambridge and this was of an inverted type. Every state school undergraduate, and they were a majority, had been brainwashed into thinking not only that they were equal to any public schoolboy, but that they were infinitely superior. I believed it myself and it took a good two years for this prejudice to die down on both sides.

Winchester did hammer home the virtues of being a good Christian gentleman. Fair enough, but occasionally it was carried through to ludicrous extremes. Due to the strange workings of a House under-sixteen soccer competition which combined both league and knockout elements,

I once computed that it would be to our advantage to lose to a side, thus barring the favourites from reaching the semi-finals. I pointed this out to our captain. He pointed it out to the House senior captain who took it to our housemaster. A remarkable compromise was passed back down to us. Only half the team were to be told this information. The other half would play as normal. I was furious and, although centre forward, spent the whole game in our own penalty area frantically trying to pass to their leading goal scorer. We won 2–1. Our goalkeeper, usually the weak link, played the game of his life, not having been told of the situation. He even saved my desperate last minute own goal attempt from three yards. Our captain, although in the know, felt that he ought at least to kick something in the right direction and made a clearance from his own half only to find that he had scored the goal of the month. We went on to lose to the favourites in the final. Never have I been so ashamed of being involved in anything so decent.

At Winchester I was taught to 'sum up' at the end of every essay. I suppose I should be doing that now, but I can't. Schoolboy judgements must, I think, be subjective. Three fifths of my time at Winchester must rank as the unhappiest days of my life. Yet a poll was taken when I was there and well over 50% of the boys said that they preferred being at school to being at home. Perhaps this was more a reflection of their homes than a vote of confidence in the school, I don't know. I could generalize. Everything was geared towards the straight and narrow. I myself was described in a report as 'typical of the ethos of the House'. I was quite offended until we checked with the family dictionary. Individuality was not encouraged. And yet the same housemaster who kept us in the rigid pattern of our forebears positively encouraged my playing in the House skiffle group. For years we happily 'Picked bales of cotton' and 'Worked on the railroad' – all in his study. And the same man who stifled any drama activities stated in another report, 'If all else fails and Tim doesn't get his "A" Levels, he can always become a film star, or as he would himself probably prefer, a music hall comedian.'

I suppose the real question is, shall I send my sons there? Assuming I shall be able to afford it and assuming they are able to pass the examination, one thing is for certain. They will not go there because I was there. They will not go there because that is the thing to do. They will go because I, my wife and the boy in question have decided that that is a marvellous thing to be able to do.

And I would check on the Latin.

Tim Brooke-Taylor (Winchester) appears regularly on television in *The Goodies* and is co-author of the Goodies' books, as well as being a pop singer.

12

By Their Speech Ye Shall Know Them

ANDREW SINCLAIR

Slang is *apartheid* by special words. The vernacular includes, argot excludes. In-talk keeps most people out. Exclusion by language in the public schools may not be as extreme as Jepthah's insistence on killing anyone who could not pronounce the word *shibboleth*. Yet their private words do create divisions between the privileged and the rest, the major public schools and the minor, the old boy and the new boy, the prefect and the fag.

The English principle has always been to divide and rule. Particular speech has been one of the most effective methods of separating the governors from the governed. The lingo of the masters is as arcane as the pidgin English of the camp followers; but only the master can converse in both tongues. If the Romans wrote, *divide et impera*, the English have always implied, *By their speech ye shall know them and obey them.*

When I went as a Colleger to Eton, I found myself immediately touched by the discrimination of language. Collegers were called *tugs* – probably derived from the *tug-meat* or bad mutton which used to be their invariable diet. To me, the word *tug* made me feel like a slow boat, squat and working and plodding and boring. Even worse was the fact that fags were called with a shout of 'Here!' or 'Boy!' Thus I was reduced to the state of the black slave, patronized from the plantation house.

After this immediate discrimination against me, I accepted a quick baptism into the new language of my clique. A test was set, by which I had to learn in a couple of weeks a list of House names and colours and Eton slang. Success was expected, failure meant a beating with a length of rubber-pipe. Even that had its special euphemism; it was called a *hosing* or *siphoning*. I succeeded in the test or *trial* like the young Hercules, for examinations at Eton were called *trials*. So I joined the discriminators and wielded the rubber-pipe myself as Captain of Chamber, the long, low, partitioned room, divided into fifteen separated stalls, where privacy was preserved by the shout of 'Stall Curtains!' At that cry, any intruder had to leave at once. It was more effective a deterrent than crucifixes and garlic are to vampires.

If the first necessity of a successful slang is the exclusion of the many, the second is the inclusion of the few. Once I had a grounding in the lingo and wore my tail-coat and white tie, I spoke and looked odd enough to become segregated from the rest of the human race. Most of my special references troubled reason and beggared sense. Each term was called a *half*, although there were evidently three terms, which meant that each of them should have been called a 'third'. *Absence* meant a roll-call which demanded my presence. A *Library* had nothing to do with books, but signified a self-electing group of boys in each House, who were sporting heroes and ran the place and never opened a book if they could help it. And as for a *ticket*, it was not the way out of Eton to the wider world, it was the way in to punishment by House or Head Master.

Some of the terms were common terms with a particular use. The *Arches* were the brick vaults beneath the Great Western Railway bridge; but Flanagan and Allan never sang 'Underneath the Arches' there, and Eton boys used them for a quick smoke in their gloom without benefit of sleeping tramp. A *bully* was not a person who tormented his mates; it was a scrum in the peculiar native sports, the Field Game and the Wall Game, in which anyone could wreak havoc on the other players. Equally, an *election* was not a democratic process except in the equality of competition – all the *tugs* were *elected* to their year in College by winning scholarships to Eton in a national examination. The survival of the brightest, really – more Darwinian selection than republican election, the choosing of the Elect in the religious sense of the word.

Three terms were close, indeed, to the industrial and penal system, for at the last resort, all public schools have something to do with workshops and reformatories. Eton boys were *marked in* or *out* for school and chapel attendance, and they *stayed out* of school when they were ill and had to have a signed *ticket* to prove their sickness. Not so far, as slang goes, from clocking in and staying out of a factory. And if a boy's work was really bad, he had to labour under his tutor's eye in *P.S.* – short for penal servitude.

Yet most of the terms were truly arcane, excluding all who were not initiates, or patronizing within the school to establish a caste system. To this day, I cannot decide whether *furking* is meaningless or obscene – I am told it signifies passing back in the Field Game. As for *pepper-boxes* and *first cut*, only those who play Eton Fives know their meaning, while *knuckling* and *calx* are reserved for those who play the Wall Game. That last desperate muddy battle has one terminal cry, 'Air!' At this call, the moiling mass of twenty boys must break apart, for somebody is being suffocated among their legs. I have seen once the death-mask of a boy imprinted in the mud at our feet. He lived, actually, but never played the game again.

Eton sports are the most exclusive and special games of all, three of them originally reserved only for present and Old Etonians – Eton Fives, the Wall Game and the Field Game. The first two depend entirely on the special architecture of the school, Fives deriving from a game by a buttress near the Chapel Steps, and the Wall being the brick wall separating the playing-fields from the Slough road, with a door as a goal at one end and a tree as a goal at the other. John Maynard Keynes was meant to have played the Wall Game as a recreation between saving the economies of the Western democracies. Perhaps the exclusive past is the last refuge from the depressive present.

As for patronage, what can be more demeaning than to be called a *scug*, that worm who has no special coloured cap for excellence at any sport at all? Bad enough to be a *sap*, a boy who studies too much. Yet no word in the Eton jargon is quite as bad as a *plop*, a term of derision used in lesser public schools for a new boy.

Of course, *tugs* and *scugs*, *saps* and *plops*, we all accepted our lowly positions meekly. Rebellion was unthinkable. Like every mother's child in hierarchic and feudal ancient Tibet, we might hope to be born the Dalai Lama himself – or to become, in our case, a member of *Pop*. That was a self-electing society of glorious young men, who wore coloured waistcoats and finely-checked trews and flowers in their button-holes, and were considered the aristocracy of the school. Solomon in all his glory was not arrayed like one of these. In the decades gone by, when Old Etonians practically controlled the Tory cabinet, not to have been in Pop meant a black mark against a politician all his life – it was nearly worse than not being a rebel at the time of Munich. All Etonians hoped to join Pop at school, few were selected, none questioned the system. Aristocracy is usually tolerable when it is open to all.

The slang of Eton could also be nostalgic and poetic. It was particularly haunting when it referred to faraway places. There was a brook called Jordan, which particularly fascinated me because the playing-fields beyond it were named Mesopotamia. They made me think of the forgotten campaigns of the First World War, as remote and melancholy as the long lists of names that covered the metal plaques I passed four times a day on my way to Chapel, the endless lists of the Etonian dead who had led over the top in the Great War, when the average life of a second lieutenant at the Front was six weeks. The special games went on in the old places, Mesopotamia and Agar's Plough, Upper Club and Sixpenny and Dutchman's Farm. The values were the same, but the generations were no longer meant to die well, but to survive in a modern and indifferent world. I never believed that Waterloo was won on the playing-fields of Eton. I could see that the Somme and the City had stuck in the mud there.

Some of the place names were affectionate. I was fondest of the *Burning Bush*, a mocking reference to the street-lamp covered with fiery ironwork that stood outside the School Library. I never saw Moses struck down in awe by the sight of it, but the threat of being impaled by it did stop the lorries in their courses round the corner of the road. The *Copper Horse* was also a nice name for the statue of George III at the end of Long Walk in Windsor Great Park – better to remember the king who lost America by his steed than by his sagacity. The *Acropolis* was also a good name to give to the little diving bank on that stretch of the river called *Athens*. Yet the choicest of the Eton names was the *Porny School*, an elementary and charity school in the High Street founded in 1802 by an Eton French master called Antoine de Pyron. He bequeathed the oldest ribald joke in the local slang, with an even longer run than the Crazy Gang.

Other private names seemed to imply that Etonians were the last of the Romans. *Divide et impera*, indeed. There was a lot of Latin in the slang. Holidays without work were called *Non Dies*, boys who had not passed their swimming tests were called *non-nants*, anyone who was not a Colleger was called an *Oppidan* or townsman. Punishments had particularly Latin names, *in piam memoriam* the law of Rome. Written penalties were called *poenas*, the longest of them being a *Georgic*, the copying out in good hand-writing of five hundred lines of one of Virgil's bucolic idylls. It was a good way of making poetry into punishment.

Yet, on another occasion, I heard punishment made into poetry. It was my first lesson in classical law, as opposed to justice. A Greek master was trying to interest us on a hot summer's day in the trial of Socrates. Attention yawned, learning dozed.

'You,' the master said, pointing at a boy at random, 'will write me out a Georgic by breakfast.'

'But I have done nothing, sir,' the boy replied.

'Exactly,' the master replied. 'That is why you will write me out the Georgic.'

After that, we listened closely to the trial of Socrates, and we understood something of the relationship between authority and justice. He was a practical man, the Greek master – or *beak*, as we used to call masters – and the rams of Greek galleys.

Slang in memory becomes fond. It loses its sense of discrimination and develops into nostalgia. It seems not so much exclusive as personal. To me, the banned ice-cream in the *sock-shop*, which was out of bounds when we were in training for our games, is almost as strong in its recall as Proust's *madeleine*. For an exclusive language also gives a fierce pride in belonging to a group. If the clique and its lingo is the enemy of the people, it is the friend of the few within it. What other people called *sending to Coventry*, we called *non-speaks*. For we tried to speak only to ourselves, excluding by our curious reference and silence those outside the bounds of our little group even within our little school.

Finally, I suppose, there can be no sense of inclusion without exclusion. The method of making nations in Europe has always been the imposition of a common language, and the local slang is the common tongue of the group or school within the nation. If it is a privileged group consisting mainly of rich men's sons, as Eton is, the private language can seem the flaunting of superiority or difference. The fiction of human brotherhood cannot survive *non-speaks*. Communication is a necessary hypothesis of equality, and we risk ourselves if we only communicate well with ourselves.

One strange and antiquated custom within Eton College showed the hypocrisy of our developed sense of the divisions of society. We felt cut off by customs and lingo not only from the tourists and visitors who stared at us as if we were dodos, but from the *beaks* who lived in an adult world of strange responsibilities and freedom. When we met one of them out of bounds, we could perform a legendary rite called *shirking*. If we held up our hands in front of our eyes like the wise monkey, the *beak* could pretend not to have noticed us because we had not noticed him. It was in his power to report us and *put us on the bill*, or else he could choose to see no evil.

Shirking was really a quality of the whole of Eton society. Like all little worlds, it was self-centred and found most of outside events irrelevant. It shirked common speech patterns, it shirked human contact with most other people. In defence of that, adolescence itself could be said to be a time of shirking between boyhood and manhood. For five years between thirteen and eighteen, we put our hands over our eyes, no longer children and hardly men, conscious of our privilege and slang under the scrutiny of those who questioned both.

Capping was another custom which showed our strong sense of hierarchy, for privilege implies humility before those greater than oneself. If we met a *beak* in the street, we had to *cap* him, raising a token forefinger in the direction of our cap or top hat or long hair. For members of *Pop*, this act of abasement became an airy wave of recognition, but for the rest of us, the *beaks* were our bosses and we *capped* them.

The only privilege we could use against the *beaks* was a *run*. If any of them were more than fifteen minutes late for school, we were allowed to *run* and leave the schoolroom empty. Then the *beak* was blamed for it, for we would blab on him. Thus the *beak* ensured that the boys arrived in school, even in the dreaded *Early School* that started at 7.30 in the morning. (If we were late twice, we had to sign a *Tardy Book* five days running before 7.25 a.m.) Yet equally, the boys watched over the *beak's* punctuality. Like all successful petty tyrannies, the rulers and the ruled kept an eye on one another and could report any mistake.

Two names particularly suggested antiquity and class. The first was the red-brick group of schoolrooms by the Burning Bush called the New Schools. They were new because they had been built as recently as 1863 – which suggested that the rest of the school was very old, as indeed it was. The other name of distinction was that all matrons of the boys' Houses were called *Dames*, as if they had received a title from the British Empire. When a boy addressed a *Dame*, he called her 'Ma'am'. It was the proud boast of the *Dames* that only the Queen and themselves were always addressed by their subjects as 'Ma'am'. They could vie with Elizabeth Arden, who was meant to have said that there were only two real Elizabeths in the world, the Queen of England and herself.

'Ma'am' to me was the figure of authority and mystery of my youth. She seemed to speak across an abyss of society and from the secret knowledge of age. Like a sibyl, she spoke of times that I never knew. Her language was speckled with old terms from Edwardian days and the Great War like 'cads' or 'Blighty'. I never understood how isolated she was in speech and time, until one day she burst into tears while she was treating a boil on my leg.

'You don't think I wanted to be Ma'am?' she said. 'My two sisters and I, we never married. Don't you think we wanted to marry? But in Cumberland, at the end of the Great War, there weren't any fellows left alive within twenty miles of us. No one alive one could possibly *marry* . . . Do you think I want to be Ma'am?'

I was embarrassed and I remembered the long plaques of the dead on the way to Chapel. I had forgotten the living, the old maids they might have left behind them.

'I'm sorry, ma'am,' I said, not knowing what to say. I supposed my wound had reminded her of the youths who had not come back to Blighty. 'Good-bye, ma'am,' I said.

At least, she was called a word that was special to her and the Queen. There must be some satisfaction in that.

Many Old Etonians still went into the Army for family reasons. It was the gold braid on the great chain of the living and the dead. Yet little of army slang filtered down to us. The only word I can remember is that we talked of *messing* together as if we were young officers. And the Cadet Force was called the *Corps*, as though no reform had touched the British Army since Ypres. The one time we were ever called out on duty was to line the route inside Windsor Castle for the funeral of George VI. By the side of the Life Guards, we looked a scruffy lot, more full of *esprit* than *Corps*.

Curiously enough, the special phrase that the boys used most was 'Yah!' They seemed incapable of saying 'Yes' to anything. It had to be 'Yah', though I have heard a dismissive 'Yup'. At first, I thought this was merely sloppiness, but later I realized that 'Yah' was a word of derision. In one of Jack London's more fearsome stories, a Melanesian island of cannibals massacre the sailors on a trading schooner except for the mate, who blasts them off with sticks of dynamite, shouting, 'Yah! Yah! Yah!' Later he returns with three schooners of traders with repeating rifles and dynamite, and they kill the cannibals in their thousands, driving them like game until the last survivors surrender. After the slaughter, the mate runs the store on the island quite alone. He can always obtain total obedience just by shouting his catch-phrase, 'Yah! Yah! Yah!'

Of course, when the Etonians say 'Yah', they do not mean to show superiority to lesser breeds. Yet this is what they are unconsciously doing. If they said 'Yes' like most other people, they might be assenting to equality. I remember as a child in the Second World War hearing my first American soldier say 'Yeah?' I found it terrifying and patronizing and relentless, as though his query could root the very truth out of my boy's mind.

I also remember that when I was at Eton, there was a shock of surprise at first reading J.D. Salinger's *The Catcher in the Rye*. That book made me realize that there could be a whole other world of slang for an adolescent, as total and inclusive as mine at Eton, which cocooned me and cossetted me and made me forget my uneasy growing pains in a casual sense of superiority over the rest of mankind. I envied Holden Caulfield because his slang was democratic unlike my own, the *lingua franca* of High School America. At that moment of truth, I knew my own private language was a restrictive practice, as obsolete as the aristocracy of brains and birth and wealth that Eton sought to teach to govern a country tired of such skills.

These thoughts of mine on the discrimination and patronage implied in the use of slang in my public school are tempered by the protection it gave me at the time of my adolescent isolation. In a curious way, that most private world was a microcosm of a lost Victorian world, which had classical values and cared as much for Greek as for its own brand of gobblygook. One custom was the weekly declamation of a *saying lesson*, a piece of Homer or Virgil or Sir Thomas Browne or Gray – the native poet whose Elegy of lost greatness suited the Eton of my time. I have never quite forgotten those ancient cadences, which have informed all my life.

Those saying lessons were actually as far from everyday speech as the school slang. Both were, in a sense, connected. The antiquated style of classical prose, which had so much to teach me, was preserved and made alive by the private language of the school, in which Latin and Greek were part of the terminology of patronage. *Kappas*, indeed, were the morons, who did not study Greek, and were even lower than the *scugs*. Yet I also remember with regret that we used to call the masses the ὁι πολλοι like any Athenian aristocrat, damning local democracy.

So slang can preserve past values, even if it denies present ones. It is the armour of the young and the insecure, as well as the brazen voice of insolence and privilege. In the public schools, it sets the boys apart from their fellows and their countrymen, although it binds them closer to their peers and their little institution. Paradoxically, slang includes only as it excludes. And with public schoolboys, it is both their special voice and their national offence. By their speech, we do know them, but we do no longer obey them.

Andrew Sinclair (Eton) is a historian and novelist and is the author of several volumes of social history and biography.

13

Facts, Theories and Emotions

LORD VAIZEY

In the great series of reforms of antique institutions that marked the middle and latter part of the nineteenth century, schools and colleges based on old charters, wills and statutes were put on a rational basis. That is why the original nine schools – ranging from Eton to St Paul's – were called public schools. (Schools run by individual proprietors were called private schools – they have now become preparatory schools, that is a preface to public schools.) They were schools that had been publicly reformed. Apart from certain administrative provisions, no uniform educational pattern was established, but one evolved from the circumstances.

But here, however, the first note of caution must be sounded. All dogs are dogs, but there is a big difference between a dachshund and an alsatian. All public schools have something in common, but they have always differed widely between themselves. All that follows should be studded with exceptions.

The organizing principle of the schools was allegiance to a Christian creed, usually originally evangelical, later high church (Lancing), Roman Catholic (Ampleforth), Quaker, Erastian (Eton), or ethical uplift. This tradition remains at the core of the public school ethos: it is allegiance, usually more than formal for many masters and boys, to the denomination to which the school belongs.

As a consequence of the renewed religious tone of the schools, a new seriousness of purpose about academic work, character and adult life informed the curriculum and the organization of the day. An understanding of the total commitment of the schoolboy's life to preparation for a life of duty and high seriousness is fundamental to any understanding of the public school. Attachment to high standards of academic achievement sprang from it and so did the serious attitude to sport. After a time, and not in all places or at all times, these became independent values – independent, that is, of the evangelical religious spirit which was their originating force. By 1900, however, the public schools became dominant academically, a position they have retained and are strengthening, and pre-eminent in those amateur games, like rowing and rugby football, which require physical toughness, a team spirit and, sometimes, an independent income.

The academic strength of the public schools lay originally in the classics, for the simple reason that the classics were then regarded as the best education. Virtually all subsequent innovations in the curriculum, from French and science to art and music, have also come from the independent sector. After 1902 most towns also had a local secondary (later a grammar) school, which was modelled academically on the public schools; their great flowering was in the inter-war years. While they rivalled and to some extent overtook the public schools in the achievement of high standards in the public school curriculum – a point noted by G.M. Trevelyan in his *English Social History* when he said: 'If we win this war [World War II], it will have been won in the primary and secondary schools' – they were not the source of major innovations in the curriculum or methods of teaching.

As part of their evangelical purpose, the newly reformed schools spread their nets wider and wider in their search for pupils. Far from being socially restrictive, they in fact became far more socially representative. Since this is contrary to common opinion and to some interpretations of the statistics, it is necessary to spell out what is meant. After the original foundation of many of the schools, predominantly for the clever sons of tradespeople – the real poor of Elizabethan times were rarely educated – the schools became for the most part corrupt and inefficient in the eighteenth century. As that century wore on, so a very wide network of private educational establishments was set up – private schools, classes and colleges – which met, more or less inadequately, the needs of an industrializing society. Again, ignoring the very poor (a high proportion of the population), most other groups had some sort of education. The reform of the public schools, including the local grammar schools which did not become famous national or regional institutions, may be seen as part of the broader social programme by which individuals or small groups set up new businesses, or seized the opportunities to reform a whole series of moribund bodies, and to revitalize them. This is what was done at Rugby, at Harrow and at Oundle. At the forefront of their minds was the propagation of the Christian faith, but that propagation required efficiency. And in so setting about these derelict establishments, they acquired new funds, and revitalized old charities. The greater part of the established funds, as well as of those that were newly acquired from benefactors, went into buildings – school rooms, boarding houses, grounds and playing fields. Contrary to widespread opinion, comparatively little charitable aid went to the well-to-do (let alone was switched from the poor) in the form of scholarships or reduced fees. By and large, pupils' families paid their own way. The reforms, of course, raised the costs of educating children, by attracting well-paid, well-qualified staff, and by adequate feeding and heating, and as a consequence the fees became high. But the purpose of the fees was not to choke off the poor. On the contrary, if a father could pay the fees, his boy could get into almost any school. By the standards of even the comparatively recent past this was democracy indeed.

It was the grammar schools that took the next step. As day schools, with bigger classes, they were cheaper than the boarding schools; as from 1902, in addition to fee-payers, they had a stream of non-fee-paying scholarship boys and girls from the elementary (now the primary) schools. By the mid-1930s, the scholarship boys and girls outnumbered the fee-payers. In 1944 entry to the grammar schools became free. At that time the Fleming Committee recommended the integration of the fee-paying public schools into the state system of education, chiefly as grammar schools.

After the great growth of the public schools and their associates, the grammar schools, in the last quarter of the nineteenth century and (in the case of the grammar schools) up to 1940, the point had been reached when the bulk of the middle class was receiving some sort of respectable education, and a proportion – a growing proportion, indeed – of the working class was also in secondary school. The rest of the population, after the early 1870s, was in elementary schools. The effect of the evangelical revival, and of the spread of the idea of academic efficiency, was to identify the public schools and the grammar schools with the better off groups, and to identify the schools with the idea of academic excellence, and academic excellence, in turn, with character building of all kinds. Until the mid-1950s, the bulk of public and grammar school pupils left school at sixteen or seventeen; they were not primarily academic forcing houses. Only a minority of their pupils were in the academic stream, and the academic stream had its own curriculum; the other children did not (by and large) have their own curriculum.

The contrast with Germany and France lay in the fact, not that the French schools were more democratic, in the sense that they drew from wider social sources, but that their schools were academic institutions, and 'character' was left to the family.

Nevertheless, in all three countries the system of education led to social segregation and its identification with academic talent. The reason for this identification of the public schools and grammar schools with social class, and with academic ability, is easy to explain in the light of modern knowledge. There is a strong positive correlation between measured intellectual ability and academic achievement, which is perhaps fairly obvious. There is also a very strong relationship between parental occupational status and measured ability. Some people hold that this relationship points to the importance of heredity in intelligence, that genetic explanations of intelligence and of other mental characteristics, like 'criminality', are the most valid. According to this sort of explanation it could well be argued that over the ages the most intelligent and able people have come to hold the higher positions in society and that in consequence the more intelligent families tend to be those with the better jobs and (inevitably) those that produce the brighter children. There seems to me little doubt that this genetic argument must have something in it, though its weakness lies in the fact that 'intelligence' is not nearly as clear-cut a characteristic as – say – the colour of eyes. The fact that 'intelligence' is a complex of characteristics lends force to the sociological argument that intelligence is not so much a genetic as an acquired characteristic. This certainly seems to a very large extent true of the motivation to succeed, and the ability to cope with academic modes of learning.

Overwhelmingly, evidence from throughout the world shows that the more favoured socio-economic classes have children who are more intelligent than average and that, once at school, these children progress faster and further than others, of equal measured ability, from different backgrounds.

This evidence is extremely powerful, indicative as it is of profound social and probably genetic processes at work which are not fully understood or comprehended. The magnitude of the distances involved is indicated by some of the following facts.

For example, in England and Wales, of those born about 1910, 37% of the sons and daughters of managerial and professional fathers had a grammar school type education, and 1% of the children of semi- and unskilled parents. Of those born in the late 1930s, the percentages had shifted to 62% and 10%. Recent evidence suggests that the gap has if anything widened since then. The Robbins Report (1963) showed that university students came to the extent of over two-thirds from the top two social groups (containing just under a fifth of the population) and only 2½% from the bottom two groups containing over a quarter of the population. Nothing has changed since then, despite major extensions of access to higher education.

International statistics show that the United Kingdom is in this respect more egalitarian than most other industrialized countries. In France, for example, it is a hundred times more likely that a Parisian child will end up in a university or one of the *Grandes Écoles* than a child from the Ardèche. Even in egalitarian Sweden, with almost universal comprehensive schools, and few private schools, Torsten Husén has shown the fantastic differences in life chances of children born in different social groups. At a conference of European education ministers, it seemed that the differences were as marked – if not more so – in the Soviet-occupied countries of Eastern Europe, despite thirty years of attacks on 'bourgeois elements'.

These sorts of irreducible brute facts are fundamental to an understanding of the public school problem. Put briefly, it is as follows. In all known industrial societies, evidence fully or partially indicates that by and large son tends to follow father; that is, professional and managerial parents tend to have children who follow their careers to a very similar degree. Of course there are some children who drop out and fall down in the social scale; but they tend to be fairly few. And there are considerable numbers of young people who rise in the social scale. The reasons for this are fairly simple. In any group of children, born to ordinary parents, some will be extremely dim and some will be extremely bright. The bright will tend to make progress up the occupational ladder. At any time, a large number of able people – including exceptionally able people – will be found among the lower occupational groups. Yet, as the size of the professional and managerial group grows, so they recruit some of the able from among the poorer groups. There is, therefore, considerable social mobility going on at any time.

The avenue for the able poor to move into the white collar, more well-heeled social groups is partly private business, setting up small factories and shops, but increasingly through education. In modern societies the accepted way into public sector employment, and employment in big business, is usually by educational attainment – degrees and certificates. Entry into those educational institutions granting those degrees and certificates is by merit; and entry to the enclosure behind the starting gate is partly by merit (in the state education system) and partly by the payment of fees in the public school system.

The criticism of the public schools as part of the social system lies then in the view that access to the better jobs is through education, and access to higher education is unduly influenced by the undoubted fact that a high proportion of those who enter higher education do so from fee-paying schools. Thus a system is set up which seems like a series of equations; family position equals fee-paying schools for the children, equals better access to the universities, equals access to jobs which maintain the family position.

There is, of course, some truth in this series of arguments. It is given added verisimilitude by the fact that almost all the clever poor who have got on in the world have done so by education, and they therefore, correctly, attribute their own success to their education. If they are critics of the system, they resent the privilege which their richer schoolfellows seem to have had; if they accept the system, they wish to democratize it so that all clever children, however poor, have access to the best schools.

More radical people, still, wish to eliminate privilege altogether, and with it the concept of academic education whose social function (it is argued) is to produce an elite.

The trouble with the argument, however, is fairly easy to spot. It is that what is true for one is not true for all. If I made a fortune by being a cat-burglar it does not follow that everybody could make a fortune by taking up burgling. The great bulk of people cannot progress through the education system to top jobs since the number of top jobs is limited. Moreover, the biggest proportion of able people, as has already been shown, are found, either by genetics or by social conditioning or by both, among the children of people already in top jobs. It follows that the only effect of either throwing the public schools open to the masses (by making them free, for example), or of abolishing them, would be that very much the same children would advance rapidly up the education system, however it were reformed, into the white collar professions. Only in countries like Russia, between 1925 and 1940, and in Mao's China, has the process been stopped by deliberately handicapping the children of bourgeois parents.

That being said, it must be established what the facts are, and what the correct chain of argument seems to be. In the first place, there is no reason whatever to doubt the well-established connection between the public schools and the seats of power. Their old boys tend to go to the better universities, and then to get to the top of various influential sectors of society – the figures produced by the Public Schools Commission are the most accurate and, moreover, they have not significantly altered, nor do they seem likely to do so, in recent times.

Over 90% of boys in public schools come from families in the top managerial and professional occupational groups. Of the intake 90% had also passed the eleven-plus – suggesting the power of the correlation between measured ability and background. Over two-fifths of the entry to the higher civil service in the 1960s came from public schools, and two-thirds of the entry to the Diplomatic Service. In 1967, three-quarters of the Directors of the Bank of England came from public schools, three-quarters of the bishops, four-fifths of the judges and QCs, 87% of the Conservative Cabinet of 1964 and two-fifths of the Labour Cabinet of 1965; two-thirds of the top doctors and three-quarters of the company directors of big companies came from public schools. This compares with about 3% of fourteen-year-olds at public schools, and 17% of undergraduates drawn from public schools.

All the signs, indeed, are that if anything this process is (from the point of view of egalitarian reformers) getting worse. The meritocratic upper civil service, lawyers, doctors, businessmen, are buying education for their children, taking the view, rightly or wrongly, that state education throughout the country has lost its standards as a consequence of the movement towards comprehensive schools, as well as the progressive onslaught on the very idea of academic standards. Indeed, as a result of the abolition of the grammar schools, the proportion of pupils from independent schools is moving upwards in the older universities, and in key faculties like medicine throughout the land.

Nevertheless, the theory of the place of education in the creation of elites has significantly shifted. Since the publication of the Coleman Report in the United States, reporting a massive study of the educationally deprived and the reasons for the lack of progress of blacks in particular, there has been a strong feeling that education does not cause social division. The conclusion from this and many other studies is that education is a *consequence*, not a *cause*, of social mobility. It follows, therefore, that though education may have a marginal effect in creating equality (and, of course, in individual cases an overwhelming effect on getting people to the top), the education system is itself derivative of the rest of the social and economic system. In other words, in this essential, it would seem that the classic Marxist position is correct. The orthodox Marxists have always argued that while reform of the education system might be a good in itself, it is an error to suppose that educational reform can alter the class structure, which is based upon the deepest economic realities of modes of production. It follows, therefore, that those who argued for a reform of the education system on the grounds that it would thus cause a social revolution were in error.

It would seem to me, however, that to conclude from this view – a view that I have come to share – that the public schools do not matter is a mistake. The conventional view that they do matter is formally incorrect, seen from the viewpoint of social theory, but from two other standpoints it is surely correct. Radical critics would take the position that the character of upper-class relationships, the mode by which the rest of society is thus dominated, spring from the survival (indeed the growth) of the public school system. 'Defenders' of the public schools would argue that they have much to offer in the defence of scholarship and of a certain attitude towards public duty. It seems to me that these two positions are not in fact incompatible, and that they are both correct in some degree.

Why? The argument so far presented is that there is a strong positive correlation between ability – including, let it be said, musical talent and physical skills – and social origin, and that this correlation is partly genetic in origin and partly environmental. The school system, while an essential vehicle for the transmission of this ability from generation to generation, is not itself sufficient for the perpetuation of the dominance of a social group. This is guaranteed, rather, by the economic and social system, of which the educational structure is derivative. This is an essential truth; but it is a truth about structures. It is not a truth about public and private values, except in so far as these are implicit in the structures.

To put it more directly, the explicit continuation of a relatively small group (or rather series of groups) is obviously closely linked not only to family, financial and social ties but also to a common educational experience. R.H.S. Crossman used to argue that the common experience of Oxford was in fact far more important in contemporary society than the public school system. Yet ordinary observation suggests that while Crossman was to some extent correct, the power of the 'old boy network' is still extremely great. What the major public schools do nationally – and what the minor public schools do regionally – is to give a common background of shared experience, shared jokes, shared relationships, in short a shared *style* which is extremely powerful in those informal attitudes and characteristics which underlie future formal relationships. It is this network, culminating in a style of speech, manners, address, behaviour, which infuriates many of those who feel excluded by it. And it would be idle to deny that there is a good deal in it. The patronizing, effortless air of Wykehamists who (more than any other group) have brought this country to its knees by their foolish advice and policies in top jobs in Whitehall, the Foreign Office and the City, has probably been responsible for more ill-feeling between the classes than anybody since the Russian aristocracy.

The particular style or manner of conduct of various groups among the old schoolboy fraternity is extremely different, to insiders; indeed, the whole point of the variability is to make the differences seem as great as possible. A great deal of social life, indeed, depends for its interest upon these nuances: where would the English novel be without them? They are the English equivalent of Sir Walter Scott's highland clans. But to the outsider, the differences seem less acute than the similarities. How far are these differences, and the overwhelming similarity (to the outsider), due to the peculiar qualities of the English public schools (to which must be added a very few in Scotland)? The answer must surely be that the tendency of the schools to be boarding schools has had an immense impact on their character and it is what gives them ultimately their objectionable qualities. It does so in several ways. First, by adding enormously to the expense of education, it has in fact made it impossible for any serious attempt to integrate the schools into the ordinary system of education to succeed – despite the fact that up to one-third of the pupils have their fees paid by governmental or quasi-governmental agencies. Next, the reason for boarding is entirely due to the historically 'rural' – that is semi-suburban – character of the English bourgeoisie, and their need to send their sons away to school to meet their social equals. It is not based upon the fact that fathers and mothers are abroad. Thirdly, as many studies have shown, the acute personal deprivation from which children sent away from home suffer leads to severe emotional problems in later life. The widespread homosexuality of the English bourgeoisie is not due so much to adolescent single sex boarding schools as to earlier emotional deprivation, according to most accepted psychiatric theory. Other nations cope with the alleged reasons for boarding far more easily; in Scotland, with a scattered rural population, hostels are attached to ordinary day schools; in America mobile parents take their children with them (as do the French); in India, the extended family system is used.

Boarding is, then, the great evil. It is ironic indeed that the majority report of the First (Newsom) Commission on Public Schools should have recommended it for more children. It is like a commission on feet problems recommending the universalization of the Chinese practice of binding feet, as in Mandarin China, to equalize handicap.

Oddly enough, the merit of the public schools has arisen by accident.

Because the academic tradition has been so powerful, they have become the major source of trained intellectual talent in the country. The reasons for this are complex. In the first instance, the schools have made little or no attempt to provide a curriculum for what are usually euphemistically described as the less able. The less intellectual boys just did the academic curriculum, badly. This appalling tradition spread to the grammar schools. The academic curriculum has been narrowly based, leading to intense specialization, with bad later consequences, largely because there has never been any national discussion of the curriculum for all pupils of differing abilities, in the context of national needs. Nevertheless, by a callous disregard of the less able boys, the schools have kept up to the mark intellectually. Secondly, the parents of their pupils, for the most part drawn from the professional and the managerial groups, have either a keen appreciation of the importance of academic achievement, or at least not too much overt hostility to it. The contrast with the position in many state schools could not be more marked. Thirdly, because of the high correlation between ability and social background, there are proportionately very many boys and girls of high ability in the schools; the masters are drawn from the same social and intellectual groups; and an academic atmosphere is generated, at least in the best schools.

Several further points are important. In the better schools the worship of games, particularly the more brutal games, has been replaced by an excellent system of sophisticated physical exercise – squash, fencing, athletics – designed to engage most people in some form of sport which they can enjoy. This enlightened practice probably spread from the state schools, but it makes the older criticisms of brutishness more out of date than many other criticisms of the schools. Next, many schools are excellent in their provision of music and art; the greater part of the players in orchestras, and of distinguished musicians playing as soloists, as well as composers, come from the public schools. (This is partly because there is a correlation between giftedness intellectually and giftedness in music.)

Lastly, perhaps, it must be said that by and large girls' boarding schools are bad, emotionally and educationally. Everybody agrees on that. They must go.

But, on balance, the case for the abolition of the public schools must now rest on a more subtle and sophisticated analysis of the way they function; and probably the game is no longer worth the candle.

Lord Vaizey (Queen Mary's Hospital School) is Professor and Head of the School of Social Sciences at Brunel University. He is the author of many books on economics, political philosophy and education.

14
The Making of a Lady
LINDA BLANDFORD

Boarding schools have always fascinated me. Whereas I have almost been able to see the rationale for sending boys away to toughen up the lips that will bear the moustache, I have never been under the impression that toughening up girls was in any way desirable. (Mind you, the dragons produced by some girls' schools also seem to bear the . . . No, perhaps that's too mean.)

There's no such thing as a girl public school type. There are only types. Many of them. Rather like species of animals, they recognize each other instantly as friend or foe by some process that's utterly bewildering to the outsider. The signals they send off are baffling until you've learned to tune in properly. Trying to stretch beyond the playground of my own school memories, I went around asking a whole lot of people what they thought of theirs. Perhaps we could start with a scene in a Knightsbridge flat one midweek afternoon.

Four young matrons are taking coffee. The furniture is sparse – a few heavy, unobtrusive antiques, family presumably. It's rather in the style of an old-established Harley Street waiting room. Initially discussion centres around the framing of an old Persian silk print. Should it be faded pink? Sage green? Pale grey? It's only a small decision but it has to be right. Four pairs of eyes assess the problem with the expert scrutiny of a cat breeder examining a champion.

Faded pink it is. Talk turns to more general topics. 'It was a lovely party. What a super choccy cake.' Yesterday, one of the matron's sons was four. 'Poor Piggy got so excited he did a poo in his pants.' They look very different, these young women in their twenties. Nicki in a severe black dress – unbuttoned to her thigh. Helen in an interesting mix of blue jeans, T-shirt, turquoise silk shirt, gold earrings, necklace and bracelet. Sal, just down from the Borders in tweed skirt, looks windswept still.

What they have in common, besides certain schoolgirl phrases delivered in precise tones of the upper register, are a certain air of assurance and the fact that they're old school chums. They're Heathfield girls.

Why were they sent there? 'I went because Mummy went.' 'Mummy's Belgian so she didn't know much about English schools. I think the fact that Princess Alexandra had gone there impressed her.' 'I was sent for the same reason many girls are. Our parents wanted to get rid of us.'

Heathfield School, Ascot (Motto: 'The merit of one is the honour of all') was founded by Miss Beatrice Eleanor Wyatt with 'the object of giving girls a sound education and a religious upbringing'. With modern wings added on to a rather fine example of a late Georgian private house, Heathfield offers such facilities as ten classrooms, six common rooms, two laboratories, twelve music rooms, five hard tennis courts, twelve grass courts, a heated swimming pool and two lacrosse and rounders pitches. Other facilities include a proximity to Eton. Heathfield girls are allowed down into Windsor but not over the bridge leading to the temptations of Eton proper. (It has not been unknown for some of the rasher Heathfield girls to sneak across.)

Heathfield is situated in 34 acres of grounds, 26 miles from London and, as the prospectus points out, it's only 13 miles from London airport (a highly relevant fact for foreign pupils). 'We've always had a cosmopolitan selection of girls there,' says Sal, by way of explanation. 'In my time there was Tamar from Iraq, and Dale from Texas and Marisa of course.' Marisa Berenson, international celebrity and actress, is a not too untypical old girl. 'They're the sort of people who are used to moving around at a society at ease with itself.'

Helen remembers (while trying to point out what makes Heathfield 'different') her first school meal. She was presented with a whole, flat white fish and tore at it clumsily. 'In front of the whole table, the head girl gave me a lesson in how to eat fish properly.' The memory of that humiliation lingers; no question of that kind of social awkwardness now. If you're looking for contrasts with state-educated girls, not many of them would describe their school days as 'like spending time in a good country house' (Nicki's words). But then not many of them would know what spending time in a good country house is like in the first place. Despite a few social-climbing cuckoos, most of the public school brigade come from the same sort of background.

There are people who believe naively that in this day and age, any girl with determination, a good eye for clothes and a good ear for vowels can lift herself up to the social level of those products of 'that potting shed of the English rose' (Katharine Whitehorn's famous description of Roedean). Can a state-school girl pass herself off as The Real Thing? There's a moment of embarrassed surprise. 'When she's young,' says Sal in a slightly strained voice, 'any pretty woman with a good figure can dress herself up and pass herself off as anything. But when she gets older, she inevitably reverts to type.' Nicki describes a well-turned-out, well-educated and ambitious state-school girl as 'a cultured pearl, not a real pearl'.

So much for the ambitions of those who aspire to join the elite of 'little darlings turned into little snobs' – one woman's summing up of her old school chums. (Public school girls, by the way, do tend to have chums not friends. It's part of the jargon.) The same woman still entered both her daughters on the lists for good schools – at birth. Why? 'Brilliant girls can always get in anywhere but you can have a real problem with the others. And of course one would send one's daughter away to school – it knocks the tiresome edges off a girl.'

Sending girls away to knock off the tiresome edges is nothing new. As long ago as the fifteenth century, noblemen's daughters were boarded out to households of the same or preferably higher (social climbing's nothing new either) standing. There they would stay under the wing of the mistress of the house until, in their early teens, they were wed. This was no life of ease or choice: there's the chilling tale of Lady Pole's 'boarder' Elizabeth Paston. She had the temerity to decline the elderly widower her mother had marked out and had to be beaten into submission.

Nor are boarding schools a modern invention. From the time of the

Wars of the Roses, girls were sent into safety in convents away from the marauding, rapacious hordes (*plus ça change* and all that). By the 1700s there were business ventures-cum-boarding schools all over the place. By the 1780s, when Mary Wollstonecraft opened hers at Newington Green, it had become the traditional resort of penniless women lacking even the meagre resources to open a shop. Mary was then in her early twenties; her famous *Vindication of The Rights of Women* was some years ahead. The feminist who was to plead with such passion for education for women offered in her own school the usual courses – reading, writing, nature study, drawing, sewing. Education then wasn't for the mind but for the manners and, at its best, for the soul. A little strumming on a musical instrument, the ability to write a charming letter, these were the skills girls needed to improve their value on the marriage market.

Mary Wollstonecraft's *Vindication* spelled out the need for women to be trained for professions and careers to liberate them from 'the bitter bread of dependence', as she put it. A hundred years later women were still pressing for education to give them that freedom.

It's against that background that the lives of two Victorian pioneers must be set. Miss Buss and Miss Beale inherited an image of girls' schools immortalized by Charlotte Bronte in *Jane Eyre*. Charlotte, bearing the scars of her ordeals (witnessing beatings, hunger, death and disease etc) at the Clergy Daughters' School, Cowan Bridge, captured her experiences there, barely camouflaged in her novel as Lowood.

There's a certain historical piquancy in the fact that of all the hundreds of schools from Charlotte Bronte's era that had closed and been long forgotten, it was to the Clergy Daughters' School that Dorothea Beale went in 1857 as head teacher. Even then, after the school had moved from Cowan Bridge to Casterton and had been morally and physically 'spring-cleaned', Miss Beale was shocked at what she found. 'There was a spirit of open irreligion and a spirit of defiance very sad to witness,' she wrote, 'but the constant restraints, the monotonous life, the want of healthy amusements were in a great measure answerable for that.'

Miss Beale soon resigned. A year later she went in a hastily-borrowed blue silk dress to be interviewed for the position of Principal of a more congenial establishment – Cheltenham Ladies' College. She was to stay and reign for nearly fifty years. It's due to her that the school that has more recently turned out other pioneers (in medicine, education, administration and welfare developments) has evolved as it has.

But in those early days, the College (founded in 1853 'for the daughters and young children of noblemen and gentlemen') was equiping girls to serve God and their husbands. 'I desire to institute no comparison between the mental abilities of boys and girls,' said Miss Beale, 'but simply to say what seems to be the right means of training girls so that they may best perform the subordinate part in the world, to which I believe they have been called.'

Miss Beale's will and mystical sense of devotion were directed at turning out young, marriageable ladies but at least they would be educated in the fullest sense. If Miss Beale felt that she was called by heaven, her friend Miss Buss heard her call on earth. She opened her school, the North London Collegiate School for Ladies, in her family house. As the family breadwinner, Frances Mary Buss knew only too well that many of her girls would have to earn a living – to support themselves and possibly ageing parents. She wanted to turn them out fully able to do so.

The foundations of the girls' public school system we know today were laid by these two women. They had to fight hard for what they believed: even teaching girls arithmetic seemed suspect to some parents. 'My dear lady,' complained one father to Miss Beale, 'if my daughters were going to be bankers, it would be very well to teach arithmetic as you do, but really there is no need.' He took his daughters away from Cheltenham and the story, as told by Miss Beale, has a fitting, if miserable, ending. The father died leaving his fortune to his daughters who, alas, hadn't a clue how to handle it. 'When I last heard of them they were involved in pecuniary difficulties.'

Cheltenham Ladies' College might be trying to teach its young gentlewomen outrageous subjects (science when it was introduced was tactfully called 'physical geography') but at least it didn't outrage the rigid class system of the time. Miss Buss horrified her critics by trying to run a democratic institution. There's the tale of a North London Collegiate teacher who upbraided a pupil for being improperly dressed. 'No lady would be seen without gloves.' 'But I ain't no lady's child,' came the answer.

Should young ladies mix with the offspring of lower orders? In 1864 the Schools' Inquiry Commission (a landmark as it happens; it was the first time education for middle-class girls was ever officially discussed) came out against the notion. Talking 'of the mixture of different classes of society in the same schools', said the Report, 'there seems to be much more agreement in the direction unfavourable to such mixture, as to girls' schools than as to boys', both from general reasons and observation, and with regard to the feeling of parents'. (Overlook the pompous phrasing and the problem hasn't changed much today: one woman expressed severe annoyance to me that her daughter's school had accepted the children of 'most offensive businessmen and even of local farmers'. She reconciled herself with the thought, 'Well, I suppose in working life, one's going to meet everyone these days.')

From the time of Miss Buss and Miss Beale until well after the Second World War, schools opened (and closed) with astonishing regularity. Whatever actually went on behind their walls only the girls themselves knew. It was part of the code that no child would own up to parents if it was all rather ghastly. Undoubtedly there were girls who loathed every moment, as there have always been and still are. In a house system, the housemistress doesn't work too well as a substitute mother when there are, maybe, seventy other girls to share her attention. The really sensitive girl can easily be crushed, her needs ignored.

But one of the reasons boarding schools acquired the happy, carefree, all-girls-together-having-a-whizzing-time image they did after the 1900s was because a new genre of girls' literature had come to the fore. From Angela Brazil's Hollies school to Enid Blyton's Mallory Towers, at least three generations of girls grew up on the exciting adventures (down secret tunnels, across playing-fields, in midnight feasts) that seemed to happen only at boarding schools. The snobs with double-barrelled names got taken down a peg or two, the poor little scholarship girls became the heroines of the hour (usually after undergoing ordeals of fire – literally. In these stories girls were forever saving each other's lives in burning houses, deep rivers, etc. etc.). Tomboys, some of them, madcaps all. The mistresses were often 'spiffing', sometimes just 'all right'. Through books and comics, girls and parents learned that the best times of all were had in boarding school.

Meanwhile the real life schools were acquiring their own individual reputations. Some quickly acquired the name for turning out girls as fierce as Boadicea, reared on hockey sticks, cold showers and long walks. For some reason Roedean was one of these. Although it's hard to see how that fitted in with another reputation it acquired – summed up by mention of one scantily-clad post-war revue at the Folies Montmartre: 'Le Drame Mysterieux de Roedean College'.

Roedean is the kind of school that inspires argument and opinion, even among people who've never met a Roedean girl, let alone seen the late-Victorian pile standing in 118 acres, facing the lonely sea, on the white cliffs (not exactly of Dover, it's just above Brighton, but you get the picture). It's the sort of school that inspires old girls to write indignantly to newspapers when some misguided fool takes their motto 'Honneur aux Dignes' to mean 'Honour with dignity' instead of 'Honour to those who are worthy of it'. (And talking of mottoes, my favourite has always been that one of the School of St Mary and St Anne, Abbots Bromley about 'That our daughters may be as the polished corners of the Temple'.) And every time Roedean crops up in the press with some reference to 'jolly hockey sticks and all that rubbish', a phrase, incidentally, last used as far as I can see by the school's headmaster, John Hunt, no end of fussed old girls will point out that the school's forte is lacrosse. Who could forget the day in 1935 when women's lacrosse history was made at Roedean? The school side gave the United States' women's team a walloping (their first game on British soil, what's more). The score: twenty-one goals to none.

Roedean, rather like mothers-in-law, has for some surely unjustified reason long been the butt of easy jokes. But times are changing. I've met people who assume the old place has closed – they haven't heard a titter about it for years.

Once upon a time, of course, jokes about Us (reasoned public school girls) didn't matter so much because they were told by Them and one never mixed with Them. Old girls stuck to other old girls as chums because they'd shared the best years of their lives together and didn't meet any other sort of girls anyway. Now they stick together as much because so many of them, in these modern times, seem hugely apologetic for having been sent to wherever they went in the first place. Benenden girls will explain without prompting that even though Princess Anne went there 'it's not grand or anything, it turns out jolly nice people'.

Turning out Jolly Nice People seems to be the trademark of boarding schools. Pulling together for the sake of the school, not letting the House down in its pursuit of the Tidiness Cup, knitting for refugees and other good causes . . . well, at the very least it makes girls awfully good at getting on with other girls. From the first few weeks, they learn to fetch and carry and knuckle under those in authority (sixth formers and prefects; staff are something else) with a cheerful smile and a willing eye. One television producer I know will only employ public school girls as secretaries if he can. He says they're the only ones who aren't too proud to do menial tasks. Working-class secretaries, he claims, are all too quick to howl 'discrimination' if they're asked to go out for his cigarettes, make his coffee or do his shopping.

And anyone still misguided enough to believe that you can't tell public school from state school should walk into any large office in the BBC. The hostility between the camps is notorious. It comes to a peak on Friday nights when the ambitious grammar school girls, living as they do on salaries in bed-sits or as flat-sharers, have to listen to the Others who are off ('orf') for the weekend to stay in Leicestershire and Warwickshire and a mass of other shires in country houses with chums. I daresay the country-house-weekenders don't mean to rub it in but they do have such well-projected voices. The result of making themselves heard in years of dorm din, perhaps.

The weekend network starts, you see, at schools. The first term may be hell. Benenden seems to be one of the few places to have thought that one out: for the first few weeks, a new girl has a slightly less new girl as a 'mother' to show her the ropes. It's a pretty well organized place all round. At one time the 'crack' system (crushes, pashes, gone-ons – the term for these emotional attachments to older girls varies with each school) was so well organized that one girl arriving a week late found herself delegated by some mysterious force to be 'cracked' on the only senior girl left, a fat, spotty prefect she couldn't stand. (Other schools aren't as fair-minded and some seniors are being 'crushed' all over the school while others are never, ever 'crushed' at all. The latter try valiantly not to show they mind; it hurts like hell.) At Benenden it was (is?) the privilege, yea duty, of the smaller girl to rush down after dinner to the room of the older girl she was 'cracked' on, turn down her bed and (treat of treats) place Polos on her pillow.

There's a lot to get used to in the first few weeks and it takes time to sort out one's bosom pals. It takes maybe even a year for friends (often for life, remember) to group together. This term's best friend may be next term's enemy but (and this is the point about weekending later) as long as the friendship lasts it involves obligatory visits in the hols.

All over England, small girls are to be seen at the beginning of the holidays, changing trains en route to other parents' homes. Where a state school girl may think a 22p bus ride is a long way to go for tea with her friend, the boarder travels hundreds of miles without question to stay with one chum or another. Later, much later, when the benefit of all this becomes clear, the young women will still be clutching their suitcases as they go off to stay in far-flung parts of the hunt counties. Where a grammar school girl might have a puddle of people who know her (and years later will talk about her) in one town, public school girls have a network of private inns the breadth of the country. There's nothing more intriguing to an outsider than to meet in Kent a woman who knows in Derbyshire a woman who went to stay with a couple in Argyllshire who went shooting in Inverness with a man who can tell you the most extraordinary tales about a woman whom you ran into at a cocktail party in London last week. And more often than not this cobweb will have first been spun at school.

At ten a public school girl has already learned how to handle servants: that particular distance that the upper classes keep from inferiors and each other is imbibed early. At school a girl soon learns that one doesn't talk to the kitchen staff; in the hols she learns how much to tip staff and how to do it unselfconsciously when she goes away (and, these days, how not to register surprise if there's no staff to tip, times being what they are). As one grander type puts it: 'You can always tell a grammar school girl who has married well by the fact that she's a fraction too familiar with her servants and rather uncomfortable with yours.'

Even today, public school girls can grow up travelling the country (and even the Continent, depending on the school and the type of girls it attracts) without ever staying in an hotel. Hotels, it seems, are the ordinary girl's substitute for other people's houses.

It's in these formative years, too, that another telling characteristic of public school girls takes shape: the writing of long, gossipy letters in large, scrawling handwriting and the forming of those perfect bread-and-butter letters to say thank you. Wolves falling on carrion are inhibited compared to girls at school scrumming around the letter racks. Letters from Mummy, from brothers and, as they get older, from friends of brothers; each as welcome as a file in a cake to a lifer in prison. They may not be the tools of escape to an outside world, but they're a reminder. They're the threads to another life, more important in their way even than exeats.

There was a time when all boarders used exeats to fill up like camels watering their humps. After weeks of Ganges' mud, dead man's leg, frogspawn, bones and barley and the occasional greased rat (if the food was awful the nicknames hardly improved it), there was an orgy in the local tea shop or restaurant. On a regular school diet of stodge, it's no wonder that sixth formers seemed to leave school weighing in at eleven stone plus despite all that fresh air and team games. (Those days are mostly gone, as it happens; some schools even have diet tables now.) But those exeats had their price: the exquisite needlepricks of shame if parents arrived in the wrong car, the wrong clothes or, worse still, with the wrong accents. Girls more than boys have always been sensitive to signposts or background.

The tyranny of the greater number can be seen at work nowhere more vividly than in a school of pubescent fillies desperately anxious for their sires and dams to look and sound exactly like whatever it is that most of the other bloodstock look and sound like. (Interestingly enough, threadbare gentility is more acceptable than ostentatious new wealth – which hurls those daughters of social climbers still further into an abyss of embarrassment.)

For every old girl who remembers endless sunny days in the dorm, there's another who remembers that tyranny at her single-sex boarding school with shudders. 'Stick girls together and they'll turn all their talents in on each other towards mutual destruction. They're like caged monkeys, waiting, preening and picking at each other one moment, snarling and attacking the next. But cast one spotty boy into a room full of these same catty girls and they'll suddenly turn into amusing, funny, civilized people.' Dances, debates, cricket matches with suitable boys' schools are like truces in the wars of the Amazons.

Most of these Amazons go in not for physical fighting but for mental and emotional torture. Small girls going through agonies at being sent to Coventry (and what did Coventry ever do to deserve its reputation?) soon learn that one doesn't step out of line, sneak to teachers, curry favour, commit gaffes or behave in any way against the laid-down *mores* of the dorm. Even schools with single rooms not dormitories provide no respite for a girl temporarily out of favour. There's no such thing as privacy. A locked lavatory is the nearest there is and there's a limit as to how long anyone seeking refuge can hole up there – sanitary fixtures being what they are in most schools, i.e. few and far between.

With boys, the early years are usually the worst. With girls the worst is all to come. It's a toss-up which is the more humiliating – to be among the first to sprout breasts or among the last to menstruate, terms after everyone else has 'gone shopping' at matron's. ('I've come shopping' means 'please may I have some sanitary towels' to matron and nothing to any nosy juniors who might be around.)

The privileges attained with each advance upwards bring a still more treacherous test – what to wear in 'home clothes'. Each school has its own rituals of growing up. For instance: first and second formers: can't go to tuck shop without sixth former, can't wear 'home shoes' with 'home clothes'. Third formers: 'home shoes' allowed. Fourth formers: can go to tuck shop in fours, go for walks on hills in fours and wear hair down with 'home clothes'. The fifths can wear make up with 'home clothes' and go to the nearest town in fours in school uniform. The lower sixth can go to the nearest town in 'home clothes' and go to a bigger town once a term. Upper sixths can wear boots, go in 'home clothes' to small and big town, have driving lessons and boyfriends to visit – if the boys write to the headmistress asking permission first (I'm surprised anyone tackles that ordeal).

It needs a will of iron for a girl to wear the wrong 'home clothes' by her own form-mates' standards. Every detail must be right. In some schools it's the snob appeal of St Laurent against St Michael. In others it's a question of aesthetics: exactly the right shade of purple. Where did the Sloane Rangers learn to conform long before they grew up to the Hermès scarf and Gucci loafers? Over the school tea table as the beady eyes looked them up and down.

Every school has its cult figures. Some, the traditional gathering places for the children of intellectuals and artists (successful architects, writers of respected, sometimes minor works etc), have one set of standards. Their heroines are those who at sixteen are opining with a kind of cultured incoherence about Le Corbusier, Stravinsky, Pevsner and ratatouille. Others are more conventional and idolize the brave, the enthusiastic, those who serve and yet can lead. Incidentally, in the headmaster's 1975–6 report for Roedean, there's a moving tribute to the girls of the VI who went on a sponsored walk for Help the Aged. 'Diana Webb walked the maximum permitted distance of twenty miles.' And more: 'in rain, wind and sea mist and said she enjoyed it.'

There's a curious twist of fate about the future of the most outstanding school heroines: their paths afterwards often lead nowhere. It seems to be a common rule that the girls who are really successful at school, trusted by the staff, peppered with awful presents by adoring juniors, demonstrating in the sixth an irrefutable excellence of style (by their peers' standards of course), well, they're the ones whose careers seem to die at seventeen. Never again do they achieve in the outside world the stardom and accolades they knew at school.

There is, however, one other small point. Girls aren't only sent away to school to learn the law of the boarding house jungle ('more like the law of organized crime in my case' has been mentioned by more than one girl). They're there to be educated. To learn things; things from textbooks that you need to know to pass exams organized by university boards to whom it doesn't matter one jot what colour of purple one wears. Maybe in the thirties academic standards didn't matter as much (although I doubt it and I'm assured it isn't true). Maybe when there was a Season and the pinnacle of a girl's ambition could be to be photographed on the occasion of her engagement for the front plate of *The Tatler*. Not any more, chums.

The academic standards vary more from school to school for girls even than for boys. But what is true is that they're mattering to prospective parents, heads and teachers more all the time. More girls press on to A-levels and universities. And, to begin with at least, if they get there they do stand out as the glittering stars, poised to take the glittering prizes. Often they've had a year off in The World that grammar school girls can't afford. They've stayed in France (with friends naturally) or in

America, been by Land Rover to India, etc. If they're pretty, can sing, dance and act – no state-school girl can match them for success. In time, of course, it evens out but at the off they're on an inside track. Apart from anything else, they know so many people. All those chums and their brothers and their own brothers' chums – meanwhile the grammar-school girl is fighting her way out of isolation. 'If you've got what it takes, you're ahead. The whole supporting structure is still yours,' as one Oxford light so bluntly puts it.

Of course it still takes a while for boarding school girls to realize what lies ahead. Swotting may be inelegant in the fourths; particular schools may have an entire history behind them of philistinism and an anti-intellectual bias but the importance of learning is seeping up through the stones of those Victorian establishments.

And where do the staff fit into this intricate web? They stand to the girls in much the same position as warders to prisoners. They can lead and direct those who co-operate and it doesn't pay to interfere too much. If that sounds an exaggeration, listen to any of the chums talking over old times. They talk of shared adventures, they gossip about other old girls, they may have a soft spot for the head (Miss Clarke, formerly head of Benenden, comes in for particular mention. Watch out for those frequent tributes to 'Celeste', Queen of the Elephants, of course; Benenden girls are famed for being big and bouncy.) Now and again some mistress crops up – 'what was her name now?'

Boys' schools seem to attract better teachers than girls'. Perhaps it's because the posts offer a man (and, most of all, his wife – if he's married) a fairly impecunious existence but a gentleman's one. While there are increasingly more married mistresses living outside school, who wants to be buried in the countryside with a mob of girls? For this and all manner of other intricate reasons, it's one of the complexities of English life that on the whole girls' schools do not harbour teachers of the same quality as the girls they're reputed to attract. Perhaps it was different in the between-Wars years with fewer respectable occupations for highly qualified women and few men left after the slaughter of 1914–18 for them to marry. Look at the lists of headmistresses and mistresses for those days – long spells of thirty, forty, nearly fifty years' devoted teaching in the same school. That's gone too.

But teaching at a girls' boarding school requires qualities of spirit and ingenuity that boys' posts don't .Without the deterrent/threat of corporal punishment, there's the simple question of law and order. There are hair-raising stories of girls hurriedly removed after outbreaks of drugs/drinking/boy smuggling (into the dorm). By and large, though, it's astonishing how little sense of anarchy there is in most schools. How can you keep discipline? By keeping errant girls in from exeats (thereby punishing parents) or by making them learn wads of Shakespeare by heart (thereby punishing the bard)? Looking back over the ten years I spent at the same school, I never recall a mistress raising her voice. I can recall breaking many rules (nothing big, mostly inconvenient) but the astounding point that I see only now is the way I never once questioned that there should be rules. I don't know how those mistresses imbued us with discipline (our motto: Honour before Honours). But maybe therein lies the skill.

Of course, my own school wasn't typical (a conviction I share with all old girls. One's own school never is). But looking at everyone else's, I still can't work out what the average girl acquires for that expense. A network of other girls with suitable brothers certainly ('Hell, it's not that,' insists one woman, 'if you come from a certain background you're going to meet them anyway'). Most people consider, and I agree with them, that on average (apart from obvious exceptions) one gets a better academic education at a good state school than at most public schools. I do see that for girls who are the first generation brains from families where there are no books, no discussions, boarding school gives a better opportunity to expand their minds away from the twin temptations of television and adolescent sex. It teaches most girls to be tidy and ordered – if you grow up with lists for everything (baths, games, meals, reading the lessons in chapel) I daresay it does induce a certain respect for organization and routine.

Still, whatever the pros and cons, it must be reassuring to have gone to a school whose Principal (one-time Head of Government Relations Department at Courtaulds) can sincerely declare, 'The school's aim is to enable each girl to develop her talents to the highest level of which she is capable and above all to help her to become a worthwhile citizen and a serene contented person.' Serene and contented old girls of Cheltenham Ladies' College doubtless look back on their time there with pleasure.

Others, from other places, might go along more readily with that declaration from Katharine Whitehorn concerning the sense of captivity: 'Never at any point in the twenty-four hours at boarding school are you free – free of the school, of the other girl's opinions, of the stiff upper lip ruling that prevented some girls who were just as unhappy as I was even telling their parents they were miserable. This is the poison gas of boarding schools.'

And that brings me back to where I came in. Speaking for myself . . . No, on second thoughts, perhaps I'd rather not.

Linda Blandford (Talbot Heath School) is a journalist and is the author of *Oil Sheikhs*.